THE A–Z GUIDE TO COLLECTING

TRIVETS

Identification

and

Value Guide

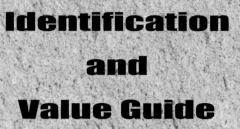

Margaret

Lynn

Rosack

COLLECTOR BOOKS

A Division of Schroeder Publishing Co., Inc.

Front cover, clockwise from top left: Dalecraft "God Bless Our Home," 1960s; "Good Luck" horseshoe plaque trivet, 1880s; Cathedral No. 4, mid to late 1800s; Ober Square No. 1, 1890s to 1916; Wilton "Heart in Hand," 1950s – 1960s; and Enterprise E, late 1800s to early 1900s.

Back cover, clockwise from top left: Streeter "Sensible," 1887; Cross Publishing Company, "Jesus Never Fails," 1940s to 1950s; Horseshoe, 1888; and Strauss " I want u" spade, 1910.

Cover design by Beth Summers   Book design by Erica Weise

Trivet photography by Edward Paul Rosack
Cover photographs by Charles R. Lynch

COLLECTOR BOOKS

P.O. Box 3009
Paducah, Kentucky 42002-3009
www.collectorbooks.com

Copyright © 2004 Margaret Lynn Rosack

Searching For A Publisher?

We are always looking for people knowledgeable within their fields. If you feel that there is a real need for a book on your collectible subject and have a large comprehensive collection, contact Collector Books.

Contents

DEDICATION

This book is dedicated to my husband, Ed Rosack, without whose tremendous patience, assistance, and encouragement it would have never been completed.

"Since few large pleasures are lent us on a long lease, it is wise to cultivate a large undergrowth of small pleasures."

Mary A. Livermore (1820 – 1905)

An 1860s era Swedish carte de visite (small, visiting card portrait), 4½" x 2½".

ACKNOWLEDGMENTS

I would like to acknowledge and thank the following persons, companies, and associations for their interest, contributions of information, and advice during the development of this book.

Bob Bamford, American Bell Association, Lawrenceville, Georgia
Matthew H. Brown, Brown Stove Works, Cleveland, Tennessee
Doris Cabral, Uncasville, Connecticut
Linda Chepyha, Canadian Fireplace Manufacturers, Mississauga, Ontario
Bill & Shirley Davis, Upper Mount Gravatt, Australia
eBay™ Inc., San Jose, California
Myrtle Eldridge, Siasconset, Massachusetts
Stephen J. Esser, President, Kutztown Publishing Company, Kutztown, Pennsylvania
George A. Fathauer, Sonoran Publishing, Chandler, Arizona
Google™ Inc., Mountain View, California
Jim and Barbara Greenawalt, PaDutchCulture, Wilmington, North Carolina
Michelle Gullia, Marketing Manager, ULEAD™ Systems, Inc., Torrance, California
Rich Hartzog, Rockford, Illinois
Mary Jo Heiar, A.Y. McDonald Manufacturing Company, Dubuque, Iowa
Bill and Peggy Heyman, Shaker Brook Farm Antique Iron Museum, Marlborough, New Hampshire
Paul J. Holt, President, John Wright Company, Wrightsville, Pennsylvania
Sherrill Hubbard, Palmdale, California
Ross Irwin, Guelph Historical Society, Guelph, Ontario, Canada
Kyle Johnston, Tucson, Arizona
Vince Katchen, Mount Bethel, Pennsylvania
Mickey Kaz, Woodland Hills, California
Maria Lampert, Patents Information, The British Library, London, England
Jennifer Lanning, Concord, North Carolina
William and Charlotte Marsh, Will-Char: The Hex Place, Paradise, Pennsylvania
Donald R. McLaughlin, Raemelton House, Mansfield, Ohio
David G. Meckley, President, Wilton Armetale, Mount Joy, Pennsylvania
Larry and Carol Meeker, Antiques of a Mechanical Nature, Somerset, California
Hazel Mitchell, Tunbridge Wells, Kent, England
Kerry A. Mohn, Historian, Ephrata Cloister, Ephrata, Pennsylvania
Jan Mosley, Corvallis, Oregon
Linda Negron, Mountaintop, Pennsylvania
Sherry Nester, Unicast Company, Boyertown, Pennsylvania
Frank Nifong, Westfield, North Carolina
D. E. Peterson, Decatur, Illinois
Emery Pineo, Antique Stove Hospital, Little Compton, Rhode Island
Becky Ross and Ellen E. Fryer, Hopewell Furnace National Historic Site, Elverson, Pennsylvania
Charles Salembier, President, Virginia Metalcrafters, Waynesboro, Virginia
William A. Sanders, Superintendent, Hopewell Furnace N.H.S., Elverson, Pennsylvania
Jeff Savage, Drexel Grapevine Antiques, Valdese, North Carolina
Richard Schlom, Charlotte, North Carolina
Adair Shepherd, Wantage, New Jersey
Thomas G. (Schroeder) Souders, Philadelphia, Pennsylvania
Arnie Stein, Morris, Minnesota
Pat Talbott, Overland Park, Kansas
Bruce L. Taylor, Erie, Pennsylvania
Joyce M. Tice, Mansfield, Pennsylvania
Robert Viguers, Harrisburg, Pennsylvania
Rita Walker, Peabody, Massachusetts
Ernest L. Wann, Jr., Florence, Alabama
Ronald W. Wyncoop, Sr., Phillipsburg, New Jersey
XE.com, Toronto, Ontario, Canada
Shirley Denton Yonce, Wichita, Kansas
Pat E. Zalba, The Chagrin Falls Historical Society, Chagrin Falls, Ohio
Leith Souders Zenowitz, Davidson, North Carolina
Gunter Zimmer, Saarbrucken, Germany
Kristin Zvonar, Charlotte, North Carolin

THE BARTHOLDI STATUE.
BEDLOE'S ISLAND.
NEW YORK HARBOR.
A GIFT FROM THE FRENCH PEOPLE TO AMERICA.
THE STATUE IS OF COPPER BRONZE, 148 FT. IN HEIGHT.
MOUNTED ON A STONE PEDESTAL 150 FT. HIGH. THE TORCH
DISPLAYS A POWERFUL ELECTRIC LIGHT.

This is the front of a 5⅝" x 3⅝" Nichol's Bark & Iron Tonic Victorian trade card. The statue, "Liberty Enlightening The World" by Frederic Auguste Bartholdi, was a joint venture between the United States, who built the stone pedestal, and France, who designed and built the copper statue. It was transported to the United States in crates, and reassembled onsite at Liberty Island in New York Harbor over a period of four months time. The poem, The New Colossus, written in 1883 by Emma Lazarus, is engraved on a tablet within the pedestal upon which Lady Liberty stands. Due to a slow fundraising effort on both sides of the Atlantic Ocean, the statue was not completed and dedicated until October 28, 1886, ten years later than originally planned.[1]

The New Colossus

Not like the brazen giant of Greek fame,
With conquering limbs astride from land to land;
Here at our sea-washed, sunset-gates shall stand
A mighty woman with a torch, whose flame
Is the imprisoned lightning, and her name
Mother of Exiles. From her beacon-hand
Glows world-wide welcome; her mild eyes command
The air-bridged harbor that twin cities frame.

"Keep, ancient lands, your storied pomp!" cries she,
With silent lips. "Give me your tired, your poor,
Your huddled masses yearning to breathe free,
The wretched refuse of your teeming shore;
Send these, the homeless, tempest-tost to me,
I lift my lamp beside the golden door!"

Emma Lazarus (1849 – 1887)

In memory of the men, women, and children who died as a result of the September 11, 2001, terrorist attacks in New York, Washington DC, and Pennsylvania.

PREFACE

By definition, the prefix tri denotes three...therefore, a trivet is a three-legged stand. Trivets originally were utilized to support cooking pots or kettles within an open hearth. Having three legs made the larger, taller stands more secure and less prone to wobble.

The first trivets were designed and hand wrought by blacksmiths. By the mid 1800s, as foundries became established in America, trivets were more commonly cast. When cooking moved from the hearth to freestanding stoves, trivets adapted in size and shape to be used on these new surfaces. Other trivets were cast and used as table protectors or as sadiron rests. The term "stand" is more appropriately used to identify those trivets used to support irons. Three legs were no longer required for stability...you'll find some trivets and stands cast with four to six legs.

With the advent of electricity in the early twentieth century, the requirement for trivets diminished. However, people still utilized them in their kitchens to protect surfaces from the heat of hot dishes, or to hang on walls as decorative accents. There was a revival of interest in cast iron during the 1950s, with many foundries promoting reproduction trivets to American housewives. Fortunately for collectors, the majority of these foundries labeled their contemporary trivets so that they would not be confused with the older originals.

Let me try and describe my fascination for trivets! They have so many appealing attributes. Most obvious would be their beauty of form. Then, there is the feel of the metal itself: strong, substantial, and enduring. And, ultimately, is the curiosity of wondering who previously owned the trivet...how old it is...where it has been... and how it was used.

This project originally began as a pamphlet describing JZH Alphabet Series trivets, thus the name "The A – Z Guide," and evolved into the book you are holding today. My goal has always been to share all I've learned about trivets and trivet collecting. My personal trivet collection currently numbers about 450, approximately 25% being contemporary trivets and 75% being pre-1940 castings. I continually collect new trivets and sell some of my others to make room, so my collection is constantly evolving. I keep digital photographs of all the trivets I purchase.

Trivet collecting is a lot like buying a car: you really need to do your homework first in order to get the best deal! Many of the trivets sold as "genuinely old" are actually reproductions. How can you tell the difference? Scarcity varies, and antique sadiron stands can differ wildly in price. Which ones are more valuable? Trivets purchased through the Internet present a unique challenge, as they cannot be personally examined beforehand. How do you make an informed purchase decision? There is an abundance of contemporary (post-1940s) trivet castings on the market. Which ones were original, copyrighted designs? Prices will eventually be adjusted, as the general public realizes the potential value of old trivets, and more are presented for sale. So, what is a fair price?

All of these questions will be addressed in this book. In addition, there is information presented regarding the cleaning of cast iron, decorating with trivets, and organizing meaningful records. Every trivet pictured within this book, unless otherwise noted, comes from my private collection.

I've tried to present an overview of trivets and trivet collecting, not attempting to reproduce the depth of information or number of trivets presented by authors Rob Roy Kelly and James Ellwood (*Trivets and Stands*, 1990). Their book is truly a classic, and should be in every serious collector's library. However, I hope you will also reserve a spot on your bookshelf for this trivet book, and that within these covers you will find some new information of value to you as a collector!

A 1950s era Wilton trivet box top, showing 34 of their different reproduction designs.

Identifying and Collecting Contemporary Trivets

Many favorite trivet designs were reproduced in the years preceding 1940. However, most of those trivets, rather than being mass produced, were cast and hand finished by smaller foundries. Some are now classified as antique in that they are already at least 100 years old. They were the common trivets and stands manufactured before the advent of electricity for everyday household use. Methods for identifying those older trivets will be discussed in Identifying Vintage and Antique Trivets. I intentionally do not include Griswold or Wagner trivets in this book, since other current references illustrate and give values for those complete lines of ironware.

Collecting contemporary trivets is often thought of as a beginning...a wayside on the journey to appreciating and collecting antique trivets. However, there are many of us who enjoy collecting this genre of trivets, and some who build their collections around contemporary trivets alone!

In this reference I classify contemporary trivets in two categories: older castings (1940 – 1970) and recent castings (after 1970). These categories include reproductions of older trivet designs as well as new, copyrighted patterns.

There are many examples of mid to late twentieth century American trivets to be found, but few have been preserved in mint condition as collectibles. Fewer still remain in their original factory packaging. Therefore, if you decide to collect contemporary trivets, remember the collector's credo: *Always buy the best you can afford.* Since the selection is ample, and prices remain reasonable, you should be buying only the nicest quality trivets you can find.

Most contemporary trivets are easy to identify by the markings on their reverse. Of course, mid-twentieth century manufacturers marked their trivets as a way of identifying their products; but for trivet collectors it has been a blessing! The majority of these trivets will feature, on the reverse, the manufacturers name, perhaps also the design name, and often a lot or stock number.

Trivets with very short feet (½") were intended for decorative wall display. Those trivets sold with rubber or plastic caps on the feet definitely postdate 1945.

Although there have been many inferior quality foreign imports since the 1940s, there were also some lovely contemporary trivets imported from overseas. Knowing when the country of origin was established gives a clue to a signed, imported trivet's age. For instance: India was established in 1947; Israel was established in 1948; Korea was divided into north and south in 1945; Occupied Japan refers to the post WWII years of 1945 to 1952; items labeled Japan date from 1952; and Taiwan was established in 1949.

You've probably noticed trivets signed Art Smithy, Brown Stove Works, Cross Publishing Company, Dalecraft, EFM, Emig, Hopewell, Iron Art, JZH, OSV, Portland Foundry, Sexton, Vermont Castings, Virginia Metalcrafters, Wilton, and John Wright. All were American made and of high quality. Although most of these trivet designs were reproductions of earlier castings, some were original, copyrighted designs.

Brown Stove Works of Cleveland, Tennessee, has been in business since 1935. Today they manufacture and distribute high-end stainless steel ranges and grills. From 1935 to 1972 they operated their own foundry, casting items such as coal heaters and stove parts. From the mid-1940s until their foundry closed, they also cast small (5" x 2¾") trivets and little ashtrays that looked like skillets, all labeled BROWN STOVE WKS, CLEVELAND, TENN on the reverse. Those items were given away as promotional items through the years.

The **Cross Publishing Company** of Elizabeth, New Jersey, remains a mystery as of the time of this book's first printing. I have searched the Internet and several New Jersey historical archive sources without success. (If any reader can provide more information on this company, I'd love to hear from you through the publisher!) The motto trivets distributed by Cross were religious in theme, which makes me believe the Cross Publishing Company was a sacred book publisher. There are several different Cross Publishing Company trivet designs pictured in Comtemporary Castings, beginning on page 150. I am estimating their era of manufacture as 1940s until I learn otherwise.

Robert Emig was a cast iron distributor who offered a line of trivets identified as **EMIG** on the reverse. His trivets were unique in that they perpetuated the more unusual antique trivet patterns. Emig trivets are lighter for their size, shallower cast and smoother than most, and have short feet for wall display. The Robert Emig Products Company was based in Reading, Pennsylvania.

Some collectors enjoy collecting **Fersommling trivets**, which are souvenirs of Pennsylvania Dutch Fersommlings (gatherings). They feature PaDutch wordings and artwork that is often enameled, and most are dated. The Unicast Division of Berkmont Industries in Boyertown, Pennsylvania, produced many of these trivets. (Unicast was formerly the Union Manufacturing Company, the maker of the JZH line of trivets.) Jim Greenawalt of Wilmington, North Carolina, who maintains a website called PaDutch Culture, has been most helpful in translating the inscriptions on my Fersommling trivets. According to Jim, Pennsylvania Dutch is actually a misnomer, as the language is more correctly termed Pennsylvania Deutch, or Old German. The earliest settlers (including his ancestors) immigrated into the Lehigh, Berks, and Northampton counties of Pennsylvania from Germany in 1830 to 1840. They formed their own small enclaves, which were named after European towns or after an influential individual. Most of the settlers were Lutheran, emigrating to escape religious persecution. They perpetuated their beloved religion, language, customs, and art while blending with their American communities. Families today continue to gather at Fersommlings, celebrating their German heritage in fun and fellowship.

Since 1954, the General Machine Corporation of Emmaus, Pennsylvania, has made 500 trivets annually as gifts for its employees and dealers. Most designs featured a trivet with a small calendar, attached with brads through two holes cast at the bottom. Included on the trivet might be the year, the letters **EFM** (for the Electric Furnace-Man Division of the company), a Pennsylvania Dutch slogan, and often enameled artwork. This company still exists in Emmaus, now known as the E.F.M. Sales Company.

Of mention is a particular cast iron trivet called **Hopewell**. This 8" x 5" trivet was actually a souvenir cast for the Hopewell Furnace National Historical Site, located in Elverson, Pennsylvania. Hopewell Furnace is an excellent example of a rural American nineteenth century foundry plantation, complete with blast furnace and ironmakers' mansion.[2] The Hopewell trivet design originates from an artifact found on the grounds of the original old foundry. It was cast, from the mid to late 1980s until 1995, for Hopewell Furnace NHS by the Unicast Company of Boyertown, Pennsylvania. Some of these trivets have the signature HOPEWELL etched on a small plate on the trivet reverse; others show the signature inscribed. Regardless, they are late twentieth century reproduction trivets. The Delvest Company of West Chester, Pennsylvania, is now providing the trivets that are for sale at the Hopewell Furnace National Historic Site.

8" x 5" Hopewell souvenir trivet (CI).

The Iron Art Company of Phillipsburg, New Jersey, in operation from 1959 to 1989, was a major distributor of cast iron products in the 1950s and 1960s. Besides trivets, **Iron Art** offered ornate bowls, mirrors, sconces, doorknockers, figurines, and match holders. Directly from their 1957 – 58 catalog, *Art Objects in Cast Iron:* "The products themselves are re-creations of valuable antiques, many of which have not been produced for generations; some are original designs, suggested from Colonial or Victorian models. All the wares have been manufactured with the desire to preserve the rich heritage of early American craftsmanship in metal." The accompanying 1957 – 58 price list offered most of their trivet line at $0.50 each, with the exception of a pair of Rooster Trivets at $1.25. It's important to note that Iron Art purchased casting patterns of the entire J.Z.H. Alphabet series from the Union Manufacturing Company, offering these trivets in their 1957 – 58 Iron Art Catalog (the last J.Z.H. Alphabet trivet was cast in 1955). Each of these reissued trivets bears an alphabet letter and the words Iron Art on the reverse.

I would like to thank a local Phillipsburg historian, Ronald W. Wynkoop, Sr., for researching and providing the following information on the Iron Art Company. A synopsis: The Phillipsburg property initially was the site of the Canavan Coal Company from 1928 to 1955. An active railroad spur led up to the building, presumably to transport coal. In 1955 the property was sold to Melvin Friedman and John Zawarski, who together established the Iron Art Company. A finishing and distribution center, located at 1400 3rd Avenue, Phillipsburg, was added in 1956. Apparently, no casting was ever performed at this location; operations included light assembly, dip painting, and drip-drying of ornamental iron objects. The property owner since 1994, Sheridan Printing Company, has since renovated the interior of this distribution center for use as a warehouse. Two other buildings also exist, for a total of three joined buildings made of concrete-block. Recent photographs of the property show a relatively modest plant, considering the scope of production and distribution attributed to the Iron Art Company during their thirty years of operation.

Don't forget that the Union Manufacturing Company, under the signature **JZH**, issued at least 40 other trivet designs in addition to the ones John Harner selected for the Alphabet Series. One of their more interesting trivets was design #16, cast in 1952, and is commonly called "Jesters." It features two animal and six jester faces intertwined to form an optical illusion. JZH also manufactured other cast iron objects, such as candleholders, figurines, and picture frames. JZH castings were made exclusively of cast iron.

Old Sturbridge Village (OSV), a 200-acre colonial reenactment town in Sturbridge, Massachusetts, provides "modern Americans with a deepened understanding of their own times through a personal encounter with the New England past."[3] They commissioned souvenir trivets from Virginia Metalcrafters. The reverse of their Old Sturbridge trivet, shows the OSV grasshopper logo in an oval, which signifies Old Sturbridge Village. VM, the Betty Lamp, and 5-21 identify Virginia Metalcrafters as the manufacturer.

The **Portland Stove Foundry** of Portland, Maine, existed from the late 1800s until they went out of business in 1984. They occasionally cast trivets; two of these trivets, featuring the outlines of the states of Maine and New Hampshire, can be viewed in Antique and Vintage Trivets and Stands.

10½" x 4¼" Old Sturbridge trivet, a 1960s era reproduction designed by Virginia Metalcrafters (CI).

Sexton produced copyrighted aluminum wall plaques and trivets. It's another mid-twentieth century distributor that I have been unable to research successfully. Personally, I like their products, and own quite a few of their items...several trivets, some smaller wall plaques, and a large eagle plaque with a 27" wingspread that oversees my horseshoe plaque trivets wall. Sexton products are marked with SEXTON, USA, the year, and a catalog number on the reverse. The products I have seen all have dates from the 1960s and 1970s. Again, if any reader can provide more information on this company, I would love to hear from you through the publisher.

Vermont Castings was founded in 1975, and at one time was the largest seller of cast iron stoves in the world. They made both wood burning and gas burning models at their former plants in Randolph (foundry) and Bethel (assembly and showroom), Vermont. Additionally, they cast small metal banks in the shape of stoves, and occasionally issued trivets. They released a large, commemorative trivet in 1978 that featured a depiction of their Randolph foundry. In the early 1980s they produced a series of square trivets in the theme of the four seasons. Canadian Fireplace Manufacturers of Mississauga, Ontario, purchased Vermont Castings in 1996. CFM subsequently merged Vermont Castings with another acquisition, the Majestic Company (a fireplace manufacturer), and this new entity continues to produce stoves and fireplaces.

Virginia Metalcrafters was founded in 1890 as the W.S. Loth Stove Company of Waynesboro, Virginia. They manufactured cast iron stoves as well as wood and coal heaters. In the mid-1920s they designed and marketed an electric stove called the Hotpoint. Their company name changed to Virginia Metalcrafters in 1938, and at that time they began to cast some small iron and brass giftware items. After World War II, when brass was once again available, production in trivets and other accessories was resumed and the gift line was expanded.[4]

As well as reproducing popular vintage designs, Virginia Metalcrafters is notable for having produced the largest number of original trivet designs of any modern manufacturer. These unique patterns are identified as such by the copyright signature on the trivet reverse. Those included several interesting cipher or monogram designs, as well as souvenir trivets made for numerous American tourist destinations. Some of the more familiar original copyrighted designs from Virginia Metalcrafters are Confederate Seal, Dogwood Blossom, and Kings Arms. Virginia Metalcrafters has made and continues to make trivets for Historic Charleston, Monticello, Mount Vernon, Mystic Seaport, Historic Newport, Old Salem, the Smithsonian Institution, Old Sturbridge Village, Colonial Williamsburg, and the Winterthur Museum. In the past, Virginia Metalcrafters has produced souvenir trivets for destinations such as Marineland and Silver Springs in Florida, and Natural Bridge and Skyline Drive in Virginia. They also made numerous other commemorative souvenirs, such as their Train series.

Please note that three designs cast by Virginia Metalcrafters are technically licensed products of Colonial Williamsburg, and are copyrighted by the Colonial Williamsburg Foundation. Those three trivet designs are Kings Arms, King George, and the Williamsburg Cypher.

Some Virginia Metalcrafters trivets were offered not only in cast iron, but also in brass and occasionally Silvertone. Just a note: Virginia Metalcrafters used a stock numbering system of a 9 or 10 followed by another number (for example: 9-18 Doodlers Dream or 10-17 Kings Arms). Those numbers had nothing to do with the date of manufacture. Virginia Metalcrafters, of Waynesboro, Virginia, is still actively casting trivets.

Wilton Products, of Mount Joy, Pennsylvania offered a large selection of reproduction trivets from the late 1940s until 1976. Signed Wilton, the product line included full-sized Early American reproductions, such as a cathedral design with 1894 on the face. Very collectible are two limited edition, oversized 12" eagle design trivets. They also reproduced many of their more popular trivet designs in a miniature 5" size. I've illustrated many of these smaller trivets in the User Guide to Trivets and Stands, as they are representational of the more popular designs offered by most of the major trivet manufacturers of the 1950s.

Wilton also manufactured motto trivets and other decorative cast iron products, similar to those offered by Iron Art and John Wright. Many of their more popular cast iron designs were also offered in brass. There is an interesting comment in their post-war 1953 catalog: "NOTE BRASS: As more brass becomes available with government releases other brass items will be introduced. Our brass line is made of hand-polished solid brass and protected with tarnish resistant lacquer."[5] The company, still operating in Mount Joy and known today as Wilton Armetale, produces beautiful hand cast, pewter-like trivets and serving ware.

I've noticed some recent Internet auctions inaccurately presenting Wilton (USA) trivets as being antique English trivets! Supposedly they are from Wilton Forge, an old English foundry that was established over 200 years ago...or from their modern-day successor, Bush & Wilton Valves of Bristol, England. However, from viewing the auction photographs it is obvious that they are 1950s era Wilton Products items, and not British antiques. Buyers beware!

Finally, the **John Wright Company**, a division of the Donsco Corporation, is still active today in Wrightsville, Pennsylvania. In fact, it is the oldest continuously operating manufacturer of cast iron products in the United States.

A three-digit number identified John Wright trivets that were issued from the late 1940s until 1970. In 1970 they expanded to a four-digit number with the addition of the suffix "4" for decorated or "0" for black. Trivets with four-digit numbers beginning in 33 date from 1983. Their more recent trivets also include the inscription John Wright Inc.

The 1974 catalog, *John Wright General Store*, 1910 – 1974, featured their then current line of trivets as well as toys, eagles, hearth items, trivets, candleholders, matchboxes, sconces, and other assorted household objects. Quoted from this catalog: "John Wright reproductions in sturdy iron and durable aluminum are made by an ancient, painstaking art called sand-casting. The same production method our forefathers used to make the originals. And John Wright craftsmen still hand-paint our Americana exactly the way it was done hundreds of years ago."[6]

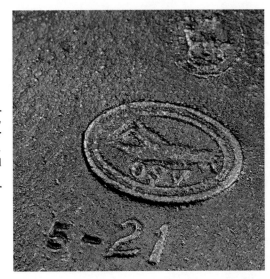

A close-up of the Virginia Metalcrafters logo, showing the design number 5-21; and their trademark, the Betty Lamp with the letters VM. The OSV grasshopper in an oval signifies Old Sturbridge Village.

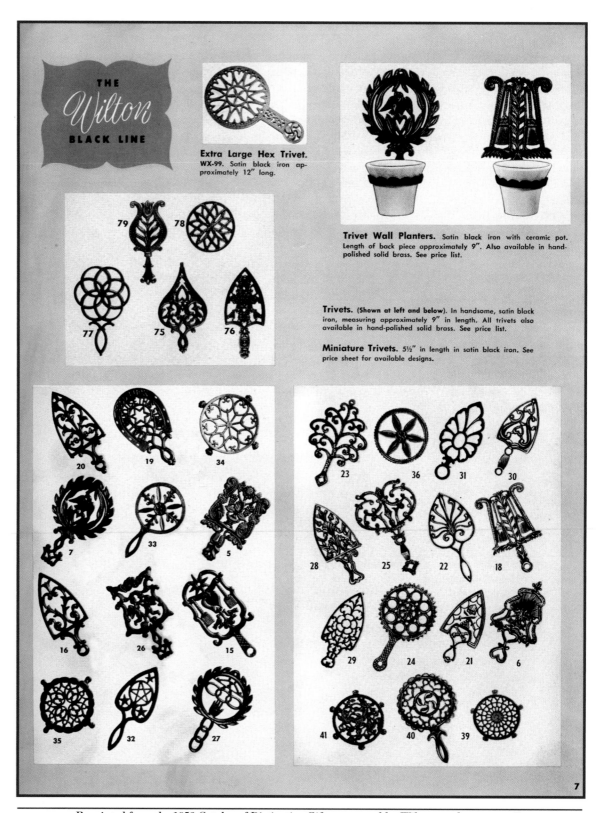

THE *Wilton* BLACK LINE

Extra Large Hex Trivet. WX-99. Satin black iron approximately 12" long.

Trivet Wall Planters. Satin black iron with ceramic pot. Length of back piece approximately 9". Also available in hand-polished solid brass. See price list.

Trivets. (Shown at left and below). In handsome, satin black iron, measuring approximately 9" in length. All trivets also available in hand-polished solid brass. See price list.

Miniature Trivets. 5½" in length in satin black iron. See price sheet for available designs.

79 78 77 75 76

20 19 34 7 33 5 16 26 15 35 32 27

23 36 31 30 28 25 22 18 29 24 21 6 41 40 39

7

Reprinted from the 1953 Catalog of Distinctive Gifts presented by Wilton products, page 7.

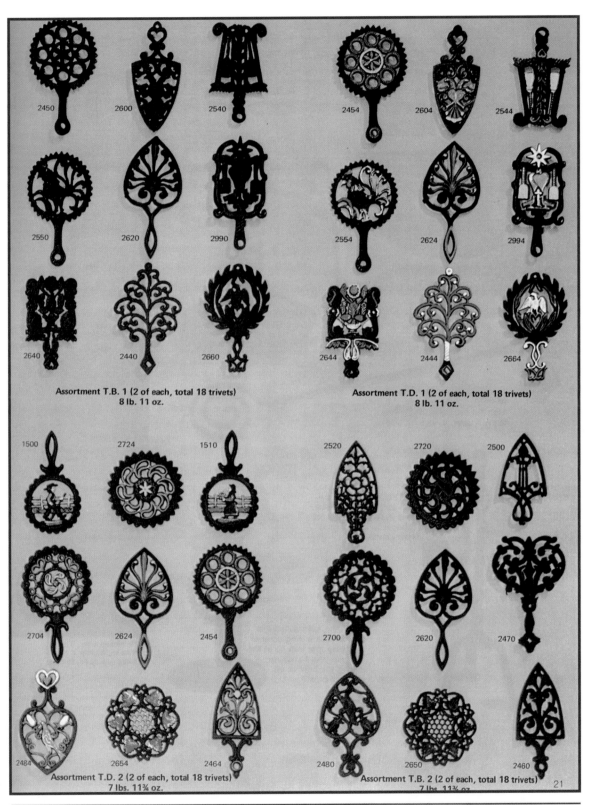

Full-sized trivets, reprinted from page 21 of the 1910 – 1974 John Wright General Store. A line of miniature trivets and several rooster wall plaques were also offered.

John Zimmerman Harner and the JZH Alphabet Series Trivets

John Zimmerman Harner (1872 – 1965) was a former owner and manager of the Union Manufacturing Company of Boyertown, Pennsylvania, which was founded in 1894. This company produced cast iron stoves, sadirons, and other ironware in its early years.

After World War II the Union Manufacturing Company expanded into trivet production. From 1944 to 1958 up to 65 different trivet designs were marketed. In 1966 the company merged and became the Unicast Foundries Division of Berkmont Industries, Inc. The Harner family sold their interest in the Unicast Division in 1981, and it has since been known as the Unicast Company. This foundry, still in Boyertown, continues to actively produce gray iron industrial items such as diesel engine parts, decorative firebacks, and other metal specialty parts.

John Harner's interest in preserving rare trivet designs led him to develop and manufacture a distinctive collection of cast iron trivets, a different design selected for each letter of the alphabet. Every trivet in the series was based on an original antique casting, and was of unsurpassed beauty and quality. Since the complete set of his alphabet trivets is becoming harder to obtain as the years go by, the best time to begin a collection is now. This reference can be utilized to help you readily identify an original alphabet trivet design.

J.Z.H., date, and alphabet letter are the only inscriptions on the back of an original issue JZH Alphabet Series trivet. However, JZH reissued some of their more popular alphabet designs. It's easy to spot these, because on the trivet reverse will be additional information, such as the design name (Sunburst); the design name and number (T-12 Cathedral); and year of re-issue, which might be different from the original manufacture year. For example, the JZH L Alphabet Series trivet was first released in 1948 and is only occasionally found; but you will find numerous reproductions labeled JZH 1955 L Cupid T-11. Compare the two trivets, noticing several differences between the two. The original issue alphabet trivet is much heavier and about ¼" longer. On the 1955 re-issued Cupid trivet, the figurative handle and the cupids face the same direction. However, on the older trivet, the handle is connected to the trivet body near the cupids' feet, and the cupids are oriented opposite to the handle.

I have come across seven re-issued JZH alphabet trivets; there may be more. So far I have found (as they are labeled on the reverse): 1945 C Rings T-36; 1955 L Cupids T-11 (discussed above); 1948 M Lyre T-35; 1948 P Hex T-9; 1955 R Cathedral T-12; 1948 U Sunburst; and 1948 V Sm. Cathedral T-46. Since most reissued designs are nearly identical to the original, it's difficult to identify a reissued alphabet trivet by design alone. You must carefully check the markings on the reverse. Original issue alphabet trivets will ultimately be of more collectible interest and value, so examine any prospective purchases carefully. (Remember also that Iron Art obtained the alphabet patterns from JZH and reissued the entire A – Z series under their company name in 1957 – 1958. Those reissues are clearly labeled Iron Art.)

I have also discovered some other oddities: F issued with and without a handle; H issued with either a solid or an open center; and P issued with either a small or a large open circle at the end of the pan handle. These variations are illustrated in Contemporary Castings.

I suspect that the some of the first trivets in the JZH Alphabet series (1944 – 1945) may have been of limited production. From my own collecting experience, A, B, and F are the most difficult trivets to obtain, and they are all from those early production years. It also would be interesting to discover why H was issued in 1955. There is nothing on the reverse of mine to suggest a reissue, and I have yet to find an H with an earlier date. Of the original twenty-six alphabet trivets, nineteen of them were released in 1948.

Please refer to Contemporary Castings for the entire catalog of the JZH Alphabet Series trivets, and good luck in obtaining a complete set for your own collection!

A picture of my contemporary trivets wall, with my collection of J.Z.H. Alphabet Series trivets in the center, surrounded by other favorite reproduction trivets by various makers.

A close-up of one John Z. Harner's basement trivet displays. In the upper right corner is the JZH casting of the "farmer picking apples," called The Gleaner that Leith Zenowitz mentions. Photograph courtesy of The Kutztown Publishing Company.

In November of 2002, I sold several JZH Alphabet trivets to a very nice woman from Concord, North Carolina, by the name of Jennifer Lanning. I was pleasantly surprised when she happened to mention that John Zimmerman Harner was a distant relative, and that she and her sister were buying JZH trivets for their mother (his great-niece) as a Christmas gift! From her email:

> "My sister (Kristin Zvonar) and I are doing this jointly. Harner was our great uncle. My mother remembers him telling jokes in Dutch, and he was very wealthy. He always gave away trivets as Christmas presents. Mom through the years has given them away and now regrets doing so! Just a bit of history for you…"

Jennifer then put me in touch with her mother, Leith Zenowitz, and I received the following message from her.

> "Hi — My daughters have bought some trivets from you — John Harner was my great uncle. My brother is more of the historian on this, so I'll give him your email address if you say it's okay, and get him to give you more details than I can.
>
> "My Great-Aunt Anna married John when they were in their sixties or so. Every year for Christmas we got either stockings (he manufactured them as well) or a trivet. Family lore has it that the stocking business went out of business because he wouldn't convert to seamless! This time frame was the 1950s. He was the typical Pennsylvania Dutchman you envision… he had many pithy sayings, in both English and Dutch. One interesting piece that my Great-Uncle John gave me was cast iron, and probably 2 or 2½ feet high, of a farmer picking apples from a tree. Another daughter has this now, and I don't remember if it had a back stamp, nor have I ever seen another one like it."

I was then contacted by Thomas G. (Schroeder) Souders of Philadelphia, Pennsylvania, who is Leith Zenowitz's brother and the unofficial family historian. He most generously contributed the following essay on his great-uncle, John Zimmerman Harner.

A 1950s photograph of John Zimmerman Harner, shown in the basement of his Boyertown, Pennsylvania, home at 600 Highland Avenue. There he maintained his personal collection of JZH castings, as well as many other Early American antiques and collectibles. Photograph courtesy of The Kutztown Publishing Company.

John Zimmerman Harner

John Zimmerman Harner, child of Benneville K. Harner and Mary Ann (Zimmerman) Harner, was born on August 4, 1872, in Berks County, Pennsylvania. He lived on a farm, which supported the family, with the best as offering at church and the surplus shared with family and those in need. His childhood was physically hard but spiritually rewarding. The work ethic and honesty of childhood served him well as he became owner of the Union Manufacturing Company (as well as Full Fashion Hosiery) in Boyertown, Pennsylvania.

After John's first wife died, he married my widowed aunt, Anna Roth. We children visited the Harners many times. I have very fond memories of the tours of the working foundry and the "museum" Uncle John had in the basement of his home in Boyertown. He had a prodigious memory and told how things were done on the farm, how the foundry worked, and could recite the minutest details from yesterday or a half century before with ease.

In reading my sister's remembrances about Uncle John's "pithy sayings" my memory was jogged, and I write these for your enjoyment (or groaning as the case may be). The following would have been uttered in his thick (and I mean thick) Pennsylvania Dutch accent.

In a diner: "I'll haf a cup of coffee wissoudt cream, und if you don't haf cream, I'll haf it wissoudt milk." In a restaurant: "I would like to haf the lobster tail, und ask the chef to leaf the pants in the kitchen." To the terrified occupants in the 1949 Nash, after spinning around about three times on an icy hill while going out to eat at Frank Reeser's Restaurant west of Reading, Pennsylvania: "Vel, it's a little bit slippery, issint it?" And, about life on the farm and the use of all products with no waste: "Ven we used the pig, we used efery part except the squeal."

John gave our Aunt Anna, his new wife, an "allowance." As our father had been killed in WW II, she offered to use this money for our college costs. This she did. I don't know how we ever would have been able to get through without her! (My father was Dr. Paul Gerhardt Schroeder, killed in action 5/11/45 aboard the USS *Bunker Hill*, CV-17, an Essex Class Aircraft Carrier. He was a flight surgeon for the 84th Air Group).

In 1954, John and Anna Harner bought a new house in Reiffton, Pennsylvania, as an investment. The real reason for this "investment purchase" was to provide a place for Anna's brother and sister-in-law, who were my grandparents, to live upon their retirement. My maternal grandfather, the Reverend Dr. Charles Edgar Roth, had no pension, working as a pastor through both World Wars and the Depression. It was a blessing supreme, to have a place to live out their years!

I feel privileged to have known these gracious people. The trivets we have are reminders of another way of life, a way of service and love. As an inveterate collector, I always took freely from the "sample" box of trivets Uncle John kept in his house and offered to guests. It has been a joy to redistribute these throughout the family. Truly, we stand on the shoulders of those who have gone before us.

Thomas G. Souders

JOHN ZIMMERMAN HARNER

Portrait of John Zimmerman Harner, from his autobiographical book, *Seedtime to Harvest*, published by The Kutztown Publishing Company, Kutztown, Pennsylvania, 1957.

The Story of the ABA Trivet

In the spring of 2002, I purchased an interesting cast iron, bell shaped trivet on eBay. The seller identified the letters "ABA" on the center front of the trivet as standing for the American Bell Association, but was unable to provide any other information on the origins or age of the trivet. By its size, feel, and design I was pretty confident that it was a product of the mid-twentieth century; but I wanted to know for sure. I asked among my other trivet collecting acquaintances, but none of them had ever had the occasion to view or handle an ABA trivet.

There was not an ABA trivet cataloged in either of Dick Hankenson's Trivet books…and I had no success finding it in Kelly & Ellwood's *Trivets and Stands* or Esther Berney's *A Collector's Guide to Pressing Irons and Trivets*. I was beginning to think that I might never learn the true identity and background of this lovely trivet!

By searching on the Internet, I learned that the A.B.A. is an international organization of bell collectors founded in 1940, whose members currently number 1,700. As defined in the American Bell Association's own online club description, "The American Bell Association International, Inc. is a group of friendly bell collectors of all ages, youth to senior, who enjoy collecting and learning about bells. Bell collectors are intrigued by the appearance, sound, and history of bells. Bell collections vary depending on member interest: brass bells; bronze bells; ceramic bells; glass bells; crystal bells; porcelain bells; wood bells; sterling and plated bells; cow bells; collectible bells; mechanical bells; tap bells; door bells; ornamental bells; religious bells; school bells; farm bells; railroad bells; sleigh bells; souvenir bells; figural bells; figurine bells; all types of bells."[7]

I contacted the Internet representative of the American Bell Association, Bob Bamford, hoping that he would be familiar with this particular trivet. Although he had no personal knowledge of their society having ever produced such a commemorative item, he began to inquire among the membership. His questioning led to a wonderful woman from Massachusetts by the name of Rita Walker, who indeed knew the history of the mysterious ABA trivet. I'll let the story reveal itself through our actual email correspondences.

From: Lynn Rosack on Friday, 6/28/2002
To: Bob Bamford, Internet Coordinator, A.B.A.

Hello! I recently purchased a trivet, which I believe is a piece of American Bell Association memorabilia. It is painted cast iron, flat in the shape of a bell, three legs, with the letters ABA on the front. The dimensions are 9¼" x 5½". Would you happen to know how old it might be? I thought perhaps it was a souvenir from one of your conventions.

I am in the process of completing a book on trivets, and wanted to include a photo of this trivet along with some information about it. Thank you for any insight you can provide on this item!

Sincerely, Lynn Rosack

From: Bob Bamford on Wednesday, 7/10/2002
To: Lynn Rosack

Lynn… Thanks for writing to ABA. I apologize for the delay in responding as I was attending our annual convention in Cincinnati. I am not aware of a trivet with the ABA letters, but I have written to a few of the older (membership-wise) members who may have the historical background to answer your question. I'll let you know what I learn, and will keep you advised if the time slips by. At each convention are many sales "booths" containing several hundred bells and bell related objects. And we have an auction of about 350 items (bells and more) each year. I've been to several conventions and have not seen a trivet among either group…yet. Is it solid or does it have cutouts as most trivets do? How are the letters "ABA" placed (center, diagonally, etc.)? Do you have a means for getting a picture online of this trivet? That might help, but in the meantime, I'm making inquires. Thanks again. I will be in touch.

Bob Bamford, Internet Coordinator, ABA

From: Lynn Rosack on Wednesday, 7/10/02
To: Bob Bamford

Dear Bob, Thanks for taking the time to research this for me! I have attached a picture with this email. The trivet is cast iron, and lightly accent painted in shades of gold (outlining the bell shape and the letters) and green (the inner filigreed work). When I first purchased it on eBay, it was identified as a trivet of your organization, although the seller did not have firsthand knowledge of that fact. Please let me know if you find out anything more.

Thanks again! Regards, Lynn

From: Bob Bamford on Monday, 7/15/02
To: Lynn Rosack

Lynn… Well, of the 1,500 or so members of ABA, I have happened to ask the only lady who had the true story of the trivet you have. What luck! I will not attempt to paraphrase her, but rather will let you read her wonderful story for yourself. She is Rita Walker of Peabody, Massachusetts (copy of email attached).

To: Bob Bamford
From: Rita Walker on Sunday, 7/14/02

Dear Bob, I have just returned from church, so I'm in a humble frame of mind. However, when I read your email, I burst out with pride. As a matter of fact my heart is still pounding from it! Do I know anything about that "ABA" trivet?? You can just bet I do! It was a Walker family project in 1966 (some 36 years ago). We had three children, ages 19, 17, and 9 at the time. We were all planning to attend the 1967 Chicago ABA Convention, and were about to purchase a travel trailer to accommodate us on the trip there. The trailer was going to cost us quite a bit, and the trip from the East Coast would be expensive for the five of us also. In addition, we knew we'd be attending the 1969 ABA Convention coming up in Pasadena, California, so we worked things out on paper and found that we could save money by eating and sleeping in our own accommodations.

Having the entrepreneurial spirit, we thought about creating something that we could sell at Convention. I always wanted a bell-shaped trivet, but I could never find one. (I hadn't even seen one). Soooo, what to do? I spoke with Ralph, my husband, and he said he'd be willing to design one, whittle it in wood to make a pattern that could then be made into a mold for casting in the foundry of the company where he worked (the company's name was United Shoe Machinery Corporation, the largest maker of shoe machinery in the world, and it was located in Beverly, Massachusetts, where we lived). By the way, I just recently presented that original mounted wood pattern to "The Belfry" Bell Museum on Nantucket Island here in Massachusetts. It's a one-of-a-kind, of course. They were thrilled to have it. I also gave them the ABA's Town Crier's costume that I had made for Ralph and which he wore for 17 years. (The ABA "Town Crier" is an individual in costume, selected to ring in the meetings and dignitaries at Conventions, using the old hand bell as in Colonial days.) They located a full-size mannequin, named him Ralph,

The American Bell Association trivet, 9¼" x 5½" in enameled cast iron as created by Ralph Walker and his family in 1966 (CI).

and dressed him up in the costume from head to toe. He stands at the door of the museum to greet all who enter, with bell in hand, I might add.

Well, back to the casting of the trivets. There were 154 of them made, and we sold them at that time for $3.50 each. We didn't make a lot of money, but it did help us to realize our dream. You will remember that I spoke of it as a "family project," and that it truly was. Following the casting, there was much burring (grinding the roughly cast edges) to be done on each piece. It was a time-consuming job because of the open scroll pattern. We all pitched in at doing this. Then Ralph dipped them in black wrought iron paint. Following this the majority of them were hand decorated with enamels. Finally, Ralph etched his signature on the back of each one. Well, needless to say, they are all in the hands of collectors now.

Well, Bob, I think I've covered all the bases, but if I've forgotten something please feel free to get back to me. I'm VERY nostalgic when it comes to things our family did together. Ralph died in 1998 while mowing our lawn. I found him there on the ground when I went to call him in for lunch. The memory of this wonderful man, along with the love I had for him for over 55 years, continue to remain in my heart. I'm so happy his craftsmanship is still admired and appreciated.

Bellfully, Rita Walker

Ralph Walker, resplendent in his Town Crier's costume. According to his wife Rita Walker, the bell he is holding was made especially for him by the Whitechapel Bell Foundry, England. It is composed of "bell metal," which is 90% copper and 10% tin.

Detail of the trivet handle reverse, showing Mr. Walker's etched signature. I recently noticed that a second ABA trivet of mine also has the initials "REW" inscribed on center of the trivet body reverse.

Identifying Vintage and Antique Trivets

I n the 1930s the U.S. Customs Office declared that an antique is any item greater than 100 years old. In this book, trivets and stands are categorized as *antique* if they *predate this publication by 100 years or more*. I label items *vintage* if they were *manufactured before 1940, but are less than 100 years old.*

It's important to learn to distinguish antique and vintage pieces from contemporary reproductions. Take advantage of every opportunity to examine an unfamiliar trivet, even though you may have no intention of purchasing it. As you gain knowledge and experience, you'll develop an appreciation and "feel" for the older metal. Here are some basic clues to age in cast trivets:

- The antique versions of trivet designs are usually larger than their vintage or contemporary reproduction counterparts. An original used as a pattern will produce a smaller trivet, as molten metal contracts as it hardens.
- When viewed from the side, you might notice a slight central bowing of the trivet body.
- Most antique pieces have legs of least 1¼" in length, as these were working trivets, meant to dissipate heat. The surface and legs may appear smooth and worn. Also, legs, especially brass, may bow inward or outward.
- The iron in an older trivet will appear darker, and the casting may be finer and lighter.
- Old cast iron may show a brownish rustiness. Beware of bright orange rust, as it usually signifies a more recently manufactured item.
- If the item is brass, green or greenish-blue verdigris will have developed over time, especially noticeable on the reverse and within the crevasses of the pattern.
- According to Kelly and Ellwood in their book *Trivets & Stands*, a trivet with a round **sprue-mark** or a rectangular **wedge-mark** (cast-marks) on the trivet reverse, at the point where the molten iron entered the mold, probably predates 1865. "Most sprue-marks are about ⁵⁄₁₆" to ½" in diameter" and "a wedge-mark is about ⅛" in width; the length varies from three-quarters to 1" or more in length."[8]
- A cast iron piece with a prominent or rough rectangular **gate-mark** likely predates 1900. If filed down, irregularly hand filed marks designate an older piece than those with regular, machine-grinding marks. Because of the softer metal, brass trivets rarely show evidence of the presence or removal of their casting marks.
- There may be **fins/finning**: small, rough cast iron projections, caused by the shifting of the pattern during sand casting
- Also, many trivets and stands have **backcoping**: areas where the metal is routed out on the reverse, in order to equalize the thickness of the casting, or to reduce the weight.
- If marked at all, the letters/numbers on antique trivets are most likely embossed or on plates. Recessed letters/numbers on the reverse are more typical of contemporary or vintage trivets. Examine the appearance of the signature, as most contemporary trivets will feature a more modern looking Condensed Gothic typeface.

Special trivets were manufactured for use on the hot stovetop. Their purpose was to modify the degree of heat transmitted to the pan in which a food item was being cooked. A **cereal trivet** rested on its rim close to the hot cook top surface, and prevented a pot of simmering food from scorching and burning. For access to the higher heat within the stove, a stove lid within the cook top could be removed and a **stove trivet** swung around and over the opening. Of most interest to collectors are those trivets with advertising lettering or logos, interesting shapes or designs, or those that are dated and/or signed. Most of these trivets were round in shape, but you will occasionally see those that were cast in oval, square, or rectangular designs.

Kitchen trivets were substantial in size and weight, and served various purposes: pot rest, stovetop trivet, or sadiron stand. Some featured intricate designs, often Pennsylvania Dutch in origin. Others patterns were simpler or more utilitarian in appearance. Most kitchen trivets were around 12" long, with legs of 1" or more.

Round trivets with three to six legs were used under coffee or teapots, or to support warm dishes on a table, and were referred to as **coffee, tea, or table stands**. Made of brass as well as cast iron, they were more delicate in structure and appearance. They commonly featured elaborate openwork designing. Some, known as Lantz trivets, always had paw feet. These dainty trivets were never intended to support heavy sadirons or large pots from the stove.

Sadiron stands were of sturdy construction, meant for use on ironing day to hold heavy, hot irons. Some mirrored the shape of an iron, while others were square, round, or oval. Sadiron stands were manufactured both with and without handles. They often featured commercial advertising designs and were sometimes sold in a set with companion sadirons. Most were made of cast iron, with an occasional brass or bronze stand to be found. Nickel plating was popular, but few of those stands exist now in their original fully plated condition.

Decorative trivets came in many shapes and sizes. If of the appropriate strength and dimensions, they also served utilitarian duty in the kitchen. Commemorative, Fraternal, horseshoe/good luck, motto, novelty, and souvenir trivets all fall within this category.

Handcrafted trivets made by cutting and piercing metal plates, or by individually hand casting the platforms and attaching legs, are desirable antiques. Most pre-date 1850, and were made of solid metals such as brass or bronze. If the finish was copper, it was usually copper plating, as only rarely was solid copper used. As I only have a few of these handcrafted trivets in my collection, it would be worthwhile for the reader to review a more comprehensive presentation of this subject, as in Kelly and Ellwood's book *Trivets & Stands*.

Hand forged trivets, blacksmith wrought, pre-date the mid to late 1800s as by then foundries predominated. Only the imagination and talent of the blacksmith limited their design! As most were used in or around the hearth, they tended to be bigger, stronger, and have three longer legs. These trivets are quite valuable, most already belonging to private collectors or in museums. Be skeptical of inexpensive wrought iron artifacts, as there are many reproductions. It's best to purchase an antique hand forged trivet from a reputable dealer or from the estate of a collector, who may have kept a recorded history of the item.

Round lattice coffee or tea stand from the late 1800s (CI).

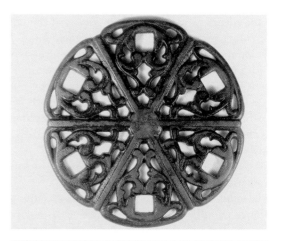

W&P Manufacturing Co. simmering cover cereal trivet with six openings for a stove-lid lifter (CI).

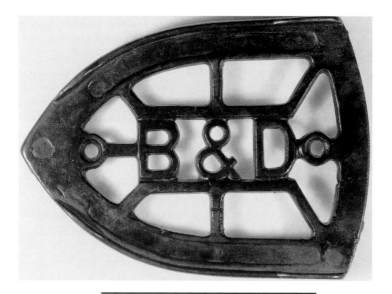

B & D (Bless & Drake) sadiron stand (CI).

"God Bless Our Home 1887" decorative horseshoe plaque trivet (CI).

Centrally located round **sprue-mark** on the trivet reverse.

Note: Remember that these two are the oldest types of cast markings, typically predating 1865.

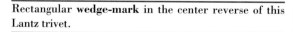

Rectangular **wedge-mark** in the center reverse of this Lantz trivet.

23

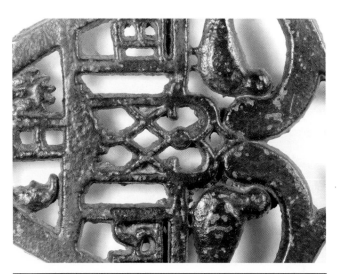

Notice this rough casting, with **finning** (rough, cast iron projections) evident.

Two unfiled rectangular **gate-marks** along the edge of this sadiron stand.

Example of extensive **backcoping** on a cathedral-designed trivet reverse.

Jenny Lind Trivets

Jenny Lind was born Johanna Maria Lind in Stockholm, Sweden, in 1820. Because her parents were unable to properly provide for her, she remained in the care of relatives for most of her early childhood. Her life story was somewhat Cinderella-like. At the age of nine, she was "discovered" while singing in her neighborhood, and was sent on to the Royal Theatre School in Stockholm for formal music training. By the age of sixteen, she was performing both popular and operatic compositions professionally. Her voice was unique in both its range and volume.

She became wildly popular in Sweden, and then throughout Europe. The famous entrepreneur P.T. Barnum persuaded her to come to America for a grand concert tour, and from 1850 to 1852 America fell under her spell. The country was gripped with what they then called "Lindomania" or "Jenny Rage," not in small part to Barnum's shrewd publicity tactics. He arranged to have over 30,000 people jamming New York Harbor as her ship arrived from Europe. In fact, P.T. Barnum organized The Great Jenny Lind Opening Concert Ticket Auction in New York City, and the very first ticket to see Jenny Lind in concert auctioned for $225, which was an enormous amount of money in those days! It was standing room only to see her wherever she performed.[9]

Jenny Lind married her German piano accompanist, Otto Goldschmidt, in Boston in 1852. They subsequently returned to England, where she entered into semi-retirement, serving as an instructor of music at the Royal College of Music and giving occasional performances for charitable causes. She died in 1887.

Her influence and legacy in America was enormous. A locomotive, The Jenny Lind, was named for her. Everything from baby cribs to children, sandwiches, sofas, perfume bottles, towns, theatres, schools, and yes, even trivets, was christened in her honor. Truly, Jenny Lind was an unforgettable inspiration throughout America for many years.

Trivets were a popular souvenir of her American tour. They date from the 1850s to 1890s. I am lucky enough to have four different versions of the Jenny Lind trivet. The first I refer to as the Jenny Lind portrait. This gorgeous cast iron trivet shows her face fashioned in bas-relief. Although the square trivet itself remains the same, it is found cast with at least three different handles, which can be viewed on p.121 of Kelly and Ellwood's *Trivets & Stands*.

The second is referred to as the Rocaille Spade Jenny Lind. This trivet has an unusual thumb hold handle, and is cast in brass. It features the traditional Jenny Lind presentation as the Greek Muse of music, Euterpe.

The third is what most collectors think of when they picture a Jenny Lind trivet. It also features the goddess Euterpe playing the harp, but with a more traditional handle that is found in several versions (Kelly and Ellwood's *Trivets & Stands*, p.114). I have only seen this style cast in iron and bronze, but would suspect that it might also have been available in brass.

The fourth trivet I have is the 1945 J.Z.H. E Alphabet Series trivet, which is representative of most Jenny Lind reproduction trivets, and of very nice quality. (Please refer back to the beginning of this chapter if you have any questions about differentiating antique from reproduction.)

So, now you know the complete story of Jenny Lind and the souvenir trivets made in her honor!

Rocaille Spade Jenny Lind trivet with an unusual handle, 7¼" x 4½" (BR).

The front of an authentic April 7, 1851, Jenny Lind concert ticket is signed P.T. Barnum.

M'lle JENNY LIND'S
FIRST GRAND
CONCERT
MONDAY,
APRIL 7th, 1851.
MOZART HALL.
No. 29
TAKE NOTICE.
This Ticket must be retained to secure possession of the seat bearing a corresponding number, which will be shown by the Ushers in attendance.
P.T. Barnum

The back identifies Louisville, Kentucky, as the concert site, and also bears the signature of the fortunate ticket holder. Photos courtesy of D.E. Peterson of Decatur, Illinois.

Jenny Lind portrait trivet, 4¾" square with 2⅝" handle (CI).

Antique print from a signed steel plate engraving of Jenny Lind, circa 1861. "Likeness from an original painting," Johnson Fry & Co. Publishers, New York.

Traditionally designed Jenny Lind trivet, 9¾" x 4½" (CI).

Horseshoe Plaque Trivets

Horseshoe plaque trivets were most prevalent from the late 1800s through the early 1900s. The one thing they all have in common is their basic horseshoe shape. The majority of them also feature a spread eagle at the top of the trivet. Beyond that, designs vary according to the theme. Some were carnival prizes, and still bear traces of glitter. Others were lodge favors, commemoratives, or were created and purchased as gifts. The backs are flat. Some collectors claim that, when turned face down, a plaque trivet could have served the dual purpose of a sadiron stand...but whether that was ever true is conjecture now!

I was fortunate enough to purchase a gilded IOOF horseshoe plaque trivet that came in the original box. Considering their inventory as listed below, this company's Beautiful Emblematic Ornaments would have been available during the late 1880s through the early 1890s. The following information was featured on the box top.

T. Jones & Sons,
Sole Manufacturers of Beautiful Emblematic Ornaments,
Are Manufactured in the Following Styles:

Benjamin Harrison	American Legion of Honor
Grover Cleveland	Ancient Order of Hibernians
Masonic	Good Luck
Independent Order of Odd Fellows	Chosen Friends
Knights of Honor	United Friends
Knights of Labor	Happy New Year
Knights of Pythias	Ind. Order Good Templers
Knights and Ladies of Honor	Brotherhood Rail Road Brakemen
Knights of Golden Eagle	Brotherhood of Locomotive Engineers
Patriotic Order Sons of America	Brotherhood of Locomotive Firemen
Grand United Order of Odd Fellows	Improved Order Red Men
Sons of Saint George	Order of Rail Road Conductors
Home Sweet Home	Junior Order United Am. Mechanics
Knights of the Macabees	Order United American Mechanics
Knights of the Mystic Chain	Catholic Mutual Benefit Association
Grand Army Republic	Cigar Makers I. U. of America
Sons of Veterans	Merry Christmas
Ancient Order of Workmen	Birthday Greeting
Ancient Order of Foresters	Switchmen's Mutual Aid Association
Royal Arcanum	

Orders By Mail Promptly Attended To.
Factory: Osborn Street, Near Blake Ave., Brooklyn, N.Y.
Office And Salesrooms, 5 And 7 Murray St., New York
AGENTS WANTED

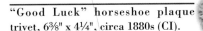

"Good Luck" horseshoe plaque trivet, 6⅜" x 4¼", circa 1880s (CI).

Examine your potential purchase carefully. It is not uncommon, especially in the more ornate horseshoe trivets, for sections to be damaged. The larger easel trivets featuring crossed branches are often found broken, with either the top or bottom branches missing beyond the horseshoe. The eagle may be missing from the top, the stump filed to resemble a filed gate mark. Also, former owners sometimes drilled mounting holes, which could possibly devalue the trivet. Finally, avoid the temptation to refinish plaque trivets...the traces of the old paint and glitter, although uneven, add charm and evidence of age to these unique relics.

Be aware that horseshoe plaque trivets were cast through the lower ends of the horseshoe. In a poor casting, the molten iron might not completely fill the mold, making the wing tips or beak of the eagle at the opposite end appear unevenly cast.[10] Also, some of these trivets appear to be brass because of the gilded paint applied. Be sure to check with a magnet before purchasing if the metallic composition is important to you.

Most plaque trivets incorporated the American Eagle within their design. Note which direction the head faces in eagles who are depicted holding arrows and olive branches in their talons. If the head faces towards the olive branches, it was a peace trivet. If facing towards the arrows, it was a war trivet.

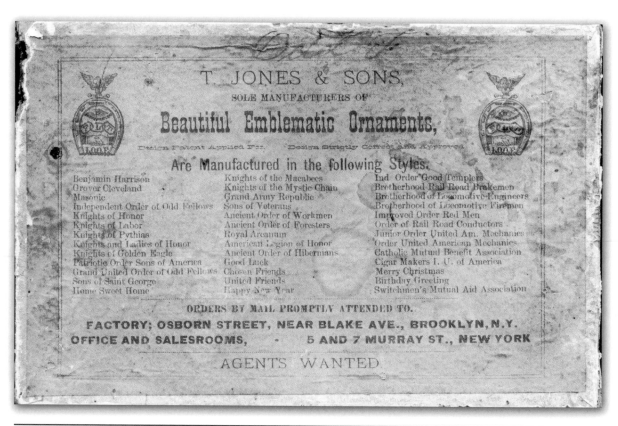

T. Jones & Sons, Beautiful Emblematic Ornaments. This is the 7" x 4½" box that held the IOOF horseshoe trivet discussed in the text. Always remember that original packaging adds to the value of any antique or collectible. Often, the packaging alone might be worth as much as or more than what is inside!

Frequently Encountered Fraternal Designs

AOH (Ancient Order of Hibernians)

The AOH was an Irish-Catholic political and fraternal society that was established in 1836. It was a militant organization in its early days, during a time when there was much anti-Catholic and anti-immigration sentiment in the eastern United States. In the late 1870s the AOH evolved into a more peaceful society, offering insurance to its members and supporting Catholic organizations and charities, both in America and overseas. In 1994 there were 191,000 members.[11] In *Trivets Book 1*, p.4, #9, Dick Hankenson shows an AOH horseshoe plaque trivet featuring the following lodge symbols: the harp, shamrocks, and the fraternal handshake. Other AOH trivets may also feature three linked rings.

AO of F (Ancient Order of Foresters)

This "Society...was established in 1834 as a means for members to band together to help one another in times of hardship, sickness and bereavement as they made their way through the Forest of Life."[12] First established in England, AO of F was brought to America in 1864. Here it remained known as the Ancient Order of Foresters until 1874, when they separated from the English lodge and changed their title to the Independent Order of Foresters. Today, one American offshoot of the Ancient Order remains, with limited membership: the Ancient Order of Foresters of the Pacific Jurisdiction, based in Hilo, Hawaii.[13] The AOF plaque trivets I have seen feature a deer running through the forest.

AOF of A (Ancient Order of Foresters of America)

A now extinct offshoot of the AO of F, it was founded in 1889. I have seen only one of these plaque trivets; in addition to the symbols above were the letters UB&C, which stood for unity, benevolence, and concord.

AOUW (Ancient Order of United Workmen)

This society existed from 1868 until 1952. It was the first of all the fraternal societies to offer and sell life insurance to its members. Also, in 1886, AOUW was instrumental in establishing the National Fraternal Congress of America, an umbrella organization for 97 member fraternal societies.[14] The symbols of this organization are Masonic in inspiration, featuring the anchor, the all-seeing eye, the Holy Bible, and the square and compass. Their motto was charity, hope, and protection.

CTAU of A (Catholic Total Abstinence Union of America)

Alcoholism was a pervasive problem in the United States during the 1800s, resulting in many premature deaths from accident and disease. This organization, established in 1872, was a Catholic temperance society, whose aim was to dissuade people from drinking alcohol by moral persuasion, rather than by legislation. It remained active until the U.S. Congress enacted Prohibition in 1919.[15] Their symbols were the harp and the cross.

F&AM (Free and Accepted Masons)

Freemasonry is the oldest of all the secret societies, having first been established in Europe in the fourteenth century. The original free masons were the nomadic tradesmen who built the medieval cathedrals, palaces, and bridges. They established lodges which served as both accommodation and meeting place. The Masonic organizations evolved through the years, and were present in America from its very beginning as a nation.[16] Familiar Masonic symbols are the all-seeing eye who the sun, moon, and stars obey; the 24" gauge and common gavel; the three steps, representing the three stages of life; Jacob's Ladder to Heaven, with the letters CHF for charity, hope, and faith; the square and compass, resting on an open Bible; and the letter G for God or for geometry.

GAR (Grand Army of the Republic)

The GAR was founded in 1866 as an organization to promote fellowship, community service, and political activism in honorably discharged Civil War veterans. Their most important annual meeting was the GAR National Encampment, which was held yearly until 1949. During these encampments both formal and informal gatherings were organized, and attendees at meetings would establish the current GAR endorsement position on political issues of the day. By 1890 the GAR had become a formidable organization, with more than 400,000 members. The GAR was instrumental in establishing May 30 as Memorial Day. The last surviving GAR member, a 109-year-old Civil War veteran, died in 1956.[17] The GAR symbols were the eagle, the American flag, and the five-point star.

IOH (Improved Order of Heptasophs)

The word Heptasoph is Latin, meaning Seven Wise Men. Organized in 1878, this society was primarily organized to provide life insurance benefits for its members, and was not as involved in fraternal activities as were other societies of the day. It merged with the Fraternal Aid Union in 1917, becoming a traditional life insurance company.[18] Its symbols were the quill, key, and laurel bough. I have seen a horseshoe plaque trivet inscribed IOH that also featured a cross.

IORM (Improved Order of Red Men)

This organization, established in 1765 and originally called the Sons of Liberty, was renamed The Order of Red Men after the Revolutionary War. The Improved Order of Red Men was established in 1834 in Baltimore. Basing their principles on the customs and terminology of the American Indians, members of the IORM promote democracy, patriotism, charitable giving, and fraternal brotherhood. The IORM has always been a non-profit patriotic fraternity and was chartered by Congress. Chapters are still active today, with over 38,000 members as of 1995. Illustrious members have included George Washington, Paul Revere, Theodore Roosevelt, Franklin D. Roosevelt, and Richard Nixon.[19] Some of their plaque trivets have the acronym TOTE, which stands for Totem of the Eagle. Their symbols revolve around the American Indian and his customs.

IOOF (Independent Order of Odd Fellows)

This organization began in England, and was brought to America by Thomas Wildey, who founded the first chapter in Boston in 1819. The original Commands of the IOOF were to visit the sick, relieve the distressed, bury the dead, and educate the orphan. They are a fraternity of men and women (women have been admitted since 1851, and are known as Rebekas) united in friendship, love, and truth (FLT). Their numbers peaked at 3½ million by 1915, declining sharply after the Depression. Lodges are still active today, with approximately a half million remaining members.[20] The most common IOOF symbols are the heart in hand and the three linked rings of FLT.

I display this beautiful wooden IOOF wall plaque along with my fraternal horseshoe plaque trivets. The Flemish Art Company of New York produced it during the Victorian era (turn of the century). Pyrography, or burnt wood art, was introduced to the public through articles in the ladies' magazines of the 1890s. It soon became a popular hobby for both men and women as handy, benzene-fueled pyrographic tools became widely available.

JOUAM (Junior Order United American Mechanics)

This fraternal and political organization was established in 1853, another of the anti-Catholic, anti-immigration secret societies. They began offering insurance to their members in 1899. Its membership never reached the proportions of other late nineteenth century fraternal organizations, reaching 200,000 at its peak in 1900. It has been in decline since then, although chapters still exist.[21] The symbols of the JOUAM include a Masonic-like Square and compass, as well as an arm holding a hammer. The word "Mechanics" refers to tradesmen or artisans.

Reverse: Close-up of the JUOAM trivet.

JOUAM trivet with original mounting loops and hanging wire.

K of P (Knights of Pythias)

In 1864 the Knights of Pythias was formed as a fraternal and service organization, not offering insurance benefits to the members until 1887. It peaked in 1923 with a membership of 908,000; however, by 1994 they were down to 80,000 members.[22] Its name was inspired by the Greek legend of Damon and Pythias: Condemned to death, Pythias was granted time from prison to arrange his mortal affairs. His friend Damon took his place, pledging his life if he did not return. When Pythias did return, as promised, both were pardoned and released. The K of P symbols include the knight in armor and shield, the open Bible, the book of law, and the American flag. Their credo is FCB, which means friendship, charity, and benevolence.

LOOM (The Loyal Order of Moose)

This "social and drinking club" was founded in 1888. Its early years were problematic, with membership declining to 246 in 1906, at which time it was successfully reorganized. Changing its name to International Moose in 1991, it boasted a four-nation membership of 1,810,000 by 1994.[23] Its symbols are the moose and the cross Pattee (a cross, similar in shape to a Maltese cross).

POS of A (Patriotic Order, Sons of America)

Irish Catholic immigration into the United States was heavy during the 1840s, with much public prejudice against this particular group. The POS of A was an anti-Catholic, anti-Irish, and anti-immigration organization that was founded in Philadelphia, Pennsylvania, around 1847 by descendents of veterans of the American Revolution. It was originally known as the Patriotic Order, United Sons of America. The group disbanded during the Civil War and reorganized in 1868, dropping "United" and becoming simply POS of A. Their main focus, upon reorganization, was the promotion of patriotism in the community and fellowship among members, although they remained anti-Catholic and anti-foreigner. The POS of A still exists, although their membership numbers are greatly diminished.[24] Their code was God, country, and order; and their symbols included a five-point star, the bust of George Washington, and a shield.

WOW (Woodmen of the World)

Due to a schism in the Modern Woodmen of America (founded in 1883) several different fraternal insurance societies resulted in 1890, two of which were Woodmen of the World and the Woodmen of the World Life Insurance Society. Both have continued to prosper through the years by absorbing smaller fraternal societies into their membership.[25] Their symbols are Masonic in flavor, and include a tree stump, a mallet, a wedge, and an Axe. I recently purchased an old easel plaque trivet that came with a 1975 newspaper article from the *Akron Beacon Journal* (Akron, Ohio). The article pictured the trivet, identified as a WOW artifact and featuring a bunch of grapes complete with leaves.

I would highly recommend the book *The International Encyclopedia of Secret Societies & Fraternal Orders* by Alan Axelrod. It is an excellent A – Z reference for anyone wishing to learn more about the origins and practices of fraternal organizations.

There are numerous Internet sites also providing complete information on fraternal societies. All you have to do is enter a search engine, such as Google, and type in the name of the organization you are researching.

If you don't know what the initials on your trivet stand for, go to Rich Hartzog's website, AAA Historical Americana — World Exonumia. His complete Internet address is in the section on Websites of Interest to Collectors, found later in this book. Rich lists literally hundreds of abbreviations for secret societies, fraternal organizations, and fraternal orders, including their slogans and mottoes when known. (In case you are unfamiliar with the term, exonumia refers to collectible items other than coins or paper money, such as medals or tokens.)

Another helpful site, Tri-County Genealogy and History is maintained by Joyce M. Tice. She has created a pictorial catalog of commemorative flagholders and plaques, many of which bear the emblems of fraternal organizations. In fact, I was finally able to identify several of my plaque trivets by similar markings seen on grave markers in her photographs! Her complete Internet address is also included in the section on Websites of Interest to Collectors.

FRIENDSHIP, LOVE AND TRUTH

An IOOF portrait, copyright 1919 by the Celebrity Art Company of Boston, Massachusetts.

Beware of broken trivets! The bottom branches are broken off below the dog.

The eagle is missing from the top of this trivet and the stump has been filed.

The British Registered Design (Rd) System

England's Registered Design system was a combination of both copyright and patent. Once registered, a design was protected from being reproduced by another manufacturer. There were two systems. The earliest, dating from 1842, was the British Rd Diamond System, comprised of a 1st and 2nd Series. This was replaced in 1884 by the British Rd Numbering System.

The earliest registration numbers (1842 – 1883) were inscribed within a diamond (also referred to as lozenge) shape on the trivet reverse. In the center of the diamond was the abbreviation Rd. In each of the four corners of the diamond were either numbers or letters signifying the day, month, year, and production bundle. Within a circle at the top was a Roman numeral identifying the class of material used in making the object. There were 13 different category classes, the most important one for us to remember being Class I, the ornamental metals category, which included trivets and stands.

It's important to understand the two different series of Rd diamond markings. In order to properly date your trivet using this system, you have to know where to find the mark signifying the year of issue. The older marking, 1st Series, included the years 1842 to 1867. In a 1st Series diamond marking, the letter indicating the year appeared in the top corner of the diamond. A 2nd Series diamond marking included the years 1868 to 1883; in this category the letter indicating the year appeared in the right corner of the diamond. I have provided diagrams of the 1st and 2nd Series Rd Diamonds so that you can interpret the numbers and letters on your own trivets and stands.

Beginning with 1884, the diamond mark system was eliminated and replaced by a system featuring an assigned sequence of numbers preceded by Rd or Rd No. (number). I have provided a chart that lists the first assigned registered number for each year from 1884 to 1931. (The numbers do continue beyond 1931, although I have not provided them.)

I personally like collecting registered British trivets; once I understood the system, it allowed me to easily and accurately date my trivets. I know this is can all seem quite complicated, especially at first. So, to simplify things, remember the following basic points:

- If the trivet has an Rd diamond or an Rd number, it was a product of The British Isles, comprised of England, Ireland, Scotland, Wales, the Channel Islands, and the Isle of Man.

- A trivet with an Rd diamond is always older than one with an Rd number.

- There will always be a letter that appears in either in the top corner or right corner of an Rd diamond, and that will determine the year. If the letter is in the top corner the trivet is older (1st Series) than if the letter is in the right corner (2nd Series).

- In trivets with an Rd number, sometimes the "d" in Rd can look like a 2, especially on a worn trivet. Use a magnifying glass, if necessary, to determine the correct registration number on your trivet or stand before proceeding to the charts.

Falkirk (Scotland) No. 5 trivet with Rd diamond. Within the top circle is the numeral I, indicating metal. The letter T, being at the top of the diamond, signifies 1st Series and thus 1867. In the left corner is A and the right corner is 29, making the casting day January 29. In the bottom corner is the batch number 4.

A = Materials

I = Metal
This is the Roman numeral found on metal objects. The numerals II through XIV identify materials such as wood, glass, ceramics, or textiles.

B = Year
Again, note the importance of the year/letter placement within the diamond. An Rd diamond with the letter in the top corner indicates an older trivet (1st Series) than if the letter is in the right corner (2nd Series). Single dates below refer to 1st Series. When there are two dates attributed to a single letter, the older is 1st Series and the other is 2nd Series.

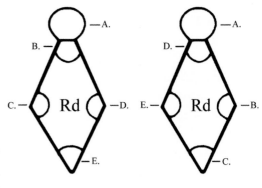

Left: 1st Series Rd Markings used 1842 to 1867.
Right: 2nd Series Rd Markings used 1868 to 1883.

A = 1845 & 1871	H = 1843 & 1869	O = 1862	V = 1850 & 1876
B = 1858	I = 1846 & 1872	P = 1851 & 1877	W = 1865
C = 1844 & 1870	J = 1854 & 1880	Q = 1866	X = 1842 & 1868
D = 1852 & 1878	K = 1857 & 1883	R = 1861	Y = 1853 & 1879
E = 1855 & 1881	L = 1856 & 1882	S = 1849 & 1875	Z = 1860
F = 1847 & 1873	M = 1859	T = 1867	
G = 1863	N = 1864	U = 1848 & 1874	

C = Month
Letter in the left corner (1st Series) or bottom corner (2nd Series) indicates the month.

A = December	B = October	C = January	D = September
E = May	G = February	H = April	I = July
K = November	M = June	R = August	W = March

D = Day of Month and E = Bundle Number
See above chart for number placement by series.

Exceptions
1857: R was used September 1 – 19.
1860: K was used to signify December.
In 1878, during March 1 – 6, W was used for the year (replacing D) and G was used for the month (replacing W).[26]

British Rd Numbering System

Beginning with 1884, the diamond mark system was eliminated and replaced by a system featuring an assigned sequence of numbers preceded by Rd or Rd No. Each number in the chart below is the first assigned number in Class I Metals for that year.[27]

The reverse of one of my Kenrick stands. You can see that it states A. KENRICK & SONS, No8, and Rd 15023. The Rd number of 15023 dates this particular trivet to 1884.

1884 1	**1896** 266237	**1908** 516375	**1920** 664869
1885 18993	**1897** 288848	**1909** 533561	**1921** 676491
1886 39547	**1898** 309956	**1910** 546084	**1922** 685412
1887 61207	**1899** 328527	**1911** 561570	**1923** 691571
1888 87266	**1900** 349120	**1912** 585707	**1924** 695944
1889 111664	**1901** 367628	**1913** 608541	**1925** 705943
1890 140481	**1902** 380979	**1914** 627887	**1926** 716386
1891 160613	**1903** 401944	**1915** 642613	**1927** 723430
1892 183259	**1904** 422489	**1916** 651079	**1928** 735899
1893 203348	**1905** 428004	**1917** 655001	**1929** 740459
1894 223861	**1906** 469160	**1918** 662576	**1930** 741336
1895 244726	**1907** 486464	**1919** 665728	**1931** 757945

There are two inconsistencies I have found in trying to authenticate the dates on Kenrick trivets. These possibly also apply to other long-established British foundries that reproduced their trivet and stand designs over many years.

Kenrick Inconsistency #1: The company name documents when the pattern was conceived. The Rd number documents when the pattern was registered.

Archibald Kenrick & Sons, Limited of West Bromwich, England, has been in business since 1791. Iron stands were but one of the many items they have produced over the years at this renowned iron foundry. Advertised as items of "Household Ironmongery," they were identified as Kenrick on the reverse by a style number, the company name, and sometimes a registration diamond or number.

Those with an Rd number or Rd diamond would seem simple to authenticate, using the previous tables provided. However, it gets a bit confusing when you realize the company name does not necessarily correspond exactly by dates to the Rd number or diamond. Through the years, the Kenrick company's name has changed as the following table shows:[28]

Evolution of the Kenrick Foundry

1791 *A. Kenrick*	1811 *A. Kenrick & Co.*
1828 *A. Kenrick & Son*	1830 *A. Kenrick & Sons*
1883 *A. Kenrick & Sons, LTD*	

Refer again to my picture of the reverse of the Kenrick trivet. The Rd number definitely registers this trivet to 1884. However, the company name A Kenrick & Sons suggests that the original pattern was conceived earlier, prior to 1883. This is because the pattern was designed while the company was still listed as A. Kenrick & Sons, but by the time the Rd number was applied for and obtained, the company name had evolved to A. Kenrick & Sons, Ltd.

I verified this through Maria Lampert, who works in Patents Information at the British Library in London, England. She checked their records, and this particular Class I Metals design was entered into the design register on October 14, 1884. The Rd number 15023 was issued to A. Kenrick & Sons Ltd. from West Bromwich, England.

Kenrick Inconsistency #2: The markings on the trivet reverse document when the pattern was conceived and registered, not necessarily when it was cast at the foundry.

In Hazel Mitchell's 1991 book, *British Iron Stands*, she includes three pages of reprinted period Kenrick advertisements. My No.8 Kenrick stand, the Rd number dating it to 1884, is advertised under two different A. Kenrick & Sons Ltd. listings from the years 1889 and 1919. Obviously, using the original pattern, manufacture of this particular design continued for some time.

And, in the book *Collecting Cast Iron* by Alex Ames, the author follows the history of a cast iron Kenrick doorknocker with a Rd lozenge dating it to 1880. It not only appeared in the 1880 Kenrick catalog, but also in their 1926 catalog. Ames cautioned, "Given the original pattern — and they were almost indestructible — manufacture could continue for many, many years."[29]

Trivets from the Isle of Man

If you have been collecting trivets for very long, you have possibly noticed a design featuring three running legs. Clad in armor and bearing spurs, it is the Trisceles, or the Three Legs of Man. This is the national symbol of independence and resilience for the Isle of Man, whose motto is Quocunque Jeceris Stabit, which translates to "Which ever way I am thrown I will stand."

Centered in the middle of the Irish Sea, between England, Ireland, Scotland, and Wales, the Isle of Man is 227 square miles in size, with a population (in 2001) of 76,000. It is uniquely self-governed and does not belong to the United Kingdom, although the UK provides for their foreign representation and defense. Its people speak English, while the native Manx Gaelic dialect has been preserved and is taught as a second language in their public schools.

The main industry of the Isle of Man is tourism. The scenic beauty of this island makes it a favorite vacation destination, as approximately 40% of the island is still uninhabited and in its natural state. There are many historic attractions to explore, and lodging is abundant. Since 1907, people have traveled there from around the world for the annual Isle of Man Tourist Trophy (TT) Motorcycle Races.[30]

Souvenir trivets from the Isle of Man have long been a popular collectible. The older souvenir trivets bear a British Rd. number. This brass Isle of Man trivet is 5¼" x ¾" with three feet. On the face: "A Present From The Isle Of Man" and the Trisceles. On the reverse is the inscription: A BAMBER, CW II, and the Rd number 168240, dating this trivet to 1891 (CI).

Sadirons, Fuel Irons, and their Companion Stands

The prefix "sad" in sadiron refers to the fact that the metal of the iron itself was heavy and solid. Sadirons came in many shapes and sizes, from small toy irons weighing mere ounces to the largest tailor's irons weighing up to sixty pounds. Housewives of that era owned several different sadirons, each specifically designed to perform a particular ironing function. The trivets that accompanied them are more accurately termed sadiron stands.

To prepare for ironing, the sadirons were placed either on the hot kitchen stove, or upon a smaller portable laundry stove. One iron would be in use as the others heated. Ironing in those days was hot, cumbersome, and hazardous. Hands often got burned, either from a chance swipe with the iron, or when a wet finger (listening for that telltale sizzle) was touched to the underside of the iron. Considering the many yards of fabric in a single Victorian dress, ironing was a tedious and unpleasant chore that consumed an enormous amount of time.

The earliest American sadirons were blacksmith wrought, with heavy bases and handles of varying sizes and designs, depending upon the whim and talent of the blacksmith. By the early to mid-1800s foundries took over many of the traditional metalworking services formerly provided by the blacksmith.

Earlier sadirons were the traditional one piece, fixed handle style; however, by the mid-1870s, a two-piece iron with a detachable, stay cool handle was popular. The sadiron base was heated separately, then the handle clipped or screwed onto it for ironing. In 1877 the Enterprise Manufacturing Company of Philadelphia manufactured a newly patented line of hollow perforated handle sadirons, which claimed to have a more natural handgrip that would remain cooler during ironing. These still necessitated using a protective hand pad. Most companies offered boxed sets, comprised of several one-piece sadirons, or of several bases, a handle, and perhaps a stand. The Enterprise Manufacturing Company of Philadelphia offered an even nicer detachable handle set, within a handsomely fashioned wooden box that included two stands, three handles, and six different sadiron bases.

Matching Howell Co. Geneva sadiron (CI).

Some housewives preferred ironing with an alternative to the sadiron called a box iron, which had an opening to insert interchangeable hot metals slugs. Another choice, the self-heating iron, was available from the late 1800s. Earlier self-heating models used burning charcoal within a hollow iron, but they were frustrating to use because the charcoal ashes frequently dirtied or burned the fabric being ironed. Later models relied on liquid fuels such as alcohol or gasoline, held in a reservoir and fed to a lit burner within the metal iron. Newer gas models actually hooked up to the home's gas light fixture, such as the Strauss IWANTU Comfort Irons, which came with their own gas line connector hose. These were much more convenient and relatively safe if used correctly. Small specialty irons, such as fluters and crimpers (which pleated fabric) were also popular for home use. Larger irons, of course, were produced for commercial laundries.

Ironing stands made by Bless and Drake (B&D), Cleveland Foundry, Colebrookdale, Enterprise, Howell, Humphrey, H.R. Ives, Ives and Allen, Ober, Strauss, N.R. Streeter, and Rosenbaum all had companion irons available.

The **Bless and Drake** Company of Newark, New Jersey, produced irons and stands from the mid-1850s until 1927. One of their trademarks was the head of Vulcan, the mythical god of fire and metalworking. This emblem differs from the trademark of William M. Crane & Company, New York, whose stands and gas irons displayed the written word "Vulcan."

"The W.H. Howell Co., Geneva, Ill." stand (CI).

The **William H. Howell** Company made a variety of pressing irons and stands in the mid to late 1800s. Their trademark was the "Howell H," prominent on many of their items. Other sadirons and stands manufactured by the Howell Company include those marketed as "GENEVA." In her book, *Pressing Irons and Trivets*, Esther Berney identifies "WAPAK" as a trademark of the Howell Company, with the WAPAK logo on the sadiron base. Those nineteenth century Howell irons are not to be confused with later sadirons produced by The Wapak Hollow Ware Company of Wapakoneta, Ohio, which was in business during the years 1903 to 1926. (On the Wapak Hollow Ware sadirons WAPAK appears on the handle, with the pound number on the base.)[31]

Hand-wrought trivet (iron).

Blacksmith wrought handle on crude sadiron (iron).

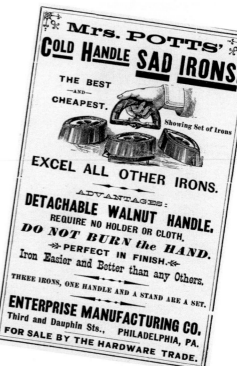

Reverse of the Mrs. Potts trade card, describing the iron's detachable handle.

Mary Florence Potts patented sadirons with "cold handles" beginning in 1871. Various manufacturers issued these popular irons. She became the worldwide spokesperson for her designs, and Victorian era Mrs. Potts trade cards were a popular collectible with housewives of that time. This card is signed "Yours Truly Ms. Florence Potts," with the legend "Inventress of Mrs. Potts Cold Handle Sad Iron."

H.R. Ives and Company was a hardware store founded in Montreal, Canada, in 1859. Their sadirons and stands predate a subsequent merger that formed the Ives and Allen Company, also of Montreal.

Nelson R. Streeter of Groton, New York, produced many different irons and stands. They manufactured the Sensible line, as well as the familiar N.R. Streeter Magic Fluter & Polisher. This rectangular, recessed stand featured the company logo embossed on its surface, and securely held a grooved hot insert. The piece of fabric to be pleated was placed on top, and then a similarly grooved roller was used to press in the pleats.

All of these products were inferior to the electric iron, which appeared in the late 1910s and completely dominated the ironing market by 1930. Once electric irons were manufactured with an inset heel rest that enabled them to sit upright, a sadiron stand or trivet was no longer strictly necessary. Of course, sadirons and trivets remained in common use until electricity was readily available, with rural and secluded areas being the last to convert to the new technology.

Simmons Special sadiron base with detachable clip handle, circa 1890s (NPCI).

Enterprise toy Star Iron from late 1870s, featuring their perforated "Stay Cool" handle (CI).

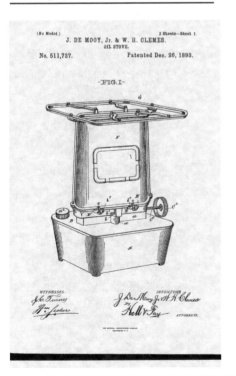

Fluting iron (unsigned) with stand, removable heatable insert, and pleat roller (CI).

Box iron with rear trap door, into which slides a heated slug (CI).

Reprint of original patent illustration for the J. De Mooy, Jr. & W.H. Clemes oil stove, December 26, 1893. This was one design typical of many of the small laundry stoves of the era. Reprinted courtesy of Bruce L. Taylor, Erie, Pennsylvania.

Ober Sadiron Stands

Ober Manufacturing

In the 1870s, two brothers by the name of John and George H. Ober founded the Ober Manufacturing Company of Chagrin Falls, Ohio. The Ober Company was predominantly a sadiron manufacturer, but the foundry also produced a variety of cast iron household products. In addition, Ober was one of the most prominent American manufacturers of toy irons in the late 1800s through the early 1900s, making little one and two pound irons sold for children's use. These were fully functional irons, and it wasn't uncommon for a mother to borrow her child's one pound pressing iron in order to iron a small or extremely delicate piece of fabric or lace.

However, the Ober brothers are perhaps best remembered today for their beautiful square, grid, and leaf patterned sadiron stands. These designs were unique to the Ober Manufacturing Company, and were not reproduced by other manufacturers. (The only exception was the Late Ober Leaf pattern, which was occasionally copied. Virginia Metalcrafters made a reproduction, which bore a stock number of 10-7). In the materials I received from the Chagrin Falls Historical Society, the Ober catalog pages show their stands as being offered in either a nickel finish or japanned. (A japanned finish protected metal by the application of a lacquered finish over a black painted surface.) The Ober foundry produced sadirons and stands until 1916, and the Ober Large Leaf design was one of their last issued sadiron stands. The Ober foundry was formally sold in 1932.

Because of their size and charm, Ober stands also doubled as coffee, tea, or table stands. Their small feet allow them to be easily displayed on a wall. Personally, I have always been intrigued by Ober sadiron stands because of their great beauty, symmetry of design, and excellence of casting. Since there were only a few issued designs, a complete set, although not inexpensive, is attainable. The Ober Manufacturing Company produced sadirons with and without detachable handles, pressing irons, sleeve irons, and toy irons; one or more of these irons would further enhance any Ober sadiron stand collection.

As you look at each of the following photographs, notice again the beautiful designing and workmanship that went into the casting of each one. A complete selection of Ober trivets is to be found in Antique and Vintage Trivets and Stands. The above letterhead graphics are courtesy of the Chagrin Falls Historical Society, Chagrin Falls, Ohio.

Ober Chagrin Falls, O., lettering on rectangle in center of grid, 4½" square (CI).

Ober Square No. 1, Ober Chagrin Falls, Ohio, around the center circle, 4⅜" square (CI).

OMCo monogram in center of grid, 4¾" square (NPCI). This design was also cast in a smaller toy version, 3⅛" square, also made of nickel plated cast iron.

Reverse of the Ober Square Leaf stand, with engraved OBER Chagrin Falls O. Mfg. Co.

Ober Square Leaf, with about 80% of the original plating remaining, 4¼" square (NPCI). Very few nickel-plated Ober stands are found today...apparently, as the original nickel finish eroded, many of these stands were refinished by their owners in a flat black.

Late Ober Leaf, 5¼" circumference (CI).

Ober Large Leaf, 6⅛" round, painted black over NPCI.

Reverse of the round Late Ober Leaf stand, showing OBER in large, embossed lettering. This OBER signature is the same as on the reverse of the round Ober Large Leaf trivet.

Houchin Alcohol Stoves and their Trivets

Beginning in the 1870s, the Houchin Manufacturing Company of New York patented a line of alcohol-burning pocket-sized stoves. The kits included a pot, a dish-like burner base, and a lid, all made of tin. There was also a decorative cast iron trivet that fit inside the cooking pan.

I was lucky enough to find one of these little stoves, not only intact, but also in the original packaging with the directions enclosed. This particular stove was patented was patented January 29, 1878. The cook pan measures 4⅜" x 2"(T), and the round trivet measures 3⅞" x 1½" (CI).

You'll occasionally find these trivets for sale in several different designs. They are easily identified as Houchin stove trivets by the company wording around the edges: HOUCHIN NY. The three legs are angled at the tips, especially made to fit into small indentations in the bottom of the tin base. It's unusual to discover a complete set as illustrated below.

A complete 1878 Houchin cook set including the round trivet, cook stove, and original packaging.

Below is the alcohol stove information is as it appears on the enclosed directions card. I'm sure this was a dandy item to have back in the nineteenth century when traveling, but I cannot imagine cooking a very big steak or chop on that 3⅞" trivet surface!

POCKET COOK STOVE.

Trademark Registered May 18, 1875.

Patented Sept. 17, 1872, May 4, 1875, July 27, 1875, and Jan'y 29, 1878.

HOUCHIN'S IMPROVED POCKET COOK STOVE. No. 668. With Boiler and gridiron on which can be broiled a Steak or Chop, Oysters, Ham, Fish, etc., or make Toast as there is neither Smell nor Smoke from the Flame. It is just the thing for Travelers, the Nursery, etc. This stove is provided with an air chamber to prevent the heat from injuring anything on which it may be placed.

If you wish a smaller flame, place the cover on the stove having first removed the small cap. **USE ONLY ALCOHOL.** Pour in slowly through the wire gauze, about two tablespoons full and light it.

We also manufacture Gas-lighting Torches, Tapers, Night Lights, Revolving Graters, Insect Powder Guns, and other specialties for Housekeeping purposes.

HOUCHIN MANUFACTURING CO., NEW YORK.

Selecting, Cleaning, and Caring for Metal Trivets and Stands

Not everyone is lucky enough to find a trivet in perfect condition, ready to display and enjoy. Many trivets will come with their share of "baggage" in the form of dirt, grease, rust, and old paint.

However, the first and foremost consideration when choosing a trivet is its structural condition. No amount of cleaning or old paint removal can improve the basic condition of a trivet that is cracked, chipped, or pitted badly from rust. So, spend a little time inspecting your potential trivet purchase... cracks can sometimes be difficult to notice. Handle the trivet, checking for any give in its structure that might indicate a defect.

If the trivet has been covered in paint, it may be hard to identify the underlying metal. Get in the habit of carrying a small magnet with you so that you can differentiate cast iron (which sticks to the magnet) from other metals. It's not unusual to discover a beautiful brass or bronze trivet under a layer of flat black paint, or a cast iron trivet painted to appear as brass. You need to know the type of metal you're working with, because you would not want to use abrasive cast iron refinishing methods on brass, as brass is a softer metal and easily scratched.

Everything you will need to renew your cast iron trivets can be found at your local hardware store. Always begin with the gentlest method. The best tool for removing dirt and rust is a stiff steel wire brush (it looks like a big toothbrush). Paper towels will come in handy. If needed, choose a paint remover specifically designed for removing paint from metal. You'll need special chemical-resistant gloves; the other types can sometimes dissolve when exposed to the paint remover. Always wear goggles whenever you are working with a cleaning product that has the potential of splashing. And, don't forget to don an apron or an old t-shirt, because you'll definitely have little flecks of rust and dirt splattering during this messy process.

The first thing to do with a dirty cast iron trivet is to wash it in soap and water. Then, if needed, take the brush (you could substitute a Brillo pad or steel wool) and go to work on the trivet; you shouldn't be able to scratch cast iron with hand scrubbing. Give extra attention to any rusty areas, and continue to scrub until your rinse water runs clear and the trivet is cleaned to your satisfaction.

Some people swear by oven cleaner as the easiest method for removing old grime and rust. Choose a product, like Easy Off, that doesn't require heat. Using gloves, apply a thick, even coat of oven cleaner to the trivet, and then place it in an airtight plastic bag overnight. At the end of that time, under running water, use your wire brush and scrub the trivet until clean. If necessary, reapply and repeat this process. (Note: Never use oven cleaner on aluminum, as it will ruin the metal.)

I once had an old horseshoe trivet that was so nasty and rusty it looked unsalvageable. After the usual cleaning steps stated above, it really didn't look much better. I bought a bottle of Naval Jelly, and, following the directions, cleaned the rust off the trivet. It took two applications, but all the rust finally came off. However, underneath, the surface was quite rough and pitted; and the use of the rust dissolver had leached quite a bit of color from the cast iron, leaving it grayish in places. At this point I applied a liquid stove and grill polish (sold under different names, such as Stove Black or Rutland Liquid Stove & Grill Polish). These polishes are a combination of wax and black pigments; they give some color and shine to the cast iron, while protecting it from further rusting. I applied the polish according to the directions on the container, then wiped it dry and baked the trivet in the oven at 300 degrees for one hour. My final result was quite acceptable, considering how the trivet looked initially.

Rusty Peerless trivet before cleaning.

If you have a painted trivet and want to remove the finish, select a paint remover especially recommended for metals. Choose a thicker solution which can be brushed or sprayed on; it will cling to the trivet surface better than a thinner liquid. Follow all product directions carefully, as these chemicals can be harmful if misused. Be sure to work in a well-ventilated area. Also, don't forget the proper gloves and eye protection. When you finish, thoroughly wash and dry your trivet.

At this point, I season my trivet, much as you would protect a treasured piece of cast iron cookware. There are many suggested ways to do this (low heat versus high heat) but this is my favorite: Preheat your oven 300 degrees F. Rinse the trivet with water one last time, and pat dry. Take some liquid cooking oil, solid shortening, or mineral oil in the palm of your hand, and rub it well into the trivet surface, taking care to cover all the crevasses. Allow this to sit for fifteen to thirty minutes, then take a paper towel and completely dry the trivet, wiping off all the oil (oil left on the trivet will cause smoking in the oven). Place the trivet in the oven directly on the oven rack, and bake for 60 minutes. You might notice some slight odor (from the oil) during the baking process. For this reason it's a good idea, if possible, to open your windows and air out the house while you season your trivet. At the end of the baking time, carefully remove the trivet from the oven (it's hot!) and cool it on a baker's rack. Your trivet should look 100% better.

I suppose that it would also be possible to bake your trivets on the upper rack within a gas grill; that would move the entire process outside, and keep your house fresh smelling. If your grill has a thermometer, you could judge the heat and the timing accordingly.

Note: If you have a cast iron trivet that has been lightly accent painted, you may find that the paint "disappears" during the baking process. Therefore, do not season/bake your trivet unless you want to take the chance of losing the painted finish.

I do not advocate the flat black painting of trivets. Following the above advice, you should be able to make all but the most neglected trivet presentable. Aesthetically speaking, I personally consider cast iron more appealing in its natural state; and older trivets, showing evidence of their age, have their own special beauty and charm.

If you are cleaning a brass trivet, remember that the metal is softer than cast iron, and easily scratched. Hardware stores carry soft nylon brushes (they also look like big toothbrushes) that are good for scrubbing crevasses in brassware. They also have a varied selection of paste or liquid brass cleaners. Often just a simple cleaning, buffing, and polishing is all it takes to bring out the concealed beauty of a brass trivet.

Once you've cleaned and/or polished your trivets and they are on display, check them every so often for developing rusty or tarnished spots. Re-polish or re-treat as necessary, following the above steps. You should not have much trouble with recurrent rust, unless you live in a very humid climate. Otherwise, a periodic dusting with a feather duster or wipe down with an aerosol furniture polish is all that will be necessary to assure that your trivets are always looking their very best.

After cleaning this Peerless stand was actually beautifully nickel plated!

Decorating Your Home with Trivets

Here are some of my personal suggestions for incorporating trivets into your home decorating scheme. Whether you are hanging one or one hundred, they make fascinating wall displays.

In the 1950s and 1960s, Virginia Metalcrafters made souvenir trivets for various U.S. vacation spots. I found six of these old trivets that tied into a theme of places we had traveled as a family...featuring Amtrak (we took the AutoTrain from Florida to Virginia), Natural Bridge, and the Skyline Drive in Virginia (we drove to Big Meadows Lodge, within Shenandoah National Park, along that lovely highway). Three others feature Florida attractions... St. Augustine, Marineland (just south of St. Augustine), and Silver Springs (Ocala). They are grouped around a framed collage of our family vacation photos.

For those with less wall space, miniature Wilton trivets (approximately 5" long) are a lot of fun to collect, and you can create a gallery of different trivet designs in a relatively small area. I have eighteen of these little Wilton trivets mounted around a doorway leading into my kitchen. I bought them all on the Internet, and spent very little for a nice mini-trivet collection. Some of the Wilton designs that are available in miniature are Heart, Plume, Rosette, Grape, Sunburst, Eagle, Dumb Dutch, Cathedral, Tassel & Grain, Military, Peacock, Family Tree, Hex, Butterfly, Cupid, Dewdrop, Tulip in Motion, Bellows, Rings, Dutch Tulip, and Miniature Handled Lantz. Most are shown in Contemporary Castings, and are excellent examples of the most commonly reproduced trivet designs.

It's nice to accent any display with other memorabilia of the era. Along a back hallway I have mounted my entire collection of antique sadiron stands, surrounding a framed photograph of a late nineteenth century laundry in operation. In another area of my home, I have my Jenny Lind trivets displayed near her framed portrait. And, in yet another wall grouping, I have all of my fraternal horseshoe plaque trivets hanging below a colorful Flemish Art Company FLT/IOOF wooden pyrography wall hanging that dates to the late 1890s.

There are many delightful trivet sconces, candleholders, and other cast iron items such as match holders, figurines, and bowls. Available from companies such as JZH, Wilton, John Wright, Iron Art, and Sexton, these lovely 1950s era items are fun to collect and add variety and appeal to any cast iron collection. Perhaps you have seen old electric trivet clocks for sale. Many of these appear to be in good condition; but if you're like me, you're not very comfortable plugging in and trusting that old 1950s wiring. I purchased a Sessions Trivet Time clock on eBay™, extracted the electric movement, and replaced it with a 3¾" diameter battery powered craft clock. Since the circumference of the new clock movement wasn't an exact match, I stretched three wide rubber bands around the clock housing before coaxing it into the cast iron trivet body. That was all it took to ensure a tight fit. There are pre-drilled hanging holes on the back of the trivet frame, which made it easy to wall mount the converted clock. I've been really pleased with how well this turned out, and how nice it looks; but, best of all, this renewed trivet clock keeps excellent time.

Sometimes it's hard to decide how to best hang or mount your trivets. I usually use a wall anchor and an appropriately sized cup hook on my walls. If the trivet design won't accommodate a cup hook or the legs are too long, then I'll use a wall anchor and place a screw through an opening in the trivet. The cup hooks are preferable, because then you're able to take your trivets down whenever you want to examine or rearrange them. If you don't want to put a lot of holes in your walls, an option is to purchase heavy-duty pegboard and mount it along the wall studs. Then, using pegboard books, you can display your trivets without undue damage to your walls. For trivets with very short feet, you can use picture hanging wire to make a small hanging loop on the back of the trivet, then mount it on a small picture hook. I hang all my horseshoe plaque trivets this way.

When I first decided to collect the JZH Alphabet Trivet series, I committed one 6' x 9' wall along a hallway for my future collection. I sketched out on paper how I wanted to arrange my trivets, and then went ahead and placed wall anchors and small hooks at each predetermined spot. I cut out 3" circles of colored paper and glued them to cardboard, punched out a hole for hanging, and used press-on metallic letters to identify each alphabet trivet. I hung these on the hooks, a reminder of which trivets I had yet to find. The colored tags came down as the trivets were located and added to the collection. Depending on the size of the trivet, some cup hooks had to be replaced with larger ones; but I started with the small 1" hooks so as not to stretch out the wall anchors unnecessarily. (A picture of this J.Z.H. trivet display appears on page 14.)

Finally, notice my antique trivets hung, by cup hooks, on a low 4' x 8' wall that divides our kitchen from the breakfast nook. They are quite a conversation piece, as it's easy to reach over from the table and take one down to examine more closely. The cup hooks were placed at predetermined intervals, and the trivets added as they were acquired. Because there is a counter overhang, there's no danger of these valuable trivets being jostled or knocked down as people walk by.

Kitchen antique trivet display.

This corner features my Jenny Lind trivets and collectibles. The small glass bottles are Jenny Lind flask reproductions by Wheaton. The center picture includes an original program page from one of her 1850s era American concerts. Interestingly, the old Atwater Kent radio was a $10 find in a Connecticut flea market back in the 1970s. My husband Ed restored it to its original appearance and working order (a shop in Groton carried a complete supply of the old radio tubes).

This is our computer station, where this book was written. Displayed is a collection of Wilton trivets, surrounding the framed Wilton box top. Notice my renovated Sessions Trivet Time clock!

A beveled corner provides a display area for some of my brass trivets, which complement an old 1920s era French gilt poem mirror, "La Promenade Du Matin" (The Walk of the Morning).

Some of my favorite sadiron stands line a back hallway of my home. The framed picture of the Stockwell Orphanage Laundry (England, circa 1880) is featured in the left center.

AMERICAN BEAUTY ELECTRIC IRONS

The American Electrical Heater Company of Detroit, Michigan, advertised itself as the "Oldest and Largest Exclusive Makers in the World" of "The Best Irons Ever Made."[32] Originally established in 1894, it merged in the early 1900s with another Detroit electric appliance company, the United Electric Heating Company. The newly established company retained the name of American Electrical Heater Company, and proceeded to successfully manufacture household and commercial irons, as well as soldering irons. The company went out of business in the early 1990s.

American Electrical Heater Company made many electric irons over the subsequent years, both for household and commercial use. However, their line of American Beauty electric irons was their most successful, and the American Beauty was considered one of the premier irons of its day.

The first time I accidentally came upon an eBay™ auction for an American Beauty iron I was intrigued by it. The sleek chrome-plated body, accented by the amber Lucite handle, was too tempting to resist; and so I purchased it, in mint condition, and in the original box. From 1951, it is No. 33-AB, with the following features as quoted from the hangtag brochure:

American Beauty adjustable-automatic Electric Iron, Thermoscope Type, CAT. No. 33-AB
- *Steel encased chrome-nickel heating element of 1000-watt input is cast in soleplate.*
- *Soleplate is of aluminum-alloy with rounded edges.*
- *Hood or cover is of steel, chrome-plated.*
- *Handle is of (amber) plastics.*
- *Weight of iron is 3 pounds.*
- *Cord is American Beauty 10,000-cycle super-flexible heater cord, 7 feet, with attachment-plug cap.*
- *Iron is listed under Re-examination Service of Underwriter's Laboratories, Inc."* [33]

Now I was hooked! I searched the Internet for more information on my iron, but little was to be found. I did learn that an American Beauty Lucite handled iron was once featured in an exhibit held at the Baltimore Museum of Art, entitled Masterpieces of American Design. I also noticed that they are a popular vintage collectible, and that they are still reasonably priced.

My friend Arnie Stein, who is an avid iron collector and an essay contributor in this book, offered the following information about these irons: "The American Beauty iron is from around 1950, give or take a year or two. I always felt it was one of the prettiest and most nicely designed irons of its era. The amber handled one you bought is harder to find than the red handled iron, especially in mint condition. Now you will need to look for the red one, unless you already have it. As far as I know, those were the only colors produced of that particular style.

"You might be interested to know that a bit later version of the American Beauty Electric was a steam-dry iron. Although somewhat different in shape, they were again produced with the ruby red or amber Lucite handles. I have both of these irons along with their boxes. They weigh three pounds each, and are both Cat. No. 81-AB. The amber iron is described as the Deluxe Model. On the inside cover of one of the boxes the former owner wrote 'bought Aug. 30th 1957.' These steam irons must be rather scarce, as I bought both of them on eBay™ in 1998, and haven't noticed any like them since."

Not long after that I found No. 79-AB, the ruby red handled iron I was searching for. Again, I was fortunate in purchasing it in mint condition, and in the original box. This version was an earlier model, circa 1947, and heavier at 4½ pounds since it contained no aluminum. The following features are quoted from the hangtag brochure:

American Beauty adjustable-automatic Electric Iron, Thermoscope Type, CAT. No. 79-AB

- *Heating element 1000 watts input and is of chrome-nickel resistance ribbon with mica insulation.*
- *Cord is American Beauty 10,000 super-flexible heater cord, 7 feet long, with attachment-plug cap.*
- *Sole-plate is of cast iron, with rounded edges and finished in a frictional-resistant chrome plate.*
- *Hood or cover is of steel, chrome-plated.*
- *Handle is of (ruby red) plastics.*
- *Weight of iron is 4½ pounds.*
- *Iron is listed under Re-examination Service of Underwriter's Laboratories, Inc."*[34]

My third American Beauty iron purchase was No. 45-AB, an American Beauty Adjustable Automatic Heat Control electric iron. I believe this one to be of mid-1940s vintage; and although in near-mint condition in the original box, it unfortunately was not accompanied by the original brochure as my other two irons were. This iron weighs 5 pounds, appears to be constructed of chrome-plated steel, and features a mustard colored Bakelite handle with an adjustable lever for three heat settings: low, intermediate, or high.

In March of 2003 I obtained an American Beauty electric irons dealer catalog labeled 9/47, which I interpret to be September 1947. Inside is a lovely description of their "newest" product, the No. 79-AB ruby red handled iron that I previously described above. Apparently, "Thermoscope Type" generated a big marketing campaign, since this was one of the first irons featuring a dial with fabric settings. The following information, regarding this new feature, is quoted from the dealer catalog:

Thermoscope Type *means that it has a thermoscope. The thermoscope is a temperature-indicating device that shows on its dial in fabric graduation — Rayon, Silk, Wool, Cotton, Linen — temperature of the ironing surface. It makes visible to the user at all times the operating temperature of the working surface of the iron. It supersedes the "wet fingertip touch" or other uncertain tests for determining ironing temperature.*

The handle is made of durable molded plastic, shaped to fit the hand comfortably and without strain to the wrist or cramping or slipping of fingers. It is removable and replaceable without removing hood or other parts of the iron. It is made in three sections, united and held together as a unit by a through-handle bolt extending from rear through center section into threaded metal insert in the front section. Should one section be broken, it is necessary to replace that section only.

Because of the perfect balance of its light weight; its cool, comfortable, molded plastic handle; its visual temperature indicating device...the thermoscope; its gliding qualities resulting from its specially finished, precision-ground, rounded-edge, sole plate; and its super-flexible heater cord, the No. 79-AB is a device that will meet requirements of the most exacting conditions."[35]

My fourth American Beauty acquisition was an interesting travel sized iron, No. 29-AB, called the Traveler. This smaller model was listed in an August 1, 1958, dealer cost schedule as selling for $12.60 each, or $7.90 each when 6 or more were purchased. The handle is inset with red Bakelite, and it folds flat to the side for ease in packing.[36]

My most recent purchase is the oldest of my five American Beauty irons: No. 6½-B, which was first introduced in 1912. It was described in a 1927 American Beauty sales catalog as weighing 6½ pounds and listing for $7.50. The iron is nickel-finished steel with a wooden handle. It came with its companion trivet, a bi-level steel stand with the American Beauty triangular emblem on top. From the catalog: "The American Beauty electric iron does the work for which it is intended easier, quicker and better and gives longer service than any other iron because of its design, mechanical and electrical construction, workmanship and the quality of materials used."[37] In the accompanying photograph of these irons you'll notice a framed advertisement from an August 25, 1923, edition of *The Saturday Evening Post*, which happens to feature this No. 6½-B American Beauty iron.

I've also purchased two old American Beauty dealer catalogs on eBay™, one from 1927 and the other from 1947. They included price lists, and have been very helpful in documenting the ages and understanding the features of each of these irons.

Finally, I was lucky enough to acquire the neatest thing: an old printer's block advertising the American Beauty iron! It's very small, only 4" x 2", and was used in typesetting advertisements for magazines and newspapers. An interesting thing about this printer's block is that there is an error in the spelling of electric: the first sentence reads, "If you want the best — an alectric iron."

Vintage electric irons are fascinating to collect, with many still available in near-mint condition. They remain reasonably priced, but surely will appreciate in value over the coming years. Those of more collectible value would include the original packaging and brochures, and be in excellent condition with the original cord. Happy Hunting!

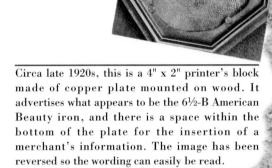

Circa late 1920s, this is a 4" x 2" printer's block made of copper plate mounted on wood. It advertises what appears to be the 6½-B American Beauty iron, and there is a space within the bottom of the plate for the insertion of a merchant's information. The image has been reversed so the wording can easily be read.

Clockwise from left: No. 29-AB Traveler (red Bakelite); No. 45-AB with box (mustard Bakelite); framed American Beauty advertisement; No. 33-AB (amber Lucite); No. 79-AB (ruby Lucite); and the No. 6½-B (wooden handle) with bi-level American Beauty trivet. My great-great grandmother crocheted these doilies.

OTHER VINTAGE DOMESTIC TREASURES

As I search for trivets, I often notice other irresistible kitchen and laundry room collectibles that would make nice accent pieces. A good, comprehensive Victorian or kitchen antiques reference book can provide more detailed information. Just remember, as with trivets, it's always prudent to buy the best quality items you can afford, because they will continue to appreciate in value over time.

In the mid-1800s, wooden framed washboards had ribbed scrubbing surfaces on which wet fabrics were rubbed until clean. The frames were made of wood or metal, and the scrubbing surfaces were formed of aluminum coated steel, brass, glass, graniteware, tin, or zinc. Those with more unusual scrubbing surfaces or legible lettering and/or graphics (that help to date the washboard) are more collectible.

Clothes wringers were attached to the washtub with steel fittings. Some models were manufactured of lovely hardwood, with either wooden (older versions) or rubber rollers and a metal hand crank. In nice condition and polished to their original sheen, they are a lovely reminder of a bygone era. Since a hardwood wringer can be quite heavy, a nice way to display it is to support its base within a larger block of wood that's been stained to match the color of the clothes wringer.

The combination of steam and heat helps to remove wrinkles from fabric. Today we've become accustomed to our electric irons with their steam and spray features. However, in the past, housewives had a sprinkler bottle at the ready to dampen the clothing as it was being ironed. These bottles varied from a simple brown bottle with a corked sprinkle insert to ones made of decorative china. Some favorite designs for collectors are a Chinese man called Sprinkle Plenty; a pink and white elephant; a clothespin; or several design variations of a painted china bottle formed in the shape of a sadiron.

18" x 8¾" wood / tin washboard advertising Victorian era bathing suits.

A large cast iron stove contributed considerable indoor heat, and not all households could afford a detached kitchen. Therefore, it wasn't long before nineteenth century housewives demanded smaller stoves created specifically for the task of heating sadirons. These smaller stoves kept the house cooler, especially in the warmer months. Laundry stoves operated with various types of fuel...coal, oil, or kerosene. Miniature stoves could warm one or two irons at a time, while larger home laundry stoves had compartments to heat several sadirons around the stove base. The largest commercial laundry stoves could heat dozens of irons at a time. Today, especially since so few exist in displayable condition, laundry stoves are highly collectible.

A metal stove damper adjusted the amount of air and exhaust flowing in and out of the cast iron cookstove flue. It was opened fully as the fire was started, closed partially during the cooking stage, and later closed even further to retain the heat of the embers. Dampers were inscribed with numbers and letters identifying the manufacturer, and in nice condition are attractive when hung on a wall.

Metal stove lid lifters were used to move stove lids, stove trivets, and cereal trivets around on the hot cookstove surface. Most were 8" to 10" long and were cast in various shapes. Newer models had openwork or coiled metal handles that stayed cooler. While some were plain and utilitarian, others featured embossed or cutout lettering or a face ("Jack Frost" is one example).

Barstow Ranges stove lid lifter, late 1800s (steel).

Have you considered a rug beater? I bought a lovely one on the Internet that has a wooden handle, engraved 1905. I have it hanging on the wall behind the table that displays my sadirons.

Made of wood, metal, glass, or pottery, match holders kept a ready supply of matches at hand for lighting the gas or wooden stove. They varied in length from several inches to a foot, and came in every shape imaginable. There were pocket, tabletop, and wall mount versions available. A revival of interest in match holders occurred in the 1950s, and several foundries, including Wilton and Iron Art, made cast iron match holder reproductions.

Victorian trade cards are quite valuable if in fine to near mint condition. Companies in the late 1870s to early 1900s distributed trade cards as promotions with products, and just about any consumer item of the time can be found advertised on a trade card. (Of particular interest to trivet collectors would be those cards advertising laundry day products such as sadirons, stoves, and laundry soaps.) The front of the cards were usually decorative, humorous, or offered some sort of political commentary; the backs were reserved for company advertising. People of that era collected the cards, gluing them into albums along with calling cards and other mementos. Collectors today prize these albums, as the valuable trade cards can be carefully soaked from the album pages and pressed, dried, and redistributed for sale. Most cards were made of a combination of paper pulp and rag, similar in composition to paper money, and have proven extremely durable.

Victorian photographs offer a fascinating glimpse into the lives and personalities of our ancestors. If you aren't lucky enough to have inherited a few of these family treasures, by all means enter an Internet auction site and browse through the many vintage tintypes, cabinet cards, and photographs offered for sale. A few of these make a charming addition to any period collection.

Since the 1940s, Jacob Zook of Pennsylvania was well known around the United States and the world for his colorful hex signs. Even after his death, they continue to be one of the most popular collectibles of Pennsylvania Dutch country. Based in Paradise, Pennsylvania, the Will-Char Company has the exclusive distribution rights to these wonderful signs, which have been hand silk printed by members of the same local family (currently the second and third generations) for over sixty years. They would be of particular interest to the trivet collector, considering the influence of Pennsylvania Dutch folk art on the development of early trivet designs.

A wonderful Victorian era prairie photograph. Itinerant photographers traveled the countryside with their cameras and props, taking portraits such as the one above.

Antique toy stoves are available, but in nice condition they are scarce and expensive. An acceptable alternative is a reproduction toy stove. I recently purchased a lovely cast iron reproduction Crescent toy stove, 12"l x 7"w x 11"h , at a roadside Cracker Barrel store. Complete with accessories, it was only $20.00! I plan to gold accent paint the Crescent logo on the oven door to more closely match the appearance of the original Crescent toy stove.

Finally, Sexton aluminum wall plaques are nice 1960s era collectibles. They come in many designs, including many with household themes, and have a hanging hook plus the Sexton mark on the reverse. Most are 6" to 14" long, and were made available in black, painted, or antiqued finishes.

1910 Horse Shoe Brand household wringer in exceptional condition.

Match holder, 10⅞" x 5⅛", featuring the bounty of the hunt, circa 1870s (CI).

Table display of a toy stove, a small sadiron heater, a rug beater, and various sadirons with their companion trivets.

Top half of the two-piece Game Junior Sadiron Heater (CI) with mica window, made by Taylor & Boggs Foundry Company, Cleveland. One sadiron at a time could be heated on the top grill of this small, portable kerosene fueled laundry stove patented in 1893. This is the design shown in the patent schematic for the Mooy & Clemes laundry stove, page 39.

Victorian trade cards featuring a laundry theme, circa 1880s

Electric Luster Starch, "The Best Laundry Starch In The World."

Bottom half of the two-piece Game Junior Sadiron Heater (CI).

Corning Stove Company. What a bathing suit!

Kendall Mfg. Company, Soapine French Laundry Soap.

Kendall Mfg. Company, French Laundry Soap. Notice the mother has hoisted the kids up in the box to keep them out of her way as she irons with her sadiron!

Empire Ringer Company, "Wringer Cats."

JACOB ZOOK ORIGINAL HEX SIGNS
(Designs Currently Available)

JZ 1 — Double Distelfink
JZ 2 — Mighty Oak
JZ 5 — Dutch Irish
JZ 6 — Sun, Rain & Fertility
JZ 7 — Love & Romance

JZ 8 — Home "Wilkum" Sign
JZ 10 — "8" Pointed Star
JZ 11 — Single Distelfink
JZ 12 — Daddy Hex
JZ 15 — Amish Carriage Horse

JZ 16 — Hereford
JZ 17 — Marriage Sign
JZ 18 — 12 Petal Rosette
JZ 19 — American Eagle
JZ 22 — Double-Headed Eagle

JZ 23 — Haus-Segen
JZ 27 — Maple Leaf
JZ 30 — Bird of Paradise "Wilkom"
JZ 31 — Bird of Paradise
JZ 33 — Friendship

JZ 34 — Bless This Child
JZ 35 — Pineapple Welcome
JZ 37 — Morning Birds
JZ 38 — Doves of Peace
JZ 39 — Willkommen

JZ 40 — Unicorn
JZ 41 — Bless This House
JZ 42 — Double Distelfink
JZ 44 — Family Blessing
JZ 45 — Tree of Life

Jacob Zook Hex Signs feature many of the familiar Pennsylvania Dutch symbols often found in classic trivet designs. They make nice decorative accents within a home trivet collection. Jacob Zook Hex Design(s), used by permission of Jacob Zook Hex Signs, 3056 U.S. Route 30 East, Paradise, Pa. 17562-0176. All Rights Reserved. www.hexsigns.com Phone # 717-687-8329

TRIVET COLLECTING AND SELLING ON THE INTERNET

I've been collecting trivets for over 25 years. For most of that time, it has meant browsing through antique shops and flea markets. Driving, walking about, rummaging through all the other antique kitchen items, then driving to other locations to repeat the process had become my frustrating routine. It was seldom that I would come upon anything exciting, and it took a long time to build up even a modest trivet collection. Most of the trivets I found were 1950s era reproductions; so that is how my trivet collection began.

Several years ago a friend introduced me to Internet shopping, and things haven't been the same since! In a single session at the computer, I can view a wider variety of antique and reproduction trivets than I could otherwise see in a year of browsing through shops. The downside is that the trivet can't be physically handled prior to purchase; but by studying the photograph(s) and emailing the seller, I can gather enough information to make a purchase decision. It's a wonderful way to buy trivets. Let me share with you some of what I've learned so far...

If you are going online to search for trivets, be sure to search under both trivet and trivets. You might also browse under the following listings: sadiron stand(s), iron stand(s), and iron rest(s). Should you be looking for horseshoe plaque trivets, the best search term is "horseshoe eagle."

I hunted unsuccessfully over a period of months for a particular trivet on both Internet auction sites and at flea markets. However, an eBay™ trivet dealer from Pennsylvania (Vince Katchen) offered to keep me in mind as he went on his buying expeditions, and my JZH A trivet was finally located. I would suggest that you also let any Internet antique/trivet dealers that you regularly buy from know what you are interested in obtaining for your own collection. Those dealers who operate in the northeastern United States (where most of the old foundries were located) often have access to the best selection of interesting trivets.

As you shop for trivets, avoid disappointment. Read the auction listing carefully, and always email the seller with your questions prior to bidding. The following are usual questions:

- *Any numbers/letters on the reverse?*
  This might help you differentiate a contemporary trivet from an antique.

- *Any excessive wear, cracks, and/or chips?*
  Sometimes there is a crack, a significant chip, or excessive wear to the trivet, but it might not be revealed in the initial auction listing.

- *What percentage of the nickel finish remains? Any paint loss to the accent painted finish?*
  It's often hard to tell the condition of the finish from auction photographs alone.

- *How long are the legs?*
  Antique trivets typically had legs of at least 1" in length.

Once I've seen a trivet on an auction site that I want for my collection, and after I've emailed the seller to clarify any concerns, I'll go ahead and place an initial minimum bid. I try to wait until the last day of the auction to make any additional bids. Bidding can become intense on the more desirable trivets, and it's always nice to purchase a lovely trivet at the lowest possible price. Decide ahead of time what your reasonable maximum bid will be, then stick to it. If you are outbid on a particularly desirable trivet, don't despair. You will often find that, soon after a particularly rare trivet sells at a high price, another just like it will come up for auction. The final bid on the second listing might possibly be lower than on that first, "one-of-a-kind" trivet. For example, in May 2002 an unusual trivet (the first one of its kind I'd ever seen) generated a lot of excitement among trivet collectors on eBay™, and auctioned for $145.61. Within a week, another one exactly like it (this one, however, without rust and in much better overall condition) was offered for auction and unbelievably sold for only $76.00.

Once you become familiar with buying trivets on the Internet, the next step is to offer your duplicate or unwanted trivets for sale to other collectors. It's a great way to make a little extra money (to put towards other trivet purchases), and it's also a terrific way to meet other trivet collectors online. Give it a try. Below are some auction listing suggestions for the novice seller.

• **Heading:** Include both words, trivet and trivets, so that potential buyers will find your auction if they browse under either term. For example: Trivet Lovers: Two Vintage Ober Trivets.

• **Description:** Include trivet dimensions, type of metal, number of legs, a description of any markings on the reverse, and the condition of the trivet (free of cracks/chips, etc.). If there are defects, be sure to reveal and describe them. Also, if there is anything special about your trivet (in the original box, casting marks visible, etc.), be sure to include that information also. The more completely you describe your trivet, the fewer email questions you'll get.

• **Photograph(s):** This is perhaps one of the most important features of your listing. Items rarely sell without a picture, and a picture of poor quality will severely limit bids on your item. A digital camera takes the best quality pictures, with the added convenience of being able to download those photos directly into your home computer and onto the Internet.

• **Price:** Remember that a trivet can sell with a single bid, so set your opening price accordingly. On trivets of value, a reserve price (lowest price you are willing to accept) will insure that your trivet will at least fetch a reasonable amount. However, you will observe sellers who consistently gamble and set their opening bids low with no reserve, trusting that the principle of supply and demand will guarantee adequate, appropriate bids.

• **Counter:** If the auction allows you to add a customer counter, do. It gives you information on how many visits you are getting to your auction, which is a reflection of either how desirable your item is, or how well you worded your heading.

• **Shipping:** Trivets should to be shipped, well padded, in a decent box. I'll assure you, if you consistently send trivets in padded mailer bags, some of your trivets will sustain damage. Trivet legs are notorious for poking through the packaging, and a sharp blow can bend or crack a valuable trivet. If your items are heavy, or you are shipping more than two trivets at a time, then choose a heavier gauge cardboard box for packaging. Can you believe I have received international shipments in Kleenex boxes, laundry detergent boxes, and even in folded paper grocery bags? It's true! I have learned to clearly specify how I want my trivets shipped (padded in a sturdy box) in order to prevent potential losses.

• **If you mail USPS™ Priority Mail,** the Post Office currently provides packaging materials free of charge. This is my method of choice, since I save money not having to purchase boxes, labels, and tape; the shipping time is faster; and the handling seems to be gentler. It's a good idea to secure the self-sealing box with some additional packing tape, since the self-stick end flaps can come unglued en route. As for padding, I usually use newspaper and peanuts to wrap and pad my boxed shipments. On more valuable trivets, I wrap in bubble wrap. (I save any bubble wrap I receive in purchases, and recycle it with subsequent mailings.) Once you know your buyer's zip code, you can go to the USPS™ website (see the next section, on websites) to determine shipping costs. For a nominal charge, I always add Delivery Confirmation so that I know when my package arrives.

• **Insurance:** I always insure my trivet purchases, and encourage others to do the same. Cast iron appears to be indestructible, but small areas of damage or rust can weaken the iron, and a sharp blow to your package in route can result in a cracked trivet. Also, old iron becomes brittle, and an antique trivet can actually shatter if dropped. And of course brass, being a softer metal, is even more easily damaged in transit. I also insure my other valuable vintage purchases, as well.

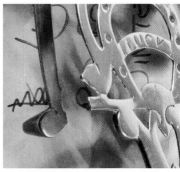

The results of an improperly packaged shipment: a ruined antique brass trivet.

• **Feedback:** The purpose of feedback on an auction site such as eBay™ is to provide information on the buying or selling practices of other members. This is important, since in Internet shopping we are usually dealing with strangers. Always keep your feedback businesslike. Remember that typing in all capital letters is interpreted as shouting, so please avoid that. Try to resolve any disagreements before filing your feedback, as it cannot be retracted once placed. If you have a good experience with a seller or buyer, please leave a positive feedback that describes what was good about the transaction. Likewise, if you have a negative experience, you also need to concisely describe that in a neutral or negative feedback. Please don't be afraid to leave neutral or negative feedback if it is warranted. It's important for everyone to be warned of the few unpleasant and/or outright dishonest buyers and sellers that exist. It's possible that you will receive a retaliatory negative feedback in return for your justified negative feedback, but keep in mind that you did the honorable thing by standing up to unethical business practices. And, of course, any inappropriate communications from a buyer or seller, such as vulgar or threatening language, should be immediately reported to the auction site, as that is probable grounds for their suspension.

At some point as a trivet collection grows, and especially as it increases in value, it's important to begin keeping accurate records. Don't forget that cast iron will melt at high temperatures, thus making a trivet collection vulnerable in the event of a fire. I've learned that most insurance companies will not issue a personal articles floater for a trivet collection, because trivets do not meet their requirements for individual value. However, they will reimburse you for damages due to loss within the framework of your homeowner's policy, as long as you can provide proof of the contents and value of your collection. I prefer to keep computer records, as they are the easiest to access and catalog. A digital photo should accompany the information on each trivet, and a copy of the disc can then be placed in a fireproof box or safety deposit box. I list the trivet name (if there is one); purchase price, seller, and approximate current value; dimensions and markings; keywords such as type of metal and maker; approximate date of manufacture; and the page it appears in a trivet reference.

In a recent Sunday edition of our newspaper's *Parade Magazine* there was an article featuring Terry and Ralph Kovel, who have been called "the Duke and Duchess of the Antiques World." I was particularly interested in Ralph Kovel's comments to author Gerri Hirshey on how eBay™ has changed the collectibles market. "It suddenly made a huge amount of things available. When millions of things appear from basements and attics and turn up online, the rare becomes commonplace. And what seemed common to you can turn out to be rare."[38]

Always keep an eye out for that scarce, valuable trivet that might turn up unexpectedly. Often, the seller may not even recognize its age or value, and on an Internet auction it may be buried under a bland heading such as "Cast Iron Trivet." The book *Trivets & Stands* currently has the most complete catalog of rare trivets, and is a good reference for looking up an unfamiliar trivet.

It's hard to predict how the advent of Internet marketing will affect the pricing of trivets. Personally, I feel that the current book appraisals are going to have to adjust, taking into consideration the prices of trivets sold online. There is currently a discrepancy between the selling prices of vintage trivets on Internet auctions (often lower) as compared to the asking prices of comparable trivets in antique shops and on antique store websites. Part of this has to do with a lack of pricing knowledge on the part of some amateur auctioneers. Another problem has to do with the fact that Internet auction sites are perceived as "online garage sales," with most customers hoping to get a bargain with their final bid, rather than being willing to bid what the trivet is actually worth. Although these factors are a boon to the serious trivet collector, who often obtains a collectible trivet at a fraction of its usual cost, they also distort the ongoing process of trivet valuation. Hopefully over time, with the volume and caliber of trivets being presented on the Internet, we will have the information needed to reach a consensus on the relative value of trivets.

Websites of Interest to Collectors

www.armetale.com — This is the website for Wilton Armetale of Mount Joy, Pennsylvania, formerly known as the Wilton Company. The history of the Wilton Company is presented on this website, as well as a catalog of their current product offerings. They have several links, one that describes the process of sand casting.

www.bl.uk — This is the website for the British Library. Entering the site, search under Searching For Registered Designs, where you will discover much information on the British Rd system. You can also contact clerks directly by email with specific questions you might have about a trivet's or stand's registration status.

www.collectibles-unlimited.com — This is the major collectibles website of Mickey Kaz of Woodland Hills, California. He offers over 6,000 collectibles for view and sale, and offers books through his BooksR4U site.

www.drexelantiques.com — Jeff Savage of Drexel Grapevine Antiques in Valdese, North Carolina, maintains this website that has wonderful information on dating English Registry Marks. He has many other helpful links, as well as his current antiques sales inventory.

www.ebay.com — Founded in 1995, eBay™ is, by definition, the world's online marketplace. I find it currently to be the best Internet site for browsing trivet and sadiron auctions. It's a great place to sell your duplicate or unwanted trivets to other collectors. There are also wonderful collector groups to join, including trivet groups.

www.exonumia.com/art/society.htm — Rich Hartzog maintains this fabulous website, AAA Historical Americana – World Exonumia. In case you are unfamiliar with the term, exonumia refers to collectible items other than coins or paper money, such as medals or tokens. He has cataloged a complete listing of fraternal organizations with their abbreviations, which really comes in handy when trying to identify initialed horseshoe plaque trivets.

www.google.com — Google™ is a fabulous Internet search engine — just type in any word or phrase, and you will immediately be linked with worldwide information. Google™ is unique among search engines in that the information is presented in order of relevance.

www.hexsigns.com — William and Charlotte Marsh of Paradise, Pennsylvania, are the sole authorized distributors for authentic Jacob Zook Hex Signs, which come directly from Pennsylvania Dutch Country. They present the History of Hex Signs, along with their online store inventory.

www.irons.com — The community page for Antique Pressing Iron Collectors is the website of Bill and Peggy Heyman of Marlborough, New Hampshire. It's a very interesting and most informative destination for collectors of irons and iron-related items. There is information on clubs, upcoming auctions, and museum sites around the country.

www.jwright.com — This is the website for the John Wright Company of Wrightsville, Pennsylvania. As they proclaim on their website, "John Wright remains America's oldest continuously operating manufacturer of cast iron products." They offer numerous products for sale in the following categories: Hearth and Home, Hardware, and Holiday.

www.PaDutchCulture.com — This is the website of Barbara and Jim Greenawalt of Wilmington, North Carolina. They offer information about anything and everything Pennsylvania Dutch. Jim was kind enough to translate the Old German wording on my Fersommling trivets. They offer links to numerous Pennsylvania Dutch sites, as well as to their online store catalog.

www.patented-antiques.com — This is the website of Larry and Carol Meeker, who own and operate Antiques of a Mechanical Nature in Somerset, California. They present a fascinating collection of mechanical antiques for sale, including trivets and sadirons. They also feature a museum collection of personal artifacts that are not for sale, but are fascinating to browse.

www.rootsweb.com/~srgp/jmtindex.htm — Joyce M. Tice has developed a wonderful website, Tri-Counties Genealogy & History, that includes a section with an extensive pictorial catalog of commemorative flagholders and plaques. A written synopsis of each organization accompanies the photographs, most of which were taken at the gravesites of deceased fraternal members.

www.ulead.com — ULEAD produces multimedia software, and sells the PhotoImpact program I use to catalog my trivets.

www.unicastco.com — This is the website for the Unicast Company, formerly the Union Manufacturing Company (JZH) of Boyertown, Pennsylvania. They offer a unique online-guided tour of their foundry, taking you from beginning to end in the casting process.

http://www.Shirbil.com — G'day from Australia! Welcome to the website of Bill and Shirley Davis, who are antique pressing iron enthusiasts. They most generously share their knowledge of flat sad irons, spirit irons, and charcoal irons. They also list their favorite website links, and maintain a guest book signed by visitors from around the world.

www.usps.gov — This is the official website for the United States Postal Service. Use their convenient postage calculator to determine shipping costs, both within the continental United States and worldwide. Remember that the USPS™ provides free shipping materials for their Priority Mail service, making this an ideal way to ship inexpensively.

www.vametalcrafters.com — This is the website for Virginia Metalcrafters of Waynesboro, Virginia. Although they no longer offer on-site factory tours, you can observe the foundry in operation through an observation window within their factory showroom. They continue to cast trivets, and their current offerings are available for sale on this Internet site.

www.xe.com/ucc — XE.com's Universal Currency Converter® is a website that can calculate exchange rates effortlessly between different currencies. It's invaluable if you are considering a transaction with someone in another country, and need to determine the current exchange rate. Universal Currency Converter is a registered trademark of the XE Corporation.

Suggested Reference Books and Magazines

A variety of wonderful reference books exists, although the majority are older and out of print. My Bibliography contains a listing of books in my personal collection that I have found useful in researching the subject of trivets. Many of the books are still available online in the resale market at a reasonable price, and they provide information often otherwise unavailable.

My all-time favorite trivet reference is *A Collector's Guide to Trivets and Stands*, 1990, by Rob Roy Kelly and James Ellwood. This 263-page hardbound book contains information on ironmaking and casting, trivet makers and distributors, trivet designs, and how to date a trivet. There are nearly 1,300 trivets pictured, along with notes on dimensions, markings, availability, and value. It's a must for every trivet collector!

The Evolution of the Sad Iron, 1970, hardbound, by A.H. "Whitey" Glissman, is a rare book find. Mr. Glissman follows the history of ironing through 282 pages, from Chinese pan irons to early seventeenth and eighteenth century sadirons, progressing on to the more modern irons of the nineteenth and twentieth century. There are some trivets and stands illustrated, most within the context of their companion irons.

Another wonderful reference is *A Collector's Guide to Pressing Irons and Trivets*, 1977, by Esther S. Berney. This 182 page hardbound book is intended primarily for the sadiron collector, but trivets are illustrated lavishly throughout, and there is one chapter concentrating solely on trivets. It's very interesting to be able to see photographs of the actual irons that were companions to many of the sadiron stands and trivets we collect.

Next on my list would have to be the self-published, softbound Dick Hankenson companion books *Trivets*, 1963 (118 pages), and *Trivets Old and Repro*, 1968 (144 pages). They show some trivets not illustrated in other references, along with personal insights by the author about trivet collecting. The Wallace-Homestead Book Company reissued these books in 1972, under the titles *Trivets Book 1* and *Trivets Book 2*. Be aware that there are copies of these books that were personally autographed by the author, and that they are of more collectible value.

If you're interested in collecting miniature trivets, try to find *Tuesday's Children — Little Irons and Trivets*, 1977, by Judy Politzer. It's a comprehensive 271 page softbound book packed with information on toy-sized irons and their matching trivets. The last chapter dedicates 51 pages to the discussion of both antique and reproduction miniature trivets. Her second book in 1986, *Early Tuesday Morning; More Little Irons and Trivets*, is 258 pages and just as highly recommended.

In 1991 *British Iron Stands* was meticulously assembled by Hazel Mitchell for the 8th International Conference of Iron Collectors in Bath, England. It's a 181 page softbound reference work describing and illustrating hundreds of British and Scottish trivets. The end of the book features reprints of old advertisements for irons and trivets. Unfortunately, only 100 numbered copies of this work were published; so if you ever get the opportunity to purchase one, do.

Finally, *Collecting Cast Iron* by Alex Ames, 1980 (288 pages), is a fabulous hardbound book, thoroughly discussing every type of cast iron object imaginable. There is information on trivets and stands, of course; but material is also presented on sadirons, stoves, grates, doorknockers, match safes, umbrella stands, urns, and toys. The following other reference books in my library that I refer to often:

• *Antique Collecting for Everyone*, 1951, hardbound, by Katherine Morrison McClinton (a nice chapter on trivets)

• *Antique Iron, Identification and Values*, 1984, softbound (there are revised editions available), by Kathryn McNerney (helpful information on cleaning cast iron)

• *Old American Kitchenware*, 1972, hardbound, by Louise K. Lantz (wonderful illustrations of all types of vintage kitchenware, including a chapter devoted to trivets)

- *Spinning Wheel's Collectible Iron, Tin, Copper & Brass*, 1974, hardbound, edited by Albert Christian Revi (several chapters on trivets, irons, and other vintage collectibles)

Old magazines with articles about trivets are intriguing to read and collect, as they often provide additional information that may not appear in any other source. Several of these older articles were written by the noted trivet experts of the time, such as Dick Hankenson and William Paley. In my Bibliography at the end of this book, I've listed 20 magazines that I've found so far that include articles on trivets. However, the following are of special interest, and deserve a place in your reference collection.

- Darmstaetter, Hugo. "Cast and Wrought Iron Beauty in Trivets for Flat-Irons and Other Hot Items." *Spinning Wheel*, September 1950: 10 – 12.
  Not only a great article, but also the trivet cover art is suitable for framing.

- Hankenson, Dick. "Old and New Cast Iron Trivets." *Spinning Wheel*, June 1962: 16.
  Another magazine with decorative cover art, accompanied by a nice article by Dick Hankenson.

- Jessup, Grace. "Trivets as My Hobby." *Hobbies*, November 1950: 107 – 109.
  The author briefly discusses her trivet collection. Notable for the beautiful cover art.

- Menard, Gene. "Trivets." *Hobbies*, October 1938: 63.
  A large collection of trivets is pictured on the cover, accompanied by a one-page article. This is my oldest magazine.

- Paley, William. "Brass Trivets: The Old and the New." *Spinning Wheel*, October 1969: 60 – 61.
  Paley discusses guidelines for determining age in brass trivets.

- Paley, William. "Flowers and Vines in Trivets." *Spinning Wheel*, September 1973: 30 – 31.
  This article discusses a variety of spade and circular trivets that feature these designs.

- Paley, William. "Trivets from A – Z." *Spinning Wheel*, March 1971: 40 – 41.
  Examples of trivets that incorporate alphabet letters or monograms into their surface design.

These collectible magazines featured articles on trivets, as well as decorative cover art.

Spinning Wheel, September 1950   *Spinning Wheel*, June 1962   *Hobbies*, November 1950   *Hobbies*, October 1938

Conversations with Other Trivet Collectors

As I concluded this book, I realized that it was missing one crucial element: an opportunity for readers to meet other collectors, and to experience trivet collecting from several different perspectives. I personally have found trivet collecting to be a somewhat solitary pursuit, as I only occasionally meet another person who collects them. However, I take great enjoyment in having my trivets displayed around my home, where I can view them on a daily basis; and as opportunities arise, I introduce as many people as possible to my fascinating hobby of trivet collecting.

When I lived in Ormond Beach, Florida, I once had my entire trivet collection displayed in the Public Library entranceway within two long, locked glass shelved display cases. I loved to linger there and listen to the comments of passers-by. Younger people invariably had no idea what trivets were, and commented on their oddity. Older folks stayed longer, reminiscing about their parents or grandparents who had used those very items in their everyday lives.

My trivet collection pales in comparison to some of the collections you are about to hear described. All of the essays to follow were contributed by people I have had the good fortune to meet through my buying and selling on eBay™. They were very generous to allow a glimpse into both their lives and their personal collections. I am so honored to share their photographs, as they contribute so much to the telling of each personal story. As you read through each one, just imagine that you could spend an afternoon with any one of these lovely people, seeing their entire collection in person and being able to discuss trivets at length.

Doris Cabral, Uncasville, Connecticut

My name is Doris Ann Cabral, and I am 58 years old. I started collecting over 20 years ago, when I happened to buy my first trivet at an antique show held at Connecticut College in New London, Connecticut. And it has been a passion ever since. I also collect other antiques, but trivets and mini bed warmers are my favorites.

This is a hobby for me, and my challenge now is to find the trivets that I don't have, which are mostly the rare ones. I have found trivets from Canada to Florida, and from the East Coast (where I live) to the West Coast...I have been all over looking...and I love the hunt! I'll have to admit, though, I've found most of my trivets in the Northeastern United States.

Just to let you know, I have a small three-bedroom ranch in southeastern Connecticut where I grew up. I have baskets, bins, and boxes full of trivets! I have brass, copper, wire, cast iron, and wrought iron...over 600 trivets. I have the iron and wire ones mounted in my kitchen, and the brass and copper ones displayed on my living room walls. I also have a sunroom with one entire wall of barn board covered with trivets. I have

Doris Cabral's favorite trivet, the British Spider and Web design, 9⅕" x 6" x 1¼" with four legs and the Rd. No. 96845 (circa 1888). Doris has over 600 trivets, many which are packed away in boxes.

many favorites, but my all-time favorite trivet is a Spider & Web design that I finally found this year in Sturbridge, Massachusetts. It's shown on page 132 of Kelly and Ellwood's book, *Trivets and Stands*. I don't know why, but just looking at these trivets on my walls gives me a warm feeling and puts a smile on my face!

An interesting experience: My husband and I went to the Brimfield Antiques Show in Massachusetts one year...that show is one of the largest and best known in the country, with over 5,000 dealers and exhibitors. They operate it for six days at a time, several times a year, and the 30,000+ visitors literally overrun the small town of Brimfield, population 3,000! Well, we both brought a fair amount of money with us...and I was just so excited by all the trivets I was finding. By the time we left, we didn't have even one dollar between the two of us! We ended up using a charge card for gas and dinner. On the drive home my hubby looked over at me, shook his head, and grinned as he said, "Doris, you are bad!"

I have met some wonderful people on eBay™ such as the author, Lynn, and Vince Katchen. I've had the pleasure of personally meeting James Ellwood, the co-author of *Trivets and Stands*, and even had the opportunity to go to his home in Scottsdale, Arizona, and view his extensive trivet collection. That was a wonderful experience, and certainly one that I will never forget!

Vince Katchen, Mount Bethel, Pennsylvania

My exposure to trivets and collecting began in Wellington, Kansas, in the late 1960s and early 1970s. A very close "second mother figure" introduced me to her old collection, which kindled an interest in trivet collecting that continued throughout the years to come, to my own benefit.

Later, again residing in Pennsylvania, I discovered that the area flea markets exhibited many different kinds of trivets; thus, I began collecting. Having moved into an old farmhouse, I had plenty of barren wall space and the free time to "hunt" for trivets. I discovered that there were many old foundries in Pennsylvania that had produced a vast number of trivets. Initially, I collected all kinds and shapes of trivets made from brass, iron, aluminum, bronze, tin, and white metal. Some were of wrought iron and proved much more expensive to acquire, as most of those were considered to be "primitives" and very collectible.

So, as time passed I began to specialize, selling those trivets I no longer wanted, primarily on eBay™. To date, I have chosen to collect only pre-World War II trivets from all nations. I especially have an interest in the older Pennsylvania designed iron, brass, and bronze trivets. At one time I had over 2,000 trivets hanging or resting about the farmhouse; but, after downsizing, I can truthfully say that it is now closer to 1,500 in number. I

Vince Katchen has an extensive trivet collection. Here are just a few of his horseshoe trivets on display at his home in Pennsylvania.

plan on publishing a book of my own someday in the near future, choosing to present primarily those early trivets not pictured in any other book.

I reside with my wife just outside of the Delaware Water Gap Recreation Area, between New Jersey and Pennsylvania. I actively continue to search for those trivets I may not have in my own collection. In addition, I continue to seek those trivets I consider to be very collectible, no matter how old. And yes, I do still sell on eBay™, using the seller name of "trivetman." My wife collects unusual and older glass/crystal bells, and also selective pieces of Cobalt Blue glass. Because of our large collections, I am occasionally told that our home will never be blown away in a windstorm or tornado!

Jan Mosley, Corvallis, Oregon

How does someone get into collecting something as obscure as black, cast iron trivets? There are so many other bright and beautiful things out there to collect and brighten the home...but heavy, metal, one-color trivets?

About seventeen years ago I began dating a wonderful man, perfect in many ways, except that he was (and is) the worst pack rat that has ever walked the planet! He adores estate, yard, and garage sales. One day he found a little owl trivet that he thought I might like, and brought it to my home. I found it very sweet, but not really anything I would've purchased for myself. Well, somehow that little trivet wormed its way into my heart, and a few months later it was joined by a second trivet, also purchased at one of our local estate sales.

Soon after, we were married and moved to our new home, which has an enormous kitchen...originally with large, blank walls. The owl and its

Jan Mosley and some of the trivets that cover her kitchen walls.

partner went up on one of the walls; and before I have had time to think about it, over 100 more trivets have joined them! My trivets now cover every available space in the kitchen, have wandered into the dining room, and have begun to creep into the family room.

I have friends, relatives, and co-workers finding and presenting new trivets to me almost monthly. Last year a co-worker called me on a Saturday to tell me about an estate sale where there were nearly 30 cast-iron, black trivets...I broke every speed law in Oregon to get there, and found 15 of them "new" to my collection. That was Heaven! I prowl antique stores and join my husband when he checks out his local sales, and I adore eBay™! A large portion of my collection has come from eBay™ purchases.

My husband and I are both on the faculty of Oregon State University. He's into potato research — crop science — and I am an administrator in engineering. I am the mature age of 56 years, and... obviously... we live in Oregon! I also half-heartedly collect miniature clocks and cat tins...and cats! I breed (very small operation cattery) the domestic breed of Bengal cats. In his spare time, my husband is an expert woodworker, restorer of "vintage" vehicles, and professional croquet player.

No one else in my family collects trivets; in fact, they often look at my collection of 100 plus and remark about the strange things people collect! It is purely a hobby, and I adore them. It is such a thrill when I can find a trivet that I do not have, and that is getting harder and harder to do...but the hunt is fun!

Linda Negron, Mountaintop, Pennsylvania

My name is Linda Negron. I'm 48 years old, and I have two wonderful, grown sons who like to indulge Mom's infatuation for trivet collecting (though they prefer to call it an obsession, which is probably true). I live on a mountain, in the Pocono Region of Pennsylvania. I acquired my first three trivets about eight years ago from an eccentric woman here in the Poconos who has, as I refer to it, "her own little flea market." Before that, I mainly collected wrought iron things, but I saw those trivets of hers and thought they were neat and different.

Then, about two years ago, I got my very first computer and found eBay™. I started buying little things here and there; and then one day I happened upon a category titled Trivets. As I searched and looked, I was amazed at just how many different trivets there were. I became fascinated with them! I came upon this one auction with two really neat trivets and thought, "Why not? I'll give this a try." Well, I won the auction; and when I received them, I was hooked on trivet collecting, and there's been no stopping me since.

Those first trivets, it so happens, came to me from Lynn herself. As a result of that first encounter, not only did I get two beautiful trivets and become determined to seriously start collecting them, but I also made a wonderful friend. She has helped me build my collection, as well as guided me with her knowledge and helpful information.

Since that first eBay™ purchase, my trivet collection has grown from five to almost one hundred and counting! Though I love them all, I do have my favorites. Besides the cast iron, I have a great collection of brass trivets, cast iron framed tile trivets, and iron rests. I have also started collecting cast iron match safes, of which I have managed to acquire a small but impressive grouping. Other collectibles that I buy are trivet candle holders (table top and sconces), electric trivet hot plates, trivet clocks, trivet wall lamps, trivet hooks, and cast iron store receipt hooks.

I have already introduced a few friends and family members to this wonderful hobby. Trivet collecting has become as much a passion for me as a business; and though I buy more than I sell, I don't see this slowing down much in the future. I've only just begun this wonderful and fascinating journey. I look forward to many more years of trivet collecting, and of the many new friends I will make along the way....

Linda Negron poses alongside some of her favorite trivets.

Adair Shepherd, Wantage, New Jersey

I am Adair Shepherd, and live with my husband Ron on a small farm in the northwest corner of New Jersey. We have twenty or so goats, mostly pygmy; two miniature donkeys and a miniature horse; and miniature Call ducks, as well as a large koi pond. We have raised eight children who are grown and out of the house, and we now take care of foster children (babies), a calling that we love. My husband is on disability and so takes care of the animals and babies during the day. I take over as soon as I get home from work, and also care for them on the weekends. We love the country and the children; they help keep us young!

Trivets and other antiques adorn Adair Shepherd's fireplace.

Trivets are my other passion. How did I pick trivets? Well, let me share with you how they became a big part of my life. Many years ago, I saw my first trivets hanging around the fireplaces of my Great-Grandmother Todd's farm, just outside of Warwick, New York. Next I visited my Grandfather Todd's sister, and she also had trivets. Many of those old trivets, including a large lazy Susan trivet, were passed down to my mother and then to me. Trivets have always been associated with warmth, hospitality, and the people I love. Some of my grown children will get my trivets when the time comes.

I have been collecting trivets, adding to the collection passed on to me, for 40 some years. Remembering where this or that trivet was found has been a standing joke between my mother (who turned 90 in December 2002) and myself for years! My trivets hang around the tops of my walls in most of my rooms, the kitchen, living room, and dining room having the most. I have well over 300 hanging right now, but there are thousands to choose from. I even have a few that "Trivetman" (Vince Katchen) doesn't have! I think that my next project will be to cover the descending staircase walls with trivets, and then call it quits.

I love to see and collect trivets from other countries, and eBay™ is perfect for finding them. I now have trivets from Australia, Wales, England, Germany, Austria, Scotland, France, Israel, and Mexico.

Arnie Stein, Morris, Minnesota

My name is Arnie Stein. I am 61 years old and my wife, Corrine, and I live in a rural farm community in western Minnesota. Our collecting interests began in 1990 and quickly expanded to a hobby of acquiring a variety of many interesting and vintage items. In 1995 we began collecting antique pressing irons from all over the world. To date we have accumulated about 1,800 old irons and the collection continues to grow.

Arnie Stein poses with a small sampling of his enormous iron and trivet collection.

Along with the irons, we acquired several trivets as well as the two trivet books by Dick Hankenson. As we studied the books, we began to look for more trivets. Since Mr. Hankenson of Maple Plain, Minnesota, had lived only 100 miles away from us, we regretted that we had never had the opportunity to meet him. Corrine and I then decided to find as many of the cast iron trivets he had illustrated in his books as we could. We now have most of them plus many others. At the present time our collection numbers about 750, consisting of good quality original pieces. With the exception of Griswold, we avoid buying reproductions such as Wilton, Virginia Metalcrafters, or JZH. Our strongest interest is in manufacturer's stands, and we take great pride in locating a companion trivet to match an iron in our collection. We also like stovepipe trivets, stove and cereal trivets, and sad iron heaters. If we see something we like, we buy it, no matter what the category. Although we concentrate on cast iron, we do have some very beautiful brass pieces as well.

One of our most gratifying moments came at an auction sale where we found a Clefton trivet complete with the Clefton carbide gas iron and gas hose, all in excellent condition, for only $10. This Clefton iron was made in Owatonna, Minnesota, around 1900. Minnesota is also famous for several liquid fuel irons made by the American Gas Machine Company of Albert Lea. We have several fine examples in our collection.

Corrine and I love going to auctions, especially those of old country estates. We have many other small collections of saws, jacks, tools, wagon wheels, corn shellers and planters, walking plows and cultivators, butter churns, coffee grinders, crocks, and glassware. We also enjoy collecting old advertising pieces from the local community. We do not, however, find many good trivets or pressing irons at local auctions. Fortunately, there are still many good pieces available on eBay™ and from other collectors. At this time we do not have our irons and trivets organized in a display, but plan to accomplish that after retirement. Hopefully we will then meet some of you folks who share our interest. Meanwhile, Happy Hunting!

Bob Viguers, Harrisburg, Pennsylvania

This is my story of trivets, and how I came to collect them. I got married in 1955 at the age of 20. Shortly after, a friend, Mr. Daniel Stephens (who knew I liked antiques) gave me one that had belonged to his wife. It was a rather common trivet, a Philadelphia Pa. Enterprise "E," and I hung it on our kitchen wall.

Trivets were one of the few antiques I felt a newly married person could afford. A short time later, I picked up a few trivets marked "Wilton" and showed them to Mr. Stephens, who said, "They aren't old! They make them in Wrightsville, Pennsylvania." Not long after that he took me to the Wilton showroom, where they had pegs displaying a dozen examples each of the various reproduction designs they produced. Retailers would come to purchase items to sell in the Lancaster County Pennsylvania Dutch souvenir shops. John Wright's showroom was just across the street, with another display of fine reproductions. One nice thing about these two companies was that they marked almost everything they made on the reverse, so collectors would know they weren't the "old" ones. (The John Wright Company used a three-digit number.)

Bob Viguers, surrounded by the trivets and stands he enjoys collecting!

We had a local weekly newspaper, and I advertised: "Interested in old trivets. Please call if you have even one." A lady called, I think her name was Mrs. Spangler; she said she was moving to what today would be called an assisted-living facility, and that she had a few things to sell, including a trivet. She mentioned that she'd had this item since childhood, and that it had been a Christmas gift. When I went to visit her, I found it to be a toy trivet and iron that came together as one. The bottom of the iron matched the trivet exactly, and they did look like they belonged together. This has become one of my favorite items.

Being interested in old items, I asked her about a rather heavy tumbler she had for sale. "Why," I asked, "would you save that?" She replied that on weekends, as a young girl, she and her friends would take the Cumberland Valley Railroad from Harrisburg, Pennsylvania, to Williams Grove, which was fifteen miles away. The rail car had a drinking fountain with one glass for everyone in that car to drink from. She stole it; and sure enough, on the bottom of the glass it had CVRR cast right into it! I bought that, too.

I've learned that very few, if any, old trivets were ever marked on the bottom. Even most of the pieces Griswold made were reproductions of much older designs. But, advertising pays! Griswold collectors proved that if you want to increase the value of something, write a book! I wish someone would do the same for Enterprise or Wilton.

The first book I saw dedicated to trivets was written by Dick Hankenson. I was so impressed that I wrote him, and we corresponded for years about trivets. (Sadly, Dick Hankenson passed away some time ago. His collection was sold piece-meal at auction.) We discussed things like what names should be assigned to trivets; the controversial Colt trivet that the firearms company denied ever producing; or how best to clean and preserve cast iron items. Dick made an oil and preservative to use on his trivets; but I find more satisfaction with the results of Stove Black, which can be bought in hardware stores; that's what your great-grandmother would have used to keep them nice. Using Stove Black, the harder you rub, the shinier your trivets will get. Grandma wouldn't have allowed some rusty pieces of junk lying around her kitchen! Here are some suggestions for how to identify old trivets.

- Look to see if it is "signed." If it is, let it sit — that is, unless you collect Wilton or Griswold or whatever.

- Remember that the rust on old castings made from ore turns a dark brown, like the rust on an old iron bridge. New iron or iron made from recycled metal rusts "orangey" because recycled metal has more oxygen in it.

- Old trivets were tools, and as such were made with long legs, to protect surfaces from hot or heavy items. These long legged trivets were hard to hang for display; so newer castings of older designs were made with shorter legs.

- Many trivets were nickel plated. I'd like to take a few of mine that have an eroded finish to a shop to get the nickel renewed, just to see what one would have originally looked like.

- Even antique trivets were made to buy and save as souvenirs of special events. For instance, the Lincoln Drape design (reproduction called Grain and Tassel by Wilton) was a souvenir for the viewing of President Lincoln's funeral train. There was a brass George Washington trivet that was a souvenir of the Philadelphia Centennial Exposition in 1876. A horseshoe that says "Christmas 1888" was probably cast as a Christmas party favor. And the Masonic and other fraternal commemoratives (P.O.E., I.O.O.F., K.G.E., etc.) were given as souvenirs of special events. Masonic trivets were often distributed to the wives on Ladies Night, or Anniversary Night, at the Lodges. I learned that in 1889, the Knights of the Golden Eagle had a convention in Philadelphia, attended by several thousand members accompanied by their wives. The horseshoe plaque trivet I have with K.G.E on it was probably a souvenir of that event.

- Several of these eagle/horseshoe plaque trivets I have still have a trace of glittery "sparkles" on them. I'm sure the majority of these were carnival or festival trophies.

And, of course, read read-read! See Dick Hankenson's *Trivets Books 1 & 2*; Kelly & Ellwood's *A Collector's Guide to Trivets and Stands*; and Esther Berney's *A Collector's Guide to Pressing Irons and Trivets*. And remember, just because someone wrote it down doesn't make it true!

Thank you for this opportunity to talk trivets, and happy collecting!

USER GUIDE TO TRIVETS AND STANDS

Naming trivets is predominantly a recent phenomenon, as most antique trivets were not appointed design names. Although some of the more popular antique trivet designs acquired names over time, the majority of trivet names we are acquainted with derive from the 1950s, when companies assigned them to their contemporary trivets. Every effort has been made to discover the most definitive, as well as any commonly used, name(s) for the trivets in the author's collection. Dick Hankenson assigned names to all the trivets in his books, and I have continued to perpetuate those names in my book. In cases where there is no generally acknowledged name, the trivet is cataloged with the best possible description as created by the author, followed by (LR).

In review, as defined by the U.S. Customs Office in the 1930s, an antique is an item greater than 100 years old. Trivets categorized as vintage are of historical or aesthetic significance, but less than 100 years old. Contemporary trivets are categorized as an older casting (1940 – 1970) or a modern casting (after 1970). Remember that, as time goes by, the numerical window for an antique, vintage, or contemporary item is constantly adjusting.

Prices were determined by reviewing price guides; by observing the interest in and sales prices of trivets on Internet auctions; and by browsing through antique shops and flea markets, discussing asking versus selling prices with dealers. Unless otherwise noted, trivets are priced in fine condition.

There can be some slight degree of variance in trivet proportions in castings by the same foundry. Therefore, all measurements are simply rounded to the closest eighth of an inch. Dimensions are listed in order of length, then width. Height, included only for antique or vintage trivets and stands or unique contemporary trivets, is measured from the table surface to the top of the trivet. If there is anything unusual about the design of the legs, for example: cleats or paw feet, it will be mentioned in the description. Trivet lengths include the handle unless otherwise stated.

Whenever possible, information on the trivets and stands cataloged in this book will include their manufacturer, intended purpose, and age. British trivets and stands, showing Rd numbers, are dated using the Registered Design numbering system. Pairing a stand with its companion sadiron, which usually had a patent date, can often most accurately identify and date an American sadiron stand. If the exact age of the trivet cannot be determined, the author has made estimation by closely examining the trivet for cast marks, leg length, and design, and then by consulting the best current references available. In that case, estimated era will be identified by the abbreviation (E).

Note: Wooden, wire, or silver trivets and metal trivets with tile inserts are not included in this reference, since I personally don't collect them.

My objective for this chapter was to present a balanced representation of the different types of trivets and stands you are most likely to encounter. I've also tried my best to discover as much information as possible about each trivet illustrated. Hopefully, there will be a future edition of this book featuring additional information and even more trivets and stands!

Value Guide

My suggested values are a reflection of age, scarcity, desirability, and condition.

$20.00 or less	— Mass-produced contemporary castings of either American or foreign origin.
$20.00 to 45.00	— Less common contemporary castings, and plentiful trivets and stands.
$45.00 to 70.00	— Scarce contemporary castings and more desirable trivets and stands.
$70.00 to 110.00	— Noteworthy trivets and stands of either American or foreign origin.
$110.00 to 150.00	— Rare trivets and stands, which are highly prized by serious collectors.
$150.00 and up	— Museum quality trivets and stands, which may be handcrafted and thus unique.

Condition Guide

A trivet or stand in fair or poor condition is acceptable in a respectable collection only if it is currently the best available representation of a particularly old or scarce trivet.

Mint — As new condition; may still be in the original packaging.

Fine — Gently used with very slight evidence of wear. If copper or nickel-plated, at least 75% of the original plating finish remains.

Good — A barely noticeable, hairline crack that doesn't affect structural integrity and/or a few small chips are acceptable in this category. Some smooth, rubbed areas of wear evident. May show slight paint fading or loss. If copper or nickel-plated, at least 50% of the plating remains.

Fair — Obvious, full surface crack(s) that doesn't affect structural integrity; larger chips in metal. Small piece of the design broken off. Partial wearing away of surface lettering and/or design detail. If plated, less than 50% of the plating remains. Significant surface pitting from rust.

Poor — The trivet has at least one full surface crack that affects its structural integrity and/or there is a significant piece missing. Surface lettering, plating, and/or design detail has worn away.

Abbreviations

A — Aluminum
BR — Brass
BZ — Bronze
CI — Cast Iron
CPCI — Copper Plated Cast Iron
NPCI — Nickel Plated Cast Iron
T — Tin

LR — Trivet name assigned by author
E — Age of trivet is estimated using the best available information.

Metal Alloys

An alloy is the mixture, by melting together, of two or more metals. Often a less valuable metal is mixed with a more valuable one, in order to increase the degree of hardness.

Brass — Yellowish metal: an alloy of copper (more than 50%), zinc, and various other metals.

Bronze — Reddish brown metal: an alloy of copper, tin, and sometimes various other trace metals.

Cast Iron — Gray-black metal, very fluid and malleable when molten: an alloy predominantly of iron, carbon (2 to 4½%), and silicon (½ to 3%).

Suggested Price — are for trivets and stands in fine or better condition. Always try to purchase the best quality pieces for your collection, and upgrade as the opportunity arises.

Stands for Ironing

A in S. NPCI, plentiful antique or vintage sadiron stand, unmarked on reverse. On face: large S and smaller A. Two smoothed gate-marks on rear edge. Manufacturer unknown. Late 1800s to early 1900s (E). 6½ x 4¼ x ½" with three feet. *$35.00*

A-Best-O. More desirable antique or vintage sadiron stand, NPCI, unmarked on reverse. On face: A-BEST-O, a trade name of the Dover Manufacturing Company, Dover, Ohio (Glissman p. 88). Sadirons with removable asbestos-lined hoods, to keep the handle cool and maintain the heat in the core, were popular in the early 1900s. Early 1900s. 7 x 4¼ x 1½" with three cleated legs. *$50.00*

Acme. More desirable antique or vintage sadiron stand, NPCI, numbered on the reverse. On face: ACME and two dragons. Front guide rail. 102 on the reverse. Possibly a companion stand to either the J.B. Mast Company Gas Iron, New York, or the Acme Self-Heating Iron Company Charcoal Iron, Ravenna, Ohio (Berney p. 86 & Irons p. 58). Late 1880s to early 1900s, depending upon manufacturer. 6½ x 3⅝ x ¾" with three feet. *$55.00*

American Beauty. Bi-level, plentiful vintage sadiron stand, pressed steel. On face: AMERICAN BEAUTY IRON and MADE BY AMERICAN ELECTRICAL HEATER CO. DETROIT USA. Made of two stands bolted together to provide a cooling space in between. Feet are hollow cups. Companion trivet to the No. 6½ B American Beauty Iron. 1920s. 7⅜ x 4¼ x 1⅜" with three cupped legs. *$25.00*

American Foundry, AF. CI, plentiful antique or vintage sadiron stand, unmarked on reverse. On face: AMERICAN. FOUNDRY. & MFG. CO. ST LOUIS MO. and their AF logo. Two very rough, unfiled gate-marks on side. Still in business, American Foundry has been casting fire hydrants since 1888. Late 1800s to early 1900s (E). 5¾ x 4¼ x ¾" with three feet. *$30.00*

B. CI, plentiful antique or vintage sadiron stand, unsigned on reverse. On face: B. Shallow side rails. Manufacturer unknown. Late 1800s to early 1900s (E). 6½ x 4⅜ x ¾" with three feet. *$35.00*

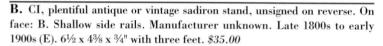

Blacksmith Wrought Circle. Noteworthy antique sadiron stand, unique item, wrought iron. Freeform design, hand wrought by a blacksmith. Early to mid 1800s (E). 6½ x 1¾" with three wrought legs. *$75.00*

Blacksmith Wrought Sadiron. Noteworthy antique item, wrought iron. Blacksmith wrought and thus unique. There is some pitting to the metal from rust and age. Handle rises 3½" above surface of iron. Early to mid 1800s (E). 6 x 4 x 1½". *$75.00*

Bless & Drake, B & D. CI, plentiful antique or vintage gas iron stand, unsigned on reverse. On face: B & D. Guide cleats on each side of platform. Two gate-marks at rear of platform. Originally manufactured by Bless & Drake, Newark, New Jersey. Hankenson commented that this plentiful trivet design was being reproduced (Book 1, Supplement p. 3). Late 1800s and beyond. 6 x 4⅜ x ⅜" with three feet. *$25.00*

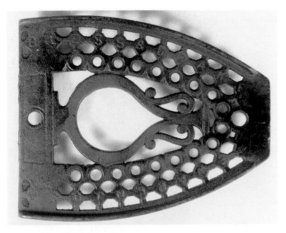

Bless & Drake, Lacy Urn Variant. CI, plentiful vintage gas iron stand, unmarked on reverse. On face: BLESS AND DRAKE NEWARK N.J. U.S.A. inscribed in small letters around the perimeter, between the first and second row of circles. Smooth shallow railing along sides. This Lacy Urn design was also cast in a version with a scalloped railing. Made in 1913 (Berney p. 82). 5⅞ x 4⅝ x 1" with three legs. *$35.00*

Bless & Drake, Lacy Urn Variant (close-up). Close-up shows where lettering appears on face of trivet... LESS & D visible in this view.

Bug, Plain. CI, plentiful antique or vintage sadiron stand, unsigned on reverse. Filed gate mark at end of platform. This style is commonly called "Bug" because the design resembles an insect. Late 1800s to early 1900s (E). 5⅝ x 3⅜ x ⅝" with three cleated feet. *$30.00*

Bug, Rochester. CI, more desirable antique sadiron stand, unmarked on reverse. On face: ROCHESTER SAD IRON. Commonly called the "Rochester Bug." Late 1800s (Irons p. 106). 5¾ x 4½ x ⅝" with three cleated feet. *$60.00*

C. CI, plentiful antique or vintage sadiron stand, unsigned on reverse. On face: C. Shallow side rails. Two filed gate-marks on rear edge. Possibly the companion stand to the Chattanooga sadiron. Late 1800s to early 1900s (E). 6¼ x 4⅛ x ¾" with three feet. *$30.00*

C in Grid (LR). CI, more desirable antique or vintage casting, numbered on reverse. On face: C in center of design. Leg supports are an extension of the rim. On reverse: the numbers 6644 and 3. Manufacturer unknown. Early 1900s (E). 5⅞ x 6⅞ x 1" with eight leg supports. *$45.00*

Carron, No. 5 Turtle. CI, more desirable vintage sadiron stand, Scottish, signed Carron. Carron and No 5 on reverse. Carron Ironworks operated in Falkirk, Scotland, from 1759 to 1985. (Earlier issues of this design often feature an Rd number or Rd diamond.) Shown in their 1932 catalog listing. 9½ x 5 x 1" with four splayed, ornamental legs. *$50.00*

Carron, No.4. CI, noteworthy antique sadiron stand, Scottish, signed Carron. On reverse: CARRON No. 4 and the Rd diamond. This diamond is from the first series, 1842 – 1867, and the letter M identifies the year of issue as 1859. Carron Ironworks operated in Falkirk, Scotland, from 1759 to 1985. 1859. 6⅝ x 5¼ x 1¼" with three splayed leg supports. *$100.00*

Cinderella Stoves & Ranges, Fancy. More desirable antique or vintage sadiron stand, NPCI, unmarked on reverse. On face: CINDERELLA STOVES AND RANGES NEVER FAIL embossed on four-leaf clover. Decorative flower edging to top and bottom areas. Also made in brass plated cast iron. Three guide cleats on each side of platform. 1890s to 1910s. 5⅜ x 4 x ¾" with three feet. *$55.00*

Cinderella Stoves & Ranges, Plain. More desirable antique or vintage sadiron stand, NPCI, unmarked on reverse. On face: CINDERELLA STOVES AND RANGES NEVER FAIL embossed on four-leaf clover. Shallow side rails. Machine grinding to a 2" area on edge of trivet rear. 1890s to 1910s. 5⅝ x 4⅛ x ⅝" with three feet. *$50.00*

Clark, J.R. CI, more desirable antique sadiron stand, unmarked on reverse. On face: THE J.R. CLARK CO. MINNEAPOLIS. A beautifully cast and very delicate stand. Late 1880s (Hankenson Book 1, p. 38). 7⅛ x 3⅞ x ⅜" with four feet. *$50.00*

Cleveland Star & Sunburst. CI, plentiful antique sadiron stand, unmarked on reverse. On face: THE CLEVELAND FOUNDRY CO., two filed gate-marks on rear edge, and ⅜" side rails. Patented June 23, 1891. 6 x 4⅜ x 1" with three legs. *$25.00*

Colebrookdale Crown & Maltese Cross No.2. CI, plentiful antique or vintage sadiron stand, unmarked on reverse. On face: COLEBROOKDALE IRON CO., POTTSTOWN, PA. Shallow side rails. My stand would be devalued due to excessive pitting from rust. Late 1890s to 1910s (Berney, p. 19). 6 x 4½ x ⅝" with three feet. *$30.00*

Colt. CI, more desirable antique gas iron stand, unmarked on reverse. On face: COLT. Large machine filed gate-mark on side. Two cleat guides on each side. This is the companion trivet to the Colt Carbide Gas Flatiron (Berney p. 80 & Glissman p. 153 – 154). I've found no evidence yet that Colt Firearms ever made this stand. Made in 1903. 6½ x 4 x ½" with three feet. *$45.00*

Crown & Maltese Cross, Plain. CI, plentiful antique or vintage sadiron stand, unmarked on reverse. Two pronounced gate-marks at rear of platform. Very common design, the basis for many variations. Late 1800s to early 1900s. 6¼ x 4⅛ x ¾" with three feet. *$25.00*

Detwiler Automatic Safety Stand. CI, more desirable antique or vintage sadiron stand, unmarked on reverse. On face: DETWILER AUTOMATIC SAFETY STAND. APP'D FOR in center circle. Filed gate-mark on side. Two guides for iron on either side. No other information yet on this manufacturer. 1900 to 1920s (E). 7½ x 4⅝ x ⅞" with three cleated feet. $65.00

Economy E. CI, more desirable antique or vintage sadiron stand, unmarked on reverse. On face: "ECONOMY" SYRACUSE, N.Y. Machine ground gate-mark on rear edge. Late 1800s to early 1900s (E). 6 x 4⅜ x ¾" with three feet. $45.00

Enterprise Bar. CI, plentiful antique sadiron stand, unmarked on reverse. On face: ENTERPRISE MFG CO PHILADELPHIA. Side rails on sides. Two gate marks at rear of platform. The Enterprise Mfg. Company was a major manufacturer of kitchen implements, such as meat grinders, coffee mills, and irons. Late 1870s and beyond (Berney p. 29). 6¼ x 4½ x ⅞" with three feet. $30.00

Enterprise E. CI, plentiful antique sadiron stand, unmarked on reverse. On face: ENTERPRISE M'F'G. CO. PHILA. USA. Two roughly filed gate-marks on rear edge. ⅜" rail on sides. Late 1800s. 6 x 4⅜ x ¼" with three feet. $20.00

Enterprise Girl's Star Toy Iron #105. CI, more desirable antique toy sadiron, signed Enterprise. Embossed on sadiron: ENTERPRISE. MFG. CO. PHILA. GIRLS STAR, PAT. OCT. 1, 57 No. 105, and PAT. JAN. 16, 77. This featured their patented "stay cool" handle with ventilation holes. 1877 and beyond. 5 x 2⅜ x 1¼". Handle rises 2⅛" above surface of iron. *$50.00*

Enterprise Girl's Star Toy Iron Stand. CI, more desirable antique toy stand, unmarked on reverse. Two rough unfiled gate-marks on lower trivet edges. Manufactured by the Enterprise Manufacturing Company, Philadelphia, Pennsylvania. Late 1870s (Berney p. 124). 5¾ x 2¾" with three small feet. *$45.00*

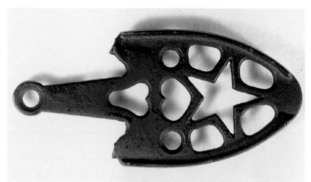

Fairy. NPCI, noteworthy antique or vintage gas iron stand, unsigned on reverse. On face: Gold accent paint to the raised lettering FAIRY and to the seal of a fairy within a circle of stars. Possibly the companion stand to the English made Fairy Prince Gas Iron. Late 1800s to early 1900s (E). 9⅜ x 4⅜ x ½" with three cleated feet. *$75.00*

Falkirk No. 5. CI, noteworthy antique sadiron stand, Rd diamond on reverse, Scottish. Two hand-filed gate-marks on edge. FALKIRK No. 5 and Rd diamond on reverse. Legend for Rd diamond: T at top signifies 1867, A in left corner and 29 in right corner signify January 29, and 4 in lower corner signifies batch number 4 for that casting. 1867. Falkirk Ironworks operated in Falkirk, Scotland, from 1819 to 1981. 9¾ x 4¼ x 1" with three splayed ornamental legs. *$90.00*

Falkirk No. 5 (reverse). Close-up detail of the Rd Diamond on the trivet reverse. Legend for Rd diamond: T at top signifies 1867, A in left corner and 29 in right corner signify January 29, and 4 in lower corner signifies batch number for that casting.

Fancy F (LR). NPCI, noteworthy antique or vintage sadiron stand, unsigned on reverse. On face: F. Recessed background behind "F" appears to have been painted a darker color at one time. Three round cast iron stops on top. Manufacturer unknown (possibly Fanner of Cleveland, Ohio). Purchased from the late Edna Glissman iron collection. Late 1800s to early 1900s (E). 6½ x 4⅜ x 1⅜" with three legs. *$75.00*

Ferrosteel Urn. CI, plentiful vintage sadiron stand, unsigned on reverse. On face: FERROSTEEL. CLEVELAND. Shallow side rails. 1915 and beyond (Hankenson Book 1, Supplement 4). 6 x 4⅜ x 1" with three legs. *$25.00*

Forged Open Spade (LR). Forged iron, French, rare antique sadiron stand, unsigned on reverse. Small chip at apex of stand where leg attaches. Hand forged and thus unique. When purchased from the late Edna Glissman iron collection, the hang tag was hand labeled "Cannes, France." Mid-1700s to mid-1800s (E). 8 x 3⅜ x 1⅝" with three twisted metal legs. *$110.00*

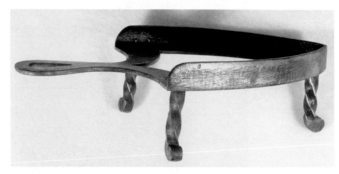

Forged Open Spade (LR), side view. Side view of trivet showing spiral legs.

General Specialty Company, H2H. CI, plentiful vintage gas iron stand, unmarked on reverse. On face, in center: H2H. Around edges: HUMPHREY GAS IRON and GENERAL SPECIALTY COMPANY. Shallow railing around platform. Manufactured in New York. Made in 1914 (Berney p. 83). 8 x 4¼ x ⅝" with four feet. *$35.00*

General Specialty Company, HGI. NPCI, plentiful vintage gas iron stand, unsigned on reverse. On face: HUMPHREY GAS IRON MFD. BY GENERAL SPECIALTY CO. Manufactured in New York. This stand is angled, with a longer front leg and two shorter back legs. Made in 1913 (Berney p. 83). 7¼ x 4⅛". My stand has a 1" front leg with two ⅜" back feet. *$35.00*

Geometric No. 3. CI, plentiful antique or vintage sadiron stand, unmarked on reverse. Shallow side rails. Two gate-marks at rear of platform. Late 1800s to early 1900s (E). 6⅛ x 4½ x 1" with three legs. *$25.00*

Harper. CI, noteworthy antique or vintage sadiron stand, unmarked on reverse. On face, twice: HARPER. File marks noted on one side edge. Harper, of Chicago, Illinois, made sadirons in the early 1900s (Irons pp. 215, 332, 343). Early 1900s. 5⅛ x 3⅝ x ⅝" with four feet. *$75.00*

Hatton Flat Iron Stand. British, CI, rare antique sadiron stand, Rd number on reverse. On face: USE THE UNIVERSAL SATIN GLAZE STARCH & AMMONIATED POWDER and W.R. HATTON & SONS WORMWOOD SCRUBS. On reverse: Rd No 250613, dating this stand to 1895. The center held a non-conducting asbestos pad. Wormwood Scrubs is an inner London suburb. Made in 1895. 10¼ x 5⅛ x 1¼" with three 1½ x 1¾" lion feet. (Length and width does not include the feet.) *$125.00*

Hazelton. CI, more desirable antique or vintage sadiron stand, signed on reverse. Plain on face. Side rails. On reverse: FRANK R. HAZELTON, ASBESTOS, and BOSTON MASS. Length does not include the unusual hanging ring on end. Early 1900s (E). 7 x 4⅜ x ⅞ " with three feet. *$50.00*

Hazelton, reverse. On reverse: FRANK R. HAZELTON, ASBESTOS, and BOSTON MASS.

Heart. Aluminum, more desirable vintage sadiron stand, unsigned on reverse. Two $\frac{5}{8}$ x $1\frac{5}{8}$" guides on each side of stand. Aluminum was long considered a precious metal due to the difficulty of extracting the ore. It didn't come into practical commercial use until the early twentieth century. Possibly handmade. 1910s to 1930s (E). $7\frac{3}{4}$ x $4\frac{7}{8}$ x $\frac{3}{4}$" with three cubed feet. *$45.00*

Heart with C, Serrated. CI, noteworthy antique sadiron stand, unsigned on reverse. On face: C. Shallow side rails. Two gate-marks visible along edge. Extensive routing on the reverse in the form of shallow, round drilled depressions. Mid to late 1800s. 8 x $3\frac{3}{4}$ x 1" with three legs. *$90.00*

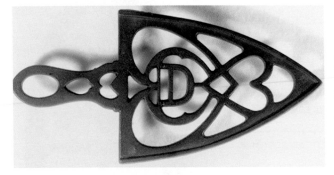

Heart with D. CI, more desirable antique sadiron stand, unmarked on reverse. On face: D, which is often mistaken for the letter A. Shallow side rails. One filed gate-mark on edge. Mid to late 1800s. 8 x $3\frac{3}{4}$ x 1" with three legs. *$60.00*

Heart with K. CI, rare antique sadiron stand, unmarked on reverse. On face: K. Shallow side rails. Two prominent, rough gate-marks along edge. Extensive backcoping on reverse. Mid to late 1800s. $7\frac{3}{4}$ x $3\frac{5}{8}$ x $1\frac{1}{8}$" with three legs. *$115.00*

Heart with W, Plain. CI, plentiful antique sadiron stand, unsigned on reverse. On face: W. Two round indentations on front of handle. Shallow side rails. Rough gate-mark on edge. Reverse: backcoping and four round indentations near center. Design known to have been produced in 1869 by Dover Stamping Company (Kelly & Ellwood p. 56). Mid to late 1800s. 8⅜ x 4 x 1" with three legs. *$40.00*

Heart with W, Serrated. CI, noteworthy antique sadiron stand, unmarked on reverse. On face: W. Seven shallow round indentations on top. Shallow side rails. Serrated edging to hearts. One entire side shows filing marks. Numerous small round drilled holes on reverse. Mid to late 1800s. 7¾ x 3¾ x 1" with three legs. *$70.00*

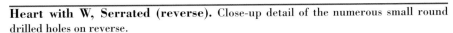

Heart with W, Serrated (reverse). Close-up detail of the numerous small round drilled holes on reverse.

Heart with W, Swirls. CI, rare antique sadiron stand, unsigned on reverse. On face: W. Shallow side rails. Filed gate-mark on rim. Backcoping behind handle. Mid to late 1800s. 9¾ x 4¾ x ⅞" with three feet. *$110.00*

Hope. CI, more desirable antique or vintage sadiron stand, unsigned on reverse. On face: HOPE inscribed below anchor. My stand would be devalued due to excessive pitting from rust. Late 1800s to early 1900s (E). 5½ x 4⅛ x ¾" with three feet. *$60.00*

Hot Cross. British, CI, rare antique charcoal box iron stand, Rd number on reverse. On face: HOT CROSS and PATENT. Rail and filed gate-mark on right side. On reverse: Rd 440821. Made by William Cross & Son, Ltd., Lyng Foundry, West Bromwich, Staffordshire, England. This was the companion stand to the "Workwell" charcoal box iron. 1905, as dated by its Rd number. 6⅞ x 4 x 1" with five legs. *$115.00*

Howell Geneva Star No. 5 Iron. CI, plentiful antique sadiron, signed Geneva. On body: the number 5 within a raised star. GENEVA in raised letters on handle. Geneva was a trademark of the W. (William) H. Howell Co., Geneva, Illinois. Mid to late 1800s. 5¼ x 3⅜ x 1½". Handle rises 3⅛" above surface of iron. *$45.00*

Howell H. CI, plentiful antique sadiron stand, unmarked on reverse. On face: THE W.H. HOWELL CO. GENEVA ILL. Scalloped railing on two sides. Two gate-marks at rear of platform. Late 1800s. 6 x 4⅜ x 1" with three legs. *$40.00*

Howell H, Left. CI, plentiful antique or vintage sadiron stand, unsigned on reverse. On face: W.H. HOWELL CO and GENEVA, ILL with the Howell wording on the *left* panel. Late 1800s to early 1900s. 5⅞ x 4¼ x ⅝" with three feet. *$25.00*

Howell H, Right. CI, plentiful antique or vintage sadiron stand, unsigned on reverse. On face: GENEVA, ILL and W.H. HOWELL CO with the Howell wording on the *right* panel. Less common version than the Howell Left. Late 1800s to early 1900s. 5⅞ x 4¼ x ⅝" with three feet. *$35.00*

Howell H, The W Howell Co. CI, plentiful antique or vintage sadiron stand, unmarked on reverse. On face: THE W H HOWELL CO GENEVA ILL. Two guide cleats for iron on each end of trivet. Different from the Howell H Left trivet because of the addition of the word *the*. Late 1800s to early 1900s. 5⅞ x 4⅜ x ¾" with three feet. *$25.00*

Howell HCo. CI, plentiful antique sadiron stand, unmarked on reverse. On face: THE W H HOWELL CO GENEVA ILL. U.S.A. and the HCo monogram. Two iron guide cleats on each side of trivet. 1870s to 1890s. 6⅛ x 4⅜ x ¾" with three feet. *$30.00*

Howell WAPAK. CI, more desirable antique sadiron stand, signed on reverse. Plain on front with two guide cleats on each side. Large machine filed gate-mark on rear of platform. WAPAK. embossed on reverse. Wapak was a trademark of the W.H. Howell Co., Geneva, Illinois. Late 1870s and beyond (Berney p. 21). 5⅝ x 4¼ x ¾" with three feet. *$45.00*

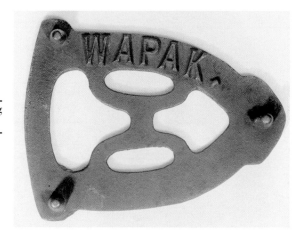

Howell WAPAK (reverse). Reverse of WAPAC trivet, showing the WAPAK signature.

ILL. CI, noteworthy vintage sadiron stand, unsigned on reverse. On face: ILL. Two gate-marks on edge. Cleated iron guides on sides. Extensive backcoping on reverse. Believed to have been a commemorative trivet celebrating the Illinois Centennial in 1918 (Paley, *Spinning Wheel*, "Trivets From A – Z"). Manufacturer unknown. 1918. 7½ x 4⅝ x 1" with three legs. *$85.00*

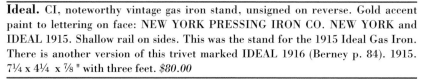

Ideal. CI, noteworthy vintage gas iron stand, unsigned on reverse. Gold accent paint to lettering on face: NEW YORK PRESSING IRON CO. NEW YORK and IDEAL 1915. Shallow rail on sides. This was the stand for the 1915 Ideal Gas Iron. There is another version of this trivet marked IDEAL 1916 (Berney p. 84). 1915. 7¼ x 4¼ x ⅞ " with three feet. *$80.00*

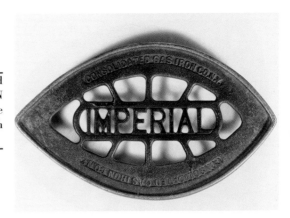

Imperial. NPCI, more desirable vintage sadiron stand, unmarked on reverse. On face: IMPERIAL and CONSOLIDATED GAS IRON CO. N.Y. Shallow railing around platform. Companion trivet to the Imperial Gas Iron. 1906 – 1915 (Berney p. 76). 8¼ x 4¾ x ⅞" with four feet. *$45.00*

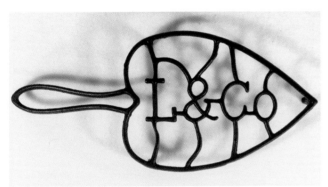

Initials: L & Co. CI, noteworthy antique sadiron stand, unsigned on reverse. On face: L & CO. Delicate casting. Cast through the rim. Manufacturer unknown. Late 1800s (E). 8¼ x 3¾ x 1" with three legs. *$85.00*

Initials: S & Co. CI, noteworthy antique sadiron stand, unsigned on reverse. On face: S & Co. Manufacturer unknown. *One fellow collector thought this might represent Schall & Company of Montgomery County, Pennsylvania.* Late 1800s (E). 7⅞ x 3½ x ⅞" with three feet. *$85.00*

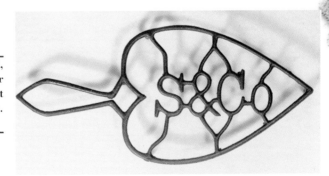

Ives, H.R. & Co. Sadiron #9. Canadian, CI, more desirable antique sadiron, signed H.R. Ives. Raised lettering, H.R. IVES & CO MONTREAL and 9 on handle. Raised star on center of base. Mid to late 1800s. 6 x 3⅞ x 1½". Handle rises 3½" above surface of iron. *$50.00*

Ives, H.R. Spider Web. Canadian, CI, plentiful antique sadiron stand, unmarked on reverse. On face: H.R. IVES & CO MONTREAL. Shallow railing along the two sides. Two gate-marks at base of trivet. H.R. Ives was a hardware store, founded in Montreal in 1859. Mid to late 1800s. 6 x 4⅜ x ⅞" with three feet. *$40.00*

Johnson. CI, rare vintage sadiron stand, unsigned on reverse. On face: JOHNSON. Shallow rail around edge. Two filed gate-marks on one side. S.C. Johnson & Son, Inc. of Racine, Wisconsin, was founded in 1886. Dick Hankenson verified that this was a promotional product for Johnson Wax (*Trivets Book 2*, p. 26). 1920s (Berney p. 148). 7⅞ x 4¼ x ½" with four small feet. *$115.00*

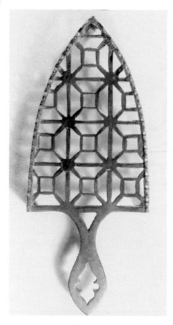

Kenrick No. 4 Style, Brass. More desirable antique or vintage sadiron stand, unmarked on reverse. Heavy trivet with lovely scalloped rim detail. 1880s to early 1900s. 11 x 4¾ x 1¼" with three legs. *$45.00*

Kenrick No. 4 Style, Cast Iron. Plentiful antique or vintage sadiron stand, unsigned on reverse. Scalloped rim detail; pitting to undersurface. (Authentic Kenrick stands are British made and signed.) 1880s to early 1900s. 10¾ x 4¾ x 1⅛" with three legs. *$40.00*

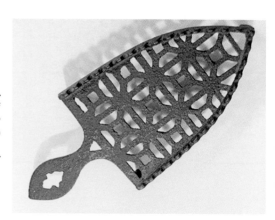

Kenrick No. 8. British, CI, noteworthy antique sadiron stand, Rd number on reverse. On reverse: A. KENRICK & SONS No. 8, and Rd 15023. Two sadiron guide posts on top of trivet. Evidence of long gate-mark on edge. Scalloped border along rim. Designed by Dr. Christopher Dresser (1834 – 1904), an influential Scottish designer. 1884 by Rd number. 9⅛ x 4⅜ x 1⅜" with three legs. *$85.00*

Koenig. CI, noteworthy vintage gas iron stand, unsigned on reverse. On face: K and KOENIG GAS IRONS 131 N. 7TH. ST PHILA. with lettering embossed in recessed panels. Koenig owned patents on gas irons beginning in 1908 (Berney p. 83). 1908 and beyond. 6¾ x 4½ x 1½" with four legs. *$80.00*

Lacy Urn, Brighton. British, CI, plentiful antique or vintage sadiron stand, signed on reverse. Decoration on urn, wavy railing, and rectangular opening plus two screw holes at base differentiate this from other Lacy Urn designs. On reverse: Brighton 8. The Brighton area of England was home to many foundries. Early 1900s (E). 5½ x 4⅜ x ¾" with three feet. *$40.00*

MJE. NPCI, more desirable antique or vintage gas iron stand, unmarked on reverse. Center of monogram is a large M, with a smaller J and E on either side. Length of rear edge filed. **Companion stand to the MJE Gas Iron.** Hankenson shows a different stand (Book 1, p. 50, #143) that also features the initials MJE. Late 1800s to early 1900s (E). 5½ x 4⅞ x ⅞" with three feet. *$50.00*

Marvel. CI, more desirable vintage charcoal iron stand, unmarked on reverse. On face: MARVEL. Rough casting. This was the companion stand to a Marvel Charcoal Iron, patented Dec. 30, 1924, that had side dampers and a lift off lid (information provided by Bill & Shirley Davis of Australia). 1924. 4 x 4¼ x ⅞" with four feet. *$55.00*

Mrs. Potts Crown, Spider Web. CI, plentiful antique or vintage sadiron stand, unsigned on reverse. On face: MRS. POTTS CROWN IRON PHILADA. Two filed gate-marks at rear of stand. Late 1870s to early 1900s (Berney pp. 28, 29 & Hankenson Book 1, Supplement p. 7). 6⅛ x 4⅜ x ⅞" with three feet. *$30.00*

Mule Shoe. CI, plentiful antique or vintage sadiron stand, unsigned on reverse. Two rough gate-marks at rear. Shallow partial side rails. Late 1800s to early 1900s. 5½ x 4⅛ x 1⅛" with three legs. *$20.00*

Muster Geschulzt. German, NPCI, more desirable antique sadiron stand, signed on reverse. On face: the sun. Shallow railing around top. Signed "Muster Geschulzt" on reverse. Made in 1870 (information provided by Gunter Zimmer of Germany). 9⅝ x 2⅞ x ⅞" with three feet. *$65.00*

Ober, Sadiron No. 6. CI with NPCI handle, more desirable vintage sadiron, signed Ober. On body: OBER 6. This iron featured a patented ornamental NPCI handle. Made in 1912 (Berney p. 23). 6 x 3¾ x 1⅜". Handle rises 3½" above surface of iron. *$65.00*

Ober, Large Leaf. NPCI, original design, painted, rare antique or vintage sadiron stand, signed Ober. On reverse: OBER embossed in large letters. Painted black over the original nickel finish. Ober trivets were made to support Ober sadirons. Late 1890s to 1916. 6⅛ x ¾" with four feet. *$160.00*

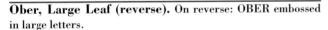

Ober, Large Leaf (reverse). On reverse: OBER embossed in large letters.

Ober, Late Ober Leaf, black finish. CI, original design, rare antique or vintage sadiron stand, signed Ober. On reverse: OBER embossed in large letters. Made by the Ober Manufacturing Company, Chagrin Falls, Ohio. Late 1890s to 1916. 5¼ x ¾" with four feet. *$125.00*

Ober, Late Ober Leaf, nickel finish. NPCI, original design, rare antique or vintage sadiron stand, signed Ober. On reverse: OBER embossed in large letters. Made by the Ober Manufacturing Company, Chagrin Falls, Ohio. Late 1890s to 1916. 5¼ x ¾" with four feet. *$135.00*

Ober, Late Ober Leaf, nickel finish (reverse). On reverse: OBER embossed in large letters. Same signature on both black and nickel-plated versions.

Ober, OMCo Full-sized Stand. CI, more desirable antique or vintage sadiron stand, original design, unmarked on reverse On face: OMCo monogram in circle on waffle front. Full-sized stand. Made by the Ober Manufacturing Company, Chagrin Falls, Ohio. Late 1890s to 1916. 4¾ x ¾" with four feet. *$45.00*

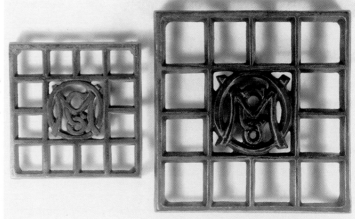

Ober, OMCo Full-sized and Toy Stands. A comparison of the toy stand next to the full sized.

Ober, OMCo Toy Stand. CI, original design, rare antique or vintage toy stand, unmarked on reverse. On face: OMCo monogram in circle on waffle front. Toy-sized stand. The Ober Manufacturing Company was also a leading American manufacturer of toy irons and stands during the late 1800s and early 1900s. Late 1890s to 1916. 3⅛ x ⅝" with four feet. *$75.00*

Ober, Sleeve Iron #801. CI with NPCI base, noteworthy antique sadiron, signed Ober. On surface of sleeve iron: 801 and THE OBER. MFG. CO. CHAGRIN FALLS, O. This is a one-piece style. In 1894 Ober sleeve irons converted to a detachable handle (Berney p. 101). Made prior to 1894. 6⅞ x 2¾ x 1". Handle rises 2¾" above surface of iron. *$75.00*

Ober, Square No. 1. CI, original design, plentiful antique or vintage sadiron stand, unmarked on reverse. On face: Ober Chagrin Falls, Ohio. in center ring. Ober designs were unique to this company. Late 1890s to 1916. 4⅜ x ⅝" with four feet. *$30.00*

Ober, Square Leaf. NPCI, original design, rare antique or vintage sadiron stand, signed Ober. Filing marks evident along one side. Ober Chagrin Falls O. Mfg. Co. on reverse. Beautifully designed nickel-plated casting. Late 1890s to 1916. 4¼ x ⅝" with four feet. *$175.00* (An extraordinarily beautiful example of this trivet, with 95% nickel plating intact, sold for an amazing $341.00 on eBay in October 2003.)

Ober, Square Leaf (reverse). Ober Chagrin Falls O. Mfg. Co. engraved in script on reverse.

Ober, Square No. 2. CI, original design, plentiful antique or vintage sadiron stand, unmarked on reverse. Plain square trivet without lettering. Made by the Ober Manufacturing Company, Chagrin Falls, Ohio. The most common of all the Ober stands. Late 1890s to 1916. 4¼ x ¾" with four feet. *$25.00*

Ober, Toy Iron #1. CI, noteworthy antique toy iron, signed Ober. On surface of iron: CHAGRIN FALLS, O., the number 1, and OBER. Late 1890s to 1916 (Politzer pp. 62, 63). 3⅜ x 2 x ¾". Handle rises 1⅝" above surface of iron. *$70.00*

Ober, Toy #1 Iron & Toy Stand. A photograph to illustrate how the toy sized stand and iron fit together.

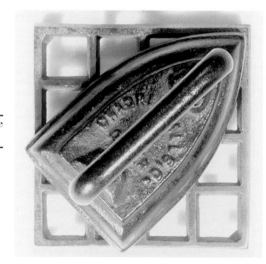

Ober, Waffle. CI, more desirable antique or vintage sadiron stand, original design, unmarked on reverse. On face, in center: OBER CHAGRIN FALLS, O. The Ober Manufacturing Company ended production in 1916. Late 1890s to 1916. 4½ x ¾" with four feet. *$55.00*

Ocean Waves. CI, plentiful antique or vintage sadiron stand, unsigned on reverse. Five ¼" round, screw-like circles noted on face. Shallow side rails that open at the point. Long, filed area on side and two filed gate-marks on rear edge. Rough, unfiled areas in casting. Manufacturer unknown. Late 1800s to early 1900s (E). 6⅜ x 4 x ⅜" with three feet. *$30.00*

Panel: American Butt Company. CI, noteworthy antique sadiron stand, unmarked on reverse. On face: AMERICAN BUTT COMPANY. Cast through the rim. The term "Butt" refers to the door hinges that were manufactured at this company. Late 1800s (E). 9¼ x 4⅛ x 1¼" with three legs. *$90.00*

Panel: Fox & Company. CI, noteworthy antique sadiron stand, numbered on reverse. On face: FOX & CO. ST. LOUIS. Two rough gate-marks on side. Shallow side rails. On reverse: No 2. Late 1800s (E). 8⅜ x 3⅜ x 1" with three legs. *$90.00*

Panel: Fox, S.R. & Company. CI, noteworthy antique sadiron stand, numbered on reverse. On face: S.R. FOX & CO. ST. LOUIS. MO. On reverse: No.1. Two rough gate-marks on side. Decorative rope edging. Note: The small acorn at the top of trivet is often found broken off on these designs. Late 1800s (E). 9¼ x 4 x 1⅛" with three legs. *$85.00*

Panel: Ives & Allen. Canadian, CI, noteworthy antique sadiron stand, unmarked on reverse. On face: IVES & ALLEN MANUFACTURERS MONTREAL. This stand is very similar to, but postdates, the H.R. Ives stand. Late 1800s (Irons, p. 102). 9 x 3⅞ x 1" with three legs. *$75.00*

Panel: Ives, H. R. Canadian, CI, noteworthy antique sadiron stand, unmarked on reverse. On face: H.R. IVES & CO MANUFACTURERS MONTREAL. Decorative rope edging. Two gate-marks on edge. Older than the similar Ives and Allen stand. Mid to late 1800s. 9 x 4 x 1¼" with three legs. *$90.00*

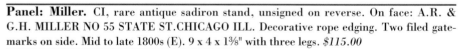

Panel: Miller. CI, rare antique sadiron stand, unsigned on reverse. On face: A.R. & G.H. MILLER NO 55 STATE ST.CHICAGO ILL. Decorative rope edging. Two filed gate-marks on side. Mid to late 1800s (E). 9 x 4 x 1⅜" with three legs. *$115.00*

Peerless. NPCI, more desirable vintage gas iron stand, unsigned on reverse. On face, in raised lettering along rim: PEERLESS IRON CO. CLEVELAND USA. Two iron guides at both upper and lower ends of stand. Shallow railing. 1914 (Berney pp. 78, 80, 92). 7¼ x 3½ x 1" with three legs. *$60.00*

Pleuger & Henger. CI, plentiful antique or vintage sadiron stand, unsigned on reverse. On face: P&H monogram and the wording PLEUGER & HENGER MFG CO ST. LOUIS, MO. Two rough gate-marks on one side. Hankenson (Book 2, p. 52) states that Pleuger & Henger became part of the American Foundry & Mfg. Co. in 1909. Pleuger & Henger was in business from 1888 to 1909. 5⅞ x 4¼ x ¾ " with three feet. *$30.00*

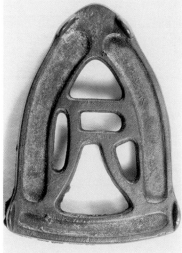

R. CI, plentiful antique or vintage sadiron stand, unsigned on reverse. On face: R. Backcoping on three sides of surface. Rough gate-marks on one side and at rear edge of platform. Flat on the reverse. Manufacturer unknown. Late 1800s to early 1900s (E). 5¾ x 4⅜ x ¾ " with three feet. *$40.00*

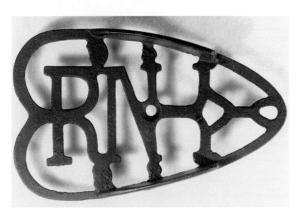

RNH. CI, noteworthy antique sadiron stand, unsigned on reverse. On face: RNH. 1" tapered guide rail on each side. Two filed gate-marks on side edge. Manufacturer unknown. Late 1800s (E). 7¼ x 4¼ x ⅝" with three feet. *$85.00*

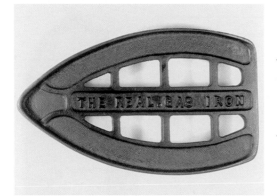

Real Gas Iron, The. CI, more desirable vintage sadiron stand, Unsigned on reverse. On face: THE REALGAS IRON. On reverse: the number 4 embossed on a raised rectangle. Manufactured by the Real Gas Iron & Stove Company, Battle Creek, Michigan (Berney p. 149). 1914. 7 x 4 x 1¼" with three legs. *$45.00*

Rosenbaum, Uneedit. NPCI, plentiful vintage gas iron stand, unsigned on reverse. On face: R and ROSENBAUM M'F'G. CO. "UNEEDIT" GAS IRON. NEW YORK. Shallow railing on top. This is the companion stand for Rosenbaum's "Uneedit" Gas Iron, pictured on this stand. 1913 to 1916 (Berney p. 84). 7 x 4 x 1⅛" with three legs. *$35.00*

Royal, Crown & Maltese Cross. NPCI, plentiful antique or vintage stand, unsigned on reverse. On face: ROYAL. Two filed gate-marks at bottom edge. 3½" long iron guides on either side. Very little nickel plating left on mine. Possibly a companion trivet for the "Royal" Gas Iron, manufactured by the Monitor Sad Iron Company (Berney p. 73). Late 1800s to early 1900s (E). Early 1900s if Monitor stand. 5¾ x 4¼ x ⅝" with three feet. *$25.00*

Schreiber & Conchar, Best On Earth. NPCI, more desirable antique sadiron stand, unsigned on reverse. On face: BEST ON EARTH embossed within panels. Two iron guides on each side. Long filed gate-mark on side. Less commonly found than the Best on Earth variation. Manufactured by Schreiber & Conchar Manufacturing Company of Dubuque, Iowa. 1897. 7⅛ x 4⅛ x ¼" with four feet. *$45.00*

Schreiber & Conchar, Best On Earth Iron. CI, more desirable antique sadiron, signed. On face of iron: BEST ON EARTH and POTTS SIZE 3. Remove the handle, and on the top of the iron where the handle attaches is PAT SEPT 28 1897. 1897. 6½ x 3⅝ x 2" base. Handle rises 2⅞" above surface of iron. *$55.00*

Schreiber & Conchar, Best On Earth, Variation. CI, plentiful antique sadiron stand, unmarked on reverse. On face: BEST ON EARTH. Raised lettering on a flat panel. Two iron guides on each side. Backcoping on reverse. Manufactured by Schreiber & Conchar Manufacturing Company of Dubuque, Iowa. 1897. 7⅜ x 4⅜ x ⅝" with four feet. *$35.00*

Schreiber & Conchar, Dubuque Potts. NPCI, plentiful antique sadiron stand, unmarked on reverse. On face: Dubuque Potts. Two rough gate-marks on side, two iron guides on each side, backcoping on reverse. Manufactured by Schreiber & Conchar Manufacturing Company of Dubuque, Iowa. Late 1800s. 7 x 4 x ⅝" with four feet. *$35.00*

Sea Company. NPCI, rare antique or vintage sadiron stand, unsigned on reverse. On face: SEA CO. S.F. CAL. Long filed gate-mark along one edge. An impressive trivet, this was my Christmas 2002 present from my husband Ed. I wish I knew more about the origins of this company. Late 1800s to early 1900s (E). 10⅞ x 3⅝ x 1½" with three legs. *$125.00*

Simmons, S. CI, more desirable antique or vintage sadiron stand, unsigned on reverse. On face: S and SIMMONS HDW CO ST LOUIS. The E.C. Simmons Hardware Company was best known for their "Keen Kutter" line of tools. Late 1800s to early 1900s. 5¾ x 4¼ x ⅝" with three feet. *$50.00*

Simmons, Special Sadiron. NPCI, more desirable antique sadiron, signed. On top of iron: SIMMONS SPECIAL. Two piece model with detachable walnut handle. Companion iron to the Simmons Special stands. Early 1900s (Bowlin p. 25). 6½ x 3½ x 2". Handle rises 2⅞" above surface of iron. *$65.00*

Simmons, Special with Embossed Letters. NPCI, More desirable antique or vintage sadiron stand, unsigned on reverse. Embossed on face: SIMMONS SPECIAL. Two guide cleats on each side. Filed gate-mark on one side. Flat on the reverse. Early 1900s. 7⅛ x 4⅛ x ⅜" with four feet. *$45.00*

Simmons, Special with Inscribed Letters. NPCI, More desirable antique or vintage sadiron stand, unsigned on reverse. Engraved on face: SIMMONS SPECIAL. Two circular openings in center panel. Two guide cleats on each side. Two pronounced gate-marks on one side. Backcoping to long panels on reverse. Early 1900s. 7⅜ x 4⅜ x ⅝" with four feet. *$45.00*

Smart, James: G In Diamond. Canadian, CI, more desirable antique sadiron stand, signed on reverse. On face: G. Long filed gate-mark at rear edge of stand. On reverse: SMART BROCKVILLE. Manufactured by the James Smart Foundry, Brockville, Ontario, Canada. The "G in a diamond" emblem appears on many of their castings. Late 1800s. 7½ x 4⅝ x ¾" with five feet. *$45.00*

Smart, James: Jas Smart or Canadian Spider Web. Canadian, CI, more desirable antique sadiron stand, signed on reverse. Plain Spider Web design on the front. Stand is identified as Jas Smart by the signature on the reverse. Manufactured by the James Smart Foundry, Brockville, Ontario, Canada. Mid to late 1800s. 5¾ x 4¼ x ¾" with three feet. *$45.00*

Smart, James: Jas Smart or Canadian Spider Web (reverse). On reverse: G in a diamond and JAS SMART MFG CO LIMITED CANADA. Their company was commonly known as "Novelty Works." This design was also cast with the inscriptions JAS SMART MFG. CO. BROCKVILLE or JAS SMART MFG. CO. MONTREAL (Hankenson Book 2, p. 30).

Spider Web. NPCI, plentiful antique or vintage sadiron stand, unsigned on reverse. Machine filed gate-mark on side. Manufacturer unknown. Very common design, the basis for many variations. Late 1800s to early 1900s (E). 6 x 4⅝ x ¾" with three feet. *$20.00*

Spider Web Variant. CI, plentiful antique or vintage sadiron stand, unsigned on reverse. Shallow side rails. Reinforcing bar around perimeter on reverse. Manufacturer unknown. Late 1800s to early 1900s (E). 5¾ x 4¼ x ¾" with three feet. *$25.00*

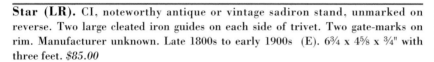

Star (LR). CI, noteworthy antique or vintage sadiron stand, unmarked on reverse. Two large cleated iron guides on each side of trivet. Two gate-marks on rim. Manufacturer unknown. Late 1800s to early 1900s (E). 6¾ x 4⅝ x ¾" with three feet. *$85.00*

Strauss, I Want U Double Point. CI, numbered on reverse, Plentiful vintage gas iron stand. On face: DOUBLE POINT "I WANT U" COMFORT IRON and STRAUSS GAS IRON CO., PHILA. PA. U.S.A. Two machine ground gate-marks on rim. Shallow top rails and small C3 on reverse. Made in 1913 (Berney p. 81). 7½ x 4¼ x 1⅜" with four legs. *$30.00*

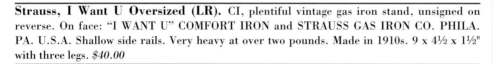

Strauss, I Want U Oversized (LR). CI, plentiful vintage gas iron stand, unsigned on reverse. On face: "I WANT U" COMFORT IRON and STRAUSS GAS IRON CO. PHILA. PA. U.S.A. Shallow side rails. Very heavy at over two pounds. Made in 1910s. 9 x 4½ x 1½" with three legs. *$40.00*

Strauss, I Want U, Spade. Brass-plated cast iron, plentiful vintage gas iron stand, unsigned on reverse. On face: "I WANT U" COMFORT IRON, STRAUSS GAS IRON CO., and PHILA. PA. U.S.A. The Strauss gas iron with hose is pictured. This particular stand is nicely brass plated; it was also offered in black and nickel-plated versions. Made in 1910 (Berney p. 81). 6½ x 4 x 1¼" with three legs. *$30.00*

Streeter, Magic Fluter, Version No. 1. CI, more desirable antique fluter bed, unsigned on reverse. On face: N. R. STREETER'S MAGIC FLUTER & POLISHER and PAT SEP 19 1876. On handle's circle: PATD JUNE 18, 1878. This recessed stand held a heated, ribbed lug; a hand roller pleated the fabric. N.R. Streeter & Co., Groton, N.Y. Mine is in fair condition. 1876. 6¾ x 3½ x ¾" with four feet. *$45.00*

Streeter, Magic Fluter, Version No. 2. CI, more desirable antique fluter bed, unsigned on reverse. On face: MRS. STREETER'S MAGIC FLUTER & POLISHER PAT SEP 19 1876. A smaller version of No.1, and in much nicer condition. 1876. 6¾ x 3½ x ⅞" with four feet. *$55.00*

Streeter, Sensible. CI, plentiful antique sadiron stand, unmarked on reverse. On face: SENSIBLE. Companion trivet to a line of Sensible sadirons. Also came in 3¼" and 4½" toy lengths to accompany toy irons. Manufactured by Nelson R. Streeter, Groton, New York. 1887 (Berney pp. 100, 167). 6⅛ x 3¾ x ¾" with four feet. *$40.00*

Sunshine-Jasper. CI, more desirable antique or vintage sadiron stand, unsigned on reverse. On face: SUNSHINE-JASPER CO. NEW YORK. U.S.A. and SUNSHINE HOME GAS IRON NO. 6 IRON STAND. Sides are wavy. Two filed gate-marks on one side. Interesting design. Late 1800s to early 1900s (E). 7⅞ x 4¼ x ¾" with four cleated feet. *$50.00*

Swastika. NPCI, plentiful antique sadiron stand, unsigned on reverse. Manufacturer unknown. Prior to being corrupted by the Nazis, this ancient swastika design symbolized the four L's: Life, Light, Love, and Luck (Internet: Lucky Mojo Curio Company, The Swastika). Late 1800s to early 1900s (E). 5½ x 4⅛ x ¾" with three feet. *$40.00*

Tailor's Harvest (LR). NPCI, more desirable antique sadiron stand, unmarked on reverse. Shallow railing on top. Oversized sadiron stand for a tailor's goose, which was a large smoothing iron. Purchased from Australia. Manufacturer unknown. Late 1800s (E). 10¼ x 3⅝ x ¾" with three feet. *$65.00*

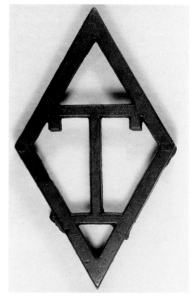

Taylor Stove Company: T in Diamond. Canadian, CI, plentiful antique sadiron stand, unsigned on reverse. On face: T. Three rough gate-marks noted. Tops of small legs visible, smooth with upper surface. Taylor Stove Company, Guelph, Ontario, Canada (Paley, *Spinning Wheel*, "Trivets A – Z"). 1880s to 1890s. 6⅞ x 4⅛ x ⅝" with four feet. *$30.00*

Taylor-Forbes: TF in Diamond. Canadian, CI, plentiful antique or vintage sadiron stand, unsigned on reverse. On face: TF. Small, post type feet. Manufactured by Taylor-Forbes, Guelph, Ontario, Canada. Early 1900s to 1920s. 7¼ x 4¼ x ⅝" with four small feet. *$40.00*

Trailing Vine. CI, plentiful antique or vintage sadiron stand, unmarked on reverse. Two gate-marks on rear edge of trivet. Two cleats on either side. Manufacturer unknown. Late 1800s to early 1900s (E). 6 x 4⅝ x ⅝" with three feet. *$35.00*

US. NPCI, more desirable antique or vintage sadiron stand, unsigned on reverse. On face: US. Two partial length side rails. Manufacturer unknown, but very similar to the Swastika stand. As a general rule, the more nickel plating remaining, the more valuable the stand. Late 1800s to early 1900s (E). 5⅜ x 4 x ¾" with three feet. *$60.00*

Vulcan. CI, more desirable vintage sadiron stand, numbered on reverse. On face: VULCAN. Shallow top rail, 674V and 3820 on reverse. The word Vulcan was the trademark of William M. Crane & Co., NY. 1921 (Berney p. 85). 6¾ x 4¼ x ⅞" with three feet. *$45.00*

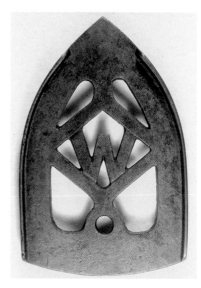

W. CI, more desirable antique or vintage sadiron stand, unsigned on reverse. On face: W. Filed gate-mark on bottom edge. Manufacturer unknown. Late 1800s to early 1900s (E). 6⅛ x 4⅛ x ¾" with three feet. *$50.00*

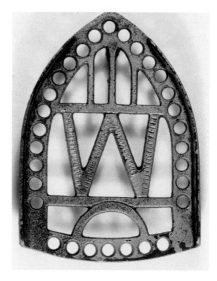

W with Holes. CI, more desirable sadiron stand, unsigned on reverse. On face: W. Shallow side rails. Machine filing along entire rear edge. Purchased from the late Edna Glissman iron collection. Late 1800s (E). 5⅝ x 4⅛ x ⅞" with three feet. *$45.00*

W, with Fox. NPCI, plentiful antique or vintage sadiron stand, unmarked on reverse. On face: W with a small fox above the W. Two iron guides atop each shallow side rail. Machine ground gate-mark on side, and backcoping on reverse. Manufacturer unknown. Late 1800s to early 1900s (E). 7⅝ x 4⅛ x ⅝" with four feet. *$25.00*

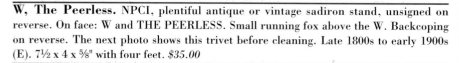

W, The Peerless. NPCI, plentiful antique or vintage sadiron stand, unsigned on reverse. On face: W and THE PEERLESS. Small running fox above the W. Backcoping on reverse. The next photo shows this trivet before cleaning. Late 1800s to early 1900s (E). 7½ x 4 x ⅝" with four feet. *$35.00*

W, The Peerless, before cleaning. An example of before and after. I did not know the trivet was beautifully nickel plated until I removed this layer of rust.

W, The Royal. NPCI, plentiful antique or vintage sadiron stand, unmarked on reverse. On face: W and THE ROYAL. Small running fox above the W. Two iron guides on each side. One machine ground gate-mark on side. Backcoping to the shield and banner. Late 1800s to early 1900s (E). 7½ x 4 x ⅝" with four feet. *$30.00*

Waffle. CI, Plentiful antique or vintage sadiron stand. Unsigned on front or reverse. Two filed gate-marks at rear of platform. Quarter inch side rails. Late 1800s to early 1900s. 6 x 4½ x ⅞" with three feet. *$20.00*

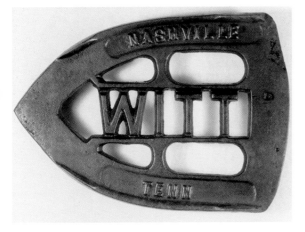

Witt. CI, plentiful vintage sadiron stand, unsigned on reverse. On face: WITT and NASHVILLE TENN. Late 1800s to early 1900s (E). 5¾ x 4 x ⅝" with three feet. *$35.00*

Spade Shaped

1880 (LR). British, brass, noteworthy antique casting, unsigned on reverse. On face: 1880. Backcoping to circles on reverse. I purchased this trivet from England. The seller stated that it originally belonged to her great-grandmother, who might have been a lady's maid to a wealthy family in Yorkshire, England. 1880. 8⅞ x 4 x 1" with three legs. *$85.00*

Beaded Hearts. CI, noteworthy antique trivet, unsigned on reverse. Heavy casting with shallow railing around top of trivet. Backcoping behind handle. Sprue mark on reverse. Mid 1800s (E). 9⅛ x 4¼ x 1¼" with three legs. *$75.00*

Birds. CPCI, plentiful antique or vintage trivet, unmarked on reverse. Copper-plated finishes were popular in the late 1800s. Late 1800s to early 1900s (E). 8 x 4¾ x ¾" with three feet. *$25.00*

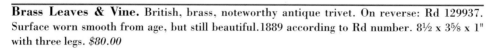

Brass Leaves & Vine. British, brass, noteworthy antique trivet. On reverse: Rd 129937. Surface worn smooth from age, but still beautiful. 1889 according to Rd number. 8½ x 3⅝ x 1" with three legs. *$80.00*

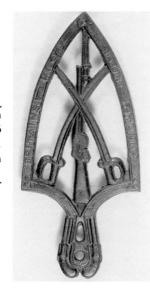

Britain's Might As Iron Stands. British, brass, noteworthy antique trivet, Rd number on front. On face: the slogan BRITAINS MIGHT AS IRON STANDS and REGD No. 352236 (worn). Features a rifle with bayonet, two swords, and a handle formed by two pistols. Smoothed gate-marks on rim. Backcoping on reverse. 1900 by Rd number. 7⅛ x 3⅜ x ⅝" with three feet. *$70.00*

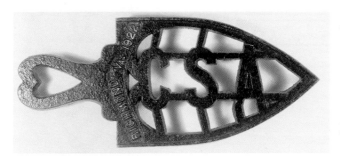

CSA. CI, rare trivet, unsigned on reverse, vintage commemorative casting. On face: CSA (Confederate States of America) and Richmond Va. 1922. Shallow side rails. Cast through the rim. Souvenir of a 1922 CSA veteran's reunion. I've heard that these were sold in 1922 to raise money for a memorial Confederate monument. 1922. 10 x 4¼ x 1" with three legs. *$90.00*

Cathedral 1894. CI, plentiful antique trivet, unsigned on reverse. On face: 1894. Two filed gate-marks on edge. Heavily backcoped on the reverse. (Note: Wilton made a reproduction in the 1960s, signed WILTON on the reverse.) 1894. 8⅝ x 3¾ x ⅞" with three feet. *$30.00*

Cathedral No. 4. CI, more desirable antique trivet, unsigned on reverse. Rough gate-marks on side where it was separated from the mold. Extensive backcoping on reverse. Frequently reproduced design. I date this one earlier by the rough gate-marks and the longer legs. Mid to late 1800s. 9⅜ x 4⅛ x 1⅛" with three legs. *$45.00*

Cathedral No. 6. CI, plentiful antique or vintage trivet, unmarked on reverse. Two pronounced gate-marks along edge. Extensive backcoping on the reverse. This design is known to have been produced in 1866 by the Reading Hardware Works of Reading, Pennsylvania (Berney p. 146). Mid 1800s to early 1900s. 8⅛ x 3½ x ⅞" with three feet. *$30.00*

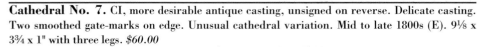

Cathedral No. 7. CI, more desirable antique casting, unsigned on reverse. Delicate casting. Two smoothed gate-marks on edge. Unusual cathedral variation. Mid to late 1800s (E). 9⅛ x 3¾ x 1" with three legs. *$60.00*

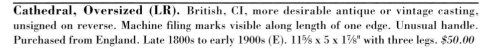

Cathedral Petals. CI, plentiful antique or vintage trivet, unsigned on reverse. Machine grinding along one edge. Late 1890s to early 1900s (E). 8⅜ x 3⅝ x ¾" with three feet. *$35.00*

Cathedral, Oversized (LR). British, CI, more desirable antique or vintage casting, unsigned on reverse. Machine filing marks visible along length of one edge. Unusual handle. Purchased from England. Late 1800s to early 1900s (E). 11⅝ x 5 x 1⅞" with three legs. *$50.00*

Cathedral, Reverse (LR). CI, more desirable antique casting, unsigned on reverse. Rough gate-mark on side. Notice the reverse direction of the larger heart, which classifies this as a reverse cathedral design. Unusual handle. Late 1800s (E). 7¾ x 3¾ x 1¼" with three legs. *$50.00*

Cathedral, Salter Style. British, brass, more desirable antique or vintage casting, unsigned on reverse. Another reverse cathedral pattern, purchased from Australia. Similar to a design produced by Englishman Thomas Salter (1893 – 1939). Quite a buildup of verdigris, especially on the reverse. Late 1800s to early 1900s (E). 8⅜ x 3⅝ x ⅞" with three feet. *$55.00*

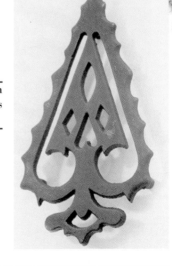

Christmas Tree (LR). CI, more desirable antique or vintage casting, unsigned on reverse. Unusual design. Reproduced by Virginia Metalcrafters in the 1950s – 1960s as Pine Tree *$9.00 – 15.00*. Early 1900s (E). 7 x 3⅞ x ⅞" with three feet. *$45.00*

Clubs and Spade (LR). Brass, rare antique casting, unsigned on reverse. Beautiful, heavy trivet. The top is similar to trivets that have been cut from sheet brass, but the legs appear to have been cast with the trivet. Early to mid 1800s (E). 9½ x 5⅛ x 1¾" with three legs. *$115.00*

Danish Spade (LR). Danish, CI, oversized, rare antique casting, unsigned on reverse. Finning noticeable. Sprue mark on reverse. Heavy casting. From the estate sale of the Edna Glissman iron collection, it was labeled as having originated in Denmark. Early to mid 1800s (E). 11¾ x 4 x 2¼" with three splayed legs. *$115.00*

Distelfink. CPCI, plentiful antique or vintage trivet, unmarked on reverse. Copper-plated finishes were popular in the late 1800s. Late 1800s to early 1900s (E). 8 x 4¾ x ⅝" with three feet. *$25.00*

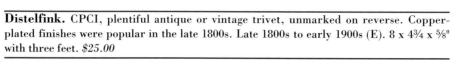

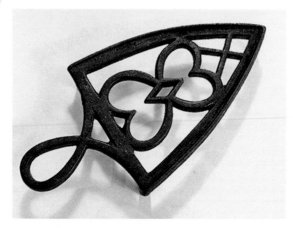

Double Heart. CI, more desirable antique casting, unmarked on reverse. ¹⁄₁₆" rail along sides. Two gate-marks on edge. Longer legs identify this as an older casting. This design is known to have been produced in 1876 by Perin & Graf Manufacturing Company (Kelly & Ellwood, p. 56). 1870s to 1900. 7¾ x 4 x 1¼" with three legs. *$45.00*

Falkirk-style Filigree (LR). British, brass, noteworthy antique trivet, unsigned on reverse. Thick casting. Sprue mark on reverse. Mid to late 1800s (E). 6½ x 3½ x 1¼" with three legs. *$75.00*

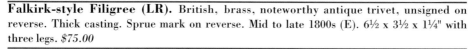

Four Hearts (LR). Brass, museum quality antique trivet, unique item, unsigned on reverse. Beautifully crafted trivet. Leg supports visible through and even with top surface. Mid 1800s or earlier. 9⅛ x 4⅝ x ⅝" with three feet. *$175.00*

Four Hearts, reverse (LR). Reverse: The bottoms of the feet are button-like in appearance. Note the verdigris and rough undersurface.

Four Stars. CI, plentiful antique or vintage trivet, unsigned on reverse. Two filed gate-marks on edge. Late 1800s to early 1900s (E). 8¼ x 3½ x ¾" with three feet. *$40.00*

Fox. British, brass, noteworthy antique trivet, unsigned on reverse. Hollow cast in brass. Downturned, scalloped edges. Mid to late 1800s (E). 8⅜ x 4⅛ x 1" with three legs. *$70.00*

Gentleman in Kharki, Version No.1. British, brass, more desirable antique trivet, unsigned on reverse. On face: A GENTLEMAN IN KHARKI. According to Mitchell (p. 79), this Boer War commemorative trivet pictures the Union flag and a British soldier, dressed in kharki, which is Afrikaans for khaki. The handle is a wreath and dagger. The Boer War was fought from 1899 to 1902. Early 1900s. 8⅝ x 4⅛ x ¾" with three feet. *$65.00*

Gentleman in Kharki, Version No. 2. The soldier design depicted in both Kharki trivets is from the painting *A Gentleman in Kharki* by A. Canton Woodville. British, brass, more desirable antique trivet, unsigned on reverse. On face: A GENTLEMAN IN KHARKI. This differs from Version No. 1 in size and by the handle, which features two rifles. Early 1900s. 6¾ x 3⅜ x ¾" with three feet. *$65.00*

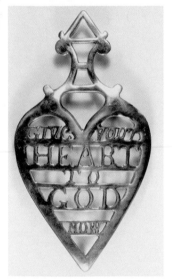

Give Your Heart To God Now. British, brass, rare antique trivet, unsigned on reverse. On face: GIVE YOUR HEART TO GOD NOW. Victorian religious design, this trivet design is also sometimes seen as "Give Your Heart To God." Gently bent in areas from age and use. Mid to late 1800s. 9½ x 5⅛ x 1" with three legs. *$110.00*

Heart & Tulip. Chiseled iron, noteworthy antique trivet, unsigned on reverse. Fragile, intricate pattern. The original Japanned finish (glossy lacquer over black paint) is peeling. Not cast, this trivet was created instead by chiseling the design through hot iron (*Spinning Wheel*, "Trivets," 9/71). Mid to late 1800s (E). 8⅞ x 4⅜ x 1⅝" with three legs. *$75.00*

Hearts & Urn Variant. Brass, oversized, plentiful antique or vintage trivet, unsigned on reverse. Extensive backcoping on reverse. Shallow railing around platform. Early 1900s. 10⅞ x 4⅝ x 1⅜" with three splayed legs. *$35.00*

Hearts & Urn or Double Hearts in Scrolls. CI, plentiful antique or vintage trivet, unsigned on reverse. Shallow rail around top. Two rough gate-marks on edge. Backcoping on handle reverse. This popular design is known to have been produced in 1911 by the Lisk Manufacturing Company (Kelly & Ellwood p. 57). Early 1900s. 9 x 4¼v x 1¼" with three legs. *$30.00*

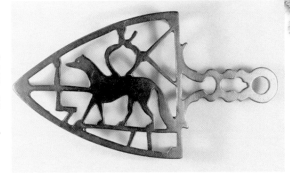

Horse. British, noteworthy antique trivet, unsigned on reverse. Heavy, solid brass. The animal is identified by Hazel Mitchell (*British Iron Stands*) to be a horse. Unusual design. Is it just me, or do I see the letters spelling the word LOVE within this trivet? Mid to late 1800s (E). 8⅜ x 4⅜ x 1⅛" with three legs. *$85.00*

Iris (LR). British, brass, noteworthy antique casting. Rd number 129938 on reverse. Front leg slightly bent inward from age. 1889. 6⅞ x 3⅛ x 1⅛" with three legs. *$90.00*

Irish Harp. British or Irish design, brass, noteworthy antique casting, unsigned on reverse. Interesting design. Heavy verdigris on reverse. According to Hazel Mitchell (*British Iron Stands*) this design is representational of an Irish harp. Mid-1800s. 9½ x 4⅜ x 1⅛" with three legs. *$90.00*

Lacy. NPCI, plentiful antique or vintage trivet, unmarked on reverse. Two gate-marks on edge. Late 1800s to early 1900s (E). 8⅜ x 3½ x ⅞" with three feet. *$25.00*

Lacy Foliage. CI, noteworthy antique casting, unsigned on reverse. ⅛" railing on top. Backcoping behind handle. Sprue mark on reverse. Mid 1800s. 9¾ x 4⅝ x 1⅝" with three legs. *$70.00*

Masonic Symbols (LR). Brass, noteworthy antique or vintage trivet, unsigned on reverse. Trivet slightly bowed in center from age. The symbols, from top to bottom: two pillars; seven-pointed mystic star; star-heart-crescent which signify divinity, sovereignty, and charity; and a square and compass resting upon an open Bible (Mitchell, p. 43). Early 1900s. 8½ x 5 x 1¼" with three legs. *$80.00*

Oak Tree with Acorns (LR). CI, rare antique casting. Sprue mark on reverse. Signed on reverse: W.P. or W.R. (lettering is worn). Unfortunately, mine is not perfect, it's missing one acorn on the right side, which devalues it somewhat. Early to mid 1800s (E). 8¼ x 4⅜ x 1¼" with three legs. *$130.00*

Oak Tree with Acorns (reverse). Close-up of the handle reverse, showing the initials W.P. or W.R., and the sprue mark farther to the right.

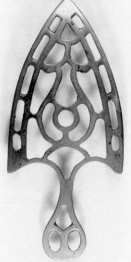

Open Geometric Lyre (LR). Probably British, brass, noteworthy antique casting, unsigned on reverse. Interesting design. Mid-1800s. 9⅜ x 4⅛ x 1" with three legs. *$90.00*

Ornate Peacock (LR). Brass, more desirable vintage trivet, signed on reverse. Heavy for size. On reverse: W G or HG SEELEY, the number 11147, and D. The light Egyptian typeface used helps to date this trivet between 1880 and 1940 (Ellwood, p. 92) Looks and feels like an early twentieth century casting. 1920s to 1930s (E). 8⅛ x 4 x ½" with three feet. *$50.00*

Peacock or Tree of Life. CI, plentiful antique trivet, unmarked on reverse. Longer legs suggest an older casting. Mid to late 1800s (E). 9⅝ x 4⅞ x 1⅝" with three legs. *$35.00*

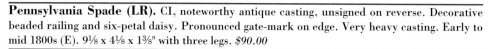

Pennsylvania Spade (LR). CI, noteworthy antique casting, unsigned on reverse. Decorative beaded railing and six-petal daisy. Pronounced gate-mark on edge. Very heavy casting. Early to mid 1800s (E). 9⅛ x 4⅛ x 1⅜" with three legs. *$90.00*

Pierced Welsh Spade. Copper plated, museum quality antique trivet, unsigned on reverse, Welsh. This piece of Welsh folk art stands on three boot-covered legs. Old repair evident to one of the legs at the point where it attaches to the body of the trivet. Early 1800s. 10⅜ x 4¾ x 1⅝" with three legs. *$225.00*

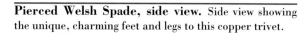

Pierced Welsh Spade, side view. Side view showing the unique, charming feet and legs to this copper trivet.

Pineapple & Bars. CI, plentiful antique or vintage trivet, unmarked on reverse. ⅛" inch top rails. Late 1800s to early 1900s (E). 7½ x 4¼ x 1½" with three legs. *$35.00*

Prince of Wales. Scottish, brass, rare antique casting, unsigned on reverse. Handle slightly bent. The seated gentleman wears a hat topped with Prince of Wales feathers, carries a hunting bow and shield, and is surrounded by the flowers of the British Isles (Mitchell p. 101). Mid to late 1800s (E). 7 x 4 x 1" with three legs. *$115.00*

Scalloped Trellis (LR). CI, noteworthy antique trivet, unsigned on reverse. One quarter inch scalloped top railing. Sprue mark on center reverse. Very heavy, somewhat heavy casting. Early to mid 1800s (E). 9 x 5 x 1" with four feet. *$80.00*

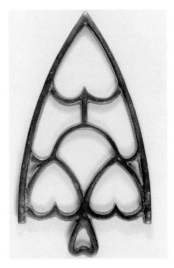

Spade Hearts (LR). Brass, more desirable antique casting, unsigned on reverse. Heavy for size. This trivet design is also found in cast iron. Late 1800s (E). 7⅝ x 4⅜ x ½" with three feet. *$70.00*

Spade Tulip. CI, noteworthy antique casting, unsigned on reverse. Finning present. Cast through the rim. Unfortunately, my trivet is worth less because of a full-surface crack near the center. Mid 1800s (E). 10¼ x 4¾ x 1⅜" with three legs. *$90.00*

Spokes & Hearts (LR). Brass with copper legs, museum quality antique trivet, unsigned on reverse. Cut and pierced pattern. The circular copper tops of the legs lie flush with the top surface of this brass trivet. Mid to late 1800s (E). 8½ x 4½ x 1¼" with three copper legs. *$175.00*

Target. CI, plentiful antique or vintage trivet, unsigned on reverse. 1⅝" long unfiled gate-mark on edge. This design is known to have been produced in 1889 by the Grey Iron Casting Company of Mount Joy, Pennsylvania (Kelly & Ellwood p. 59). Late 1800s to early 1900s. 8 x 4 x ¾" with three feet. *$25.00*

Twig & Bluebird. British, CI, accent painted, more desirable vintage trivet, Rd number on reverse. Bird is accent painted gold. Rd 623836 dates this trivet to 1913. 5⅞ x 3⅝ x ¾" with three feet. *$65.00*

UCM. French, plentiful antique or vintage trivet, tinned sheet metal, unsigned on reverse. Half-inch high scalloped side rails. Black wash to metal. These appear to be Masonic symbols. Early 1900s to early 1930s (E). 9¼ x 4¾ x 1¼" with three bent metal legs. *$35.00*

Valentine (LR). CI, noteworthy antique casting, unsigned on reverse. Delicate casting. Two gate marks on edge. Backcoping on reverse. Mid to late 1800s (E). 7¼ x 3⅛ x ⅝" with three feet. *$85.00*

Welsh Harp, Left. British or Welsh, brass, noteworthy antique trivet, unsigned on reverse. Long legs, bent inward from age. Sprue mark on reverse. From the estate sale of the Edna Glissman iron collection. Mid to late 1800s (E). 10⅜ x 4¼ x 1⅝" with three legs. *$85.00*

Welsh Harp, Right. British or Welsh, brass, noteworthy antique trivet, oversized, unsigned on reverse. Verdigris on reverse. From the estate sale of the Edna Glissman iron collection. Mid to late 1800s (E). 9 x 3⅞ x 1⅝" with three legs. *$80.00*

Circular and Stove Trivets

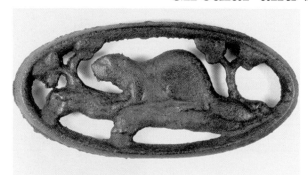

Beaver. CI, rare antique casting, unsigned on reverse. Rough casting with finning present. Gate-mark visible on edge. Animal themes in trivets are rare because they were much more difficult to cast (Berney p. 141). Mid 1800s (E). 6½ x 3⅛ x ¾" with three feet. *$125.00*

Bonzo the Dog, Ornamental Legs. British, CI, noteworthy vintage casting, unsigned on reverse. Englishman George Studdy (1878 – 1948) created the cartoon character Bonzo in 1922. The ornamental legged trivet is slightly harder to come by. I have also seen this Bonzo design in brass with 1" high ornamental legs. 1920s. 5¾" round with three 3" legs. *$80.00*

Bonzo the Dog, Ornamental Legs, side view. The three 3" ornamental legs screw into the platform of the trivet.

Bonzo the Dog, Splayed Legs. British, CI, noteworthy vintage casting, unsigned on reverse. This version of the Bonzo trivet, with three splayed legs, has two extra loops in the rope, one on either side of the dog's head. 1920s. 5¾" round with three 2" legs. *$70.00*

Bonzo the Dog, Splayed Legs, side view. The splayed legs are an extension of the body.

Cloverdale Meat Products. Die-cut aluminum, less common vintage or contemporary trivet, signed on face. On face: CLOVERDALE MEAT PRODUCTS, ALWAYS THE BEST, NICHOLS-FOSS PACKING CO. and FRANKFURTERS, RING BOLOGNA, POLISH & SMOKED PORK SAUSAGE. A very lightweight trivet, I'm not sure of it's practical use other than advertising. Cloverdale has been in business since 1918, based in Mandan, North Dakota. Age of this trivet unknown. 6" round with three 1⅛" feet. $20.00

Colonial Tableau (LR). CI, more desirable antique casting, painted, unsigned on reverse. Two gate-marks on edge. Painted in a muted brick red. Late 1800s (E). 5 x ½" with four feet. $60.00

Cup Of Peace & Plenty That Cheers, The (brass). Scottish, brass, noteworthy antique trivet, signed on reverse. On face: THE CUP OF PEACE & PLENTY THAT CHEERS. On reverse: GREENLEES GLASGOW. Small sprue mark on center reverse. This is how my brass trivet appeared after removing a tremendous amount of black paint (see next photo). Late 1800s (E). 6⅛ x ⅜" with three splayed feet. $75.00

Cup Of Peace & Plenty That Cheers, The (painted brass). This is how my brass Peace & Plenty trivet looked when first purchased as "cast iron." Using the magnet test, it did not stick to the metal underneath. I used a paint remover to take this flat black overcoat off (see previous photo).

Handle: Aslan of Narnia (LR). CI, numbered on reverse, painted, scarce vintage casting. A22 on the reverse in Gothic typeset. Two large, machine filed gate-marks on side. This trivet reminded me of the Narnia legend, with the four flowers representing the four children. However, CS Lewis did not publish his first book until 1950! Still, this feels like a 1940s or earlier piece. 9¾ x 6¾ x ⅞" with three feet. $50.00

Handle: Eagle with Long Handle. Brass, more desirable antique casting, unsigned on reverse. Front legs lean forward. Unusual interpretation of a very common design, Thin casting. I might be wrong, but I am dating this trivet to the mid to late 1800s due to the early, docile appearance of the eagle and the long handle. 11 x 6 x ⅞" with three feet. $65.00

Handle: Early Rooster (LR). CI, noteworthy antique casting, unsigned on reverse. Rough casting, smooth handle and finning of iron. Very old example of this design. Early to mid 1800s (E). 8¼ x 5⅛ x ¾" with three feet. $75.00

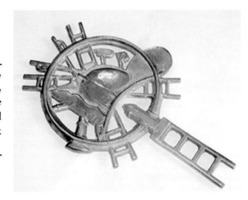

Handle: Firefighting. Brass, numbered on reverse, plentiful trivet, vintage commemorative casting. Roughly cast. Symbols: fire hat, ladders, fire hydrant, water hose, tools. Looks like a 2 on the reverse. More commonly found in cast iron, painted red. The first fire hydrants appeared in the early 1800s; fire trucks in the early 1900s. Early 1900s to 1940. 10¾ x 6¾ x ½" with four feet. *$45.00*

Handle: Freeform Scrolls (LR). British, CI, more desirable antique casting. On reverse: Rd No 237023, which dates this trivet to 1894. Also, on the reverse of the handle is the number 1476. 1894. 9 x 5½" with two 1" front supports and one center bracket support which can attach this trivet to a fireplace firebar. *$50.00*

Handle: Kansas Sunflower. CI, more desirable vintage trivet, unsigned on reverse. On face: KANSAS, THE SUNFLOWER STATE. Heavy casting. Filed gate-mark along side of circle. Feels and looks like an older vintage casting. The sunflower became the state flower in 1903. The state flag, with a sunflower, was adopted in 1927. Vintage, pre-1940 (E). 7⅞ x 4¾ x ¾" with three feet. *$45.00*

Handle: Lacy Round with Handle. Brass, noteworthy antique casting, unsigned on reverse. Casting is heavy for its size. Legs resemble little bowling pins, and screw into base. Late 1800s (E). 7¼ x 4 x 1" with three legs. *$70.00*

Handle: Odd Fellows or Heart in Hand. CI, plentiful antique or vintage trivet, unsigned on reverse. Rough gate-mark on side of handle. Probably an early reproduction, as the feet are less than 1" in length. An IOOF (Independent Order of Odd Fellows) design, this is also sometimes called Heart in Hand. Early 1900s to 1940 (E). 8 x 5⅜ x ⅞" with four feet. *$20.00*

Handle: Seven Hearts. CI, plentiful trivet, unsigned on reverse, vintage casting. Two rough gate-marks on edge. This is most probably a vintage era reproduction. The original is slightly larger with longer legs. Pre-1940 (E). 6⅝ x 4⅝ x ¾" with three feet. *$20.00*

Handle: Six Hearts. CI, oversized, rare antique casting, unmarked on reverse. Beautifully cast. I donated this trivet in 2001 to eBay's Auction For America, a September 11th fundraiser. Pre-1880. 12 x 6⅝ x 1⅞" with three legs. *$110.00*

Isle of Man 1891, Brass. Noteworthy antique trivet. On face: A PRESENT FROM THE ISLE OF MAN. On reverse: Rd 168240, signifying 1891, and the letters A. BAMBER, and GW and D, which stands for George Wolliscroft of Douglas, Isle of Man. 1891. 5¼" in diameter with three ¾" feet. *$75.00*

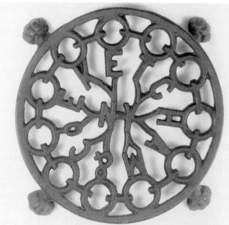

Isle of Man 1891, Cast Iron. Noteworthy antique casting. On face: A PRESENT FROM THE ISLE OF MAN. On reverse: GWD and Rd 168240, which dates this trivet to 1891. 5½" in diameter with three ½" feet. *$70.00*

Isle of Man 1895. CI, noteworthy antique trivet, painted. On face: A PRESENT FROM THE ISLE OF MAN and QUOCUNQUE JECERIS STABIT, meaning, "Which ever way I am thrown I will stand." On reverse: Rd No 254460, dating this trivet to 1895. 5½" in diameter with three ¼" feet. *$70.00*

Ketcham. CI, antique casting, more desirable coffee or tea stand, unsigned on reverse. On face: E KETCHAM & CO NY. Gate-mark on rim. Late 1800s. 5½" in diameter with four Lantz style paw feet. *$65.00*

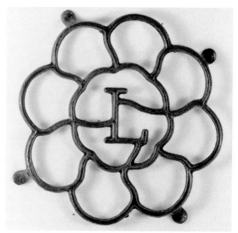

L with Pad Feet (LR). NPCI, more desirable antique or vintage casting, unsigned on reverse. Cast through the rim. Delicate casting. Late 1800s to early 1900s (E). 4⅝ x ⅜" with four smooth pad feet. *$65.00*

Lantz No. 4. Brass, plentiful antique or vintage coffee or tea stand, unsigned on reverse. Casting is bowed centrally from use. Two gate-marks on edge. Late 1800s to early 1900s. 4¾ diameter with four pad feet. *$40.00*

Lantz No. 5. CI, plentiful vintage coffee or tea stand. Decorative edging. Cast through the rim. Number 3 on reverse. Probably an early reproduction. Early 1900s. 4⅞ x ½ with five paw feet. *$35.00*

Lantz No. 7. CI, plentiful antique or vintage coffee or tea stand, unsigned on reverse. Roughly cast through the rim. Late 1800s to early 1900s. 5⅛ x ½" with four Lantz style paw feet. *$35.00*

Lantz Variant. CI, more desirable antique coffee or tea stand, unsigned on reverse. Large wedge mark on center reverse. This is my oldest Lantz trivet. One broken pattern circle reduces the value of mine somewhat. Early to mid 1800s. 5¼ x ⅜" with six Lantz style paw feet. *$55.00*

OES (Order of Eastern Star). CI, more desirable antique or vintage casting, unsigned on reverse. On face: OES. Four machine filed gate-marks on scalloped edges between one pair of feet. OES is a religious, Masonic affiliated organization formed in 1867. A representative of the General Grand Chapter OES identified this as an Eastern Star trivet. Late 1880s to early 1900s (E). Grand Chapter OES unable to assist in dating this trivet. 4⅞ x ½" with four pad feet. *$55.00*

Our Ain Fireside. Scottish, brass, noteworthy antique trivet, signed on reverse. On face: OUR AIN FIRESIDE, a teakettle, and fireside tools. On reverse: GREENLEES GLASGOW. Late 1800s (E). 6¼ x ¾" with three splayed legs. *$75.00*

Queen Spirit Stove. CI, antique casting, more desirable trivet for alcohol stove. On face: QUEEN SPIRIT STOVE, On reverse: S & Co NY and Pat Apd For. This company was possibly Savery and Company, New York. I'm still searching for the cook stove that rests on this base. Late 1800s. 6 x 2½" with three ornamental legs, which are riveted onto the trivet. *$55.00*

Round Lattice. CI, plentiful antique trivet, unsigned on reverse. Delicate casting. Several gate-marks on edge. Each cleated foot imprinted with a fleur de lis. This stand is known to have been produced in 1889 by the Grey Iron Casting Company, Mt. Joy, Pennsylvania (Kelly & Ellwood, p. 59). Late 1880s to 1900. 5⅛ x ⅜" with four feet. *$35.00*

Six Petal. CI, plentiful antique or vintage casting, unmarked on reverse. Center of petals recessed. Heavy casting. (Wilton made a signed reproduction called Star Wheel.) Early 1900s. 4¾ x ⅞" with three feet. *$25.00*

Stove or Cereal Trivet: 1889. CI, noteworthy antique stove trivet, signed on reverse. Pretty design. All the markings are on the reverse. On reverse: 1889 N T EC. 7. 8. and Q EC. 78. I am dating this trivet to 1889 due to the markings. 6" diameter with three 1½" legs and a fourth post that attached to the stove. *$70.00*

Stove or Cereal Trivet: 1889, reverse. On reverse: 1889 N T EC. 7. 8. and Q EC. 78.

Stove or Cereal Trivet: Cereal No. 2. CI, plentiful antique or vintage cereal trivet, signed on reverse. On face: RAISE REGISTER AND CEREALS WILL NEVER BURN. Opening for stove lid lifter. On reverse: HIGH SIMMERING COVER REGISTER. Other numbers/letters unreadable. Late 1800s to early 1900s (E). 6¾" diameter with no feet. *$35.00*

Stove or Cereal Trivet: Heart & Circles (LR). CI, less common antique or vintage stove trivet, signed on reverse. Finning present. On reverse: PATENT APPLIED FOR. Trivet attached to stove by post, and probably pivoted to area needed. This was one of a set of two. Late 1800s to early 1900s (E). 12½ x 7⅜", no legs, but has one ⅜" stove post. *$40.00*

Stove or Cereal Trivet: Jewel Stoves and Ranges. CI, less common antique or vintage stove trivet. On front: JEWEL STOVES AND RANGES and DETROIT STOVE WORKS, LARGEST STOVE PLANT IN THE WORLD (Detroit, Michigan). On reverse: 82 16 LJ 1904, and the number 21. Unsure if this was a stove trivet or just an embellishment for the stove. 1904. 7⅛ x 6⅝", sits on raised rim. *$35.00*

Stove or Cereal Trivet: K-6 NEW PIC. NPCI, plentiful antique or vintage cereal trivet. On reverse: K-6 78. Front: four square openings for the stove lid lifter. Late 1800s to early 1900s. 7⅞" diameter with four ⅝" stove leg supports. *$35.00*

Stove or Cereal Trivet: K S & R Co. CI, less common vintage stove trivet, unmarked on reverse. On face: K S & R Co., which stands for King Stove and Range Company of Florence, Alabama. 1912 to 1930s. Information courtesy of Ernest Wann, Jr. 7" diameter. *$25.00*

Stove or Cereal Trivet: Maple Leaf Stoves & Ranges. NPCI, more desirable antique or vintage stove trivet, unsigned on reverse. On front: MAPLE LEAF STOVES & RANGES. Lip attachment for stove. Does anyone know anything more about this early company? Late 1800s to early 1900s (E). 6½" square with stove attachment. *$50.00*

Stove or Cereal Trivet: Slow Cooking Cover. CI, more desirable antique or vintage cereal trivet, signed on reverse. On face: SLOW COOKING COVER. On reverse: W in a circle. Four openings for a stove lid lifter. Late 1800s to early 1900s. 7½" square, 9" from corner to corner; a cleat at each corner. *$45.00*

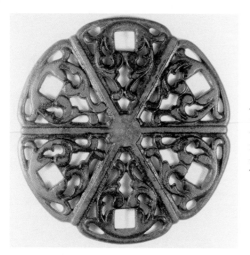

Stove or Cereal Trivet: W. & P. Mfg. Co. CI, more desirable antique cereal trivet, unsigned on reverse. Six openings for stove lid lifter. Large raised round cast mark on reverse. Late 1800s to early 1900s (E). 7½" round with three cleats. *$65.00*

Thayer Universal Tool. CI, noteworthy antique kitchen gadget, signed. Signed PAT. MAY 24. 81 BY WM. H. THAYER. Many uses: trivet, hot pan or stove lid lifter, meat hook or tenderizer, and candleholder. 1881. 5¼ x 4" with no feet. *$75.00*

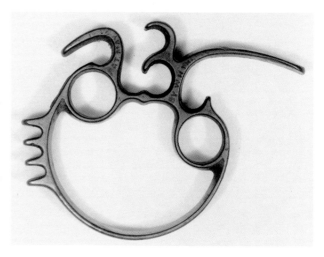

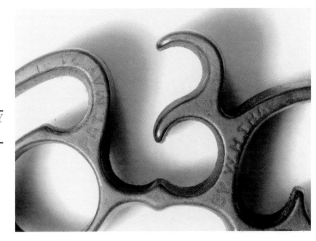

Thayer Universal Tool, signature, close-up PAT. MAY 24. 81 BY WM. H. THAYER on surface near finger grips.

Tiny Cameo (LR). Antique or vintage casting, unsigned on reverse, white metal. On front: cameo of woman. This is cast of some sort of very soft white metal and may be a one-of-a-kind item. Pre-1940. May be quite a bit older. 2⅜ x ⅜" with three feet. *$45.00*

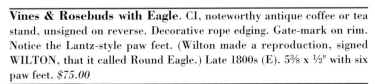

Vines & Rosebuds with Eagle. CI, noteworthy antique coffee or tea stand, unsigned on reverse. Decorative rope edging. Gate-mark on rim. Notice the Lantz-style paw feet. (Wilton made a reproduction, signed WILTON, that it called Round Eagle.) Late 1800s (E). 5⅜ x ½" with six paw feet. *$75.00*

Vines & Rosebuds with Star. CI, more desirable antique coffee or tea stand, unsigned on reverse. Decorative rope edging. Wedge mark on center reverse. Notice the Lantz-style paw feet. Mid 1800s. 5½ x ½" with six paw feet. *$65.00*

Horseshoe Shaped

Easel, Dog. CI, horseshoe easel trivet, more desirable antique casting, unsigned on reverse. Filed gate-mark on lower edge, under dog. On reverse: backcoping to horseshoe and dog. Mid to late 1800s (E). 12¼ x 7¼" without feet. *$70.00*

Easel, Dog (broken). Beware of trivets that may appear intact, but that are actually broken. The lower branches were broken off, and the rough areas filed down to resemble gate-marks.

Easel, Good Luck GAR (Grand Army of the Republic). CI, horseshoe easel trivet, noteworthy antique casting, unmarked on reverse. On face: GOOD LUCK and GAR. Filed gate-mark on lower edge, under dog. On reverse: backcoping to horseshoe and dog. The GAR was founded in 1866 and was active until the late 1940s. Mid to late 1800s (E). 11¾ x 7⅛" without feet. *$90.00*

Easel, Woodsmen of the World. CI, horseshoe easel trivet, noteworthy antique casting, unsigned on reverse. On face: GOOD LUCK still faintly visible at arch of horseshoe. On reverse: two mounting screws and a crude metal support. The Woodmen of the World, a fraternal life insurance society, was founded in 1890 and is still active today. 1890s and beyond. 13 x 7⅛" without feet. *$95.00*

Easel, Woodsmen of the World, reverse. Reverse view shows mounting screws and metal support that allows this piece to stand upright.

GAR Centennial (Grand Army of the Republic). CI, museum quality antique commemorative horseshoe, unmarked on reverse. On face: 1788 OHIO CENTENNIAL 1888, 22nd NATIONAL ENCAMPMENT, and GAR COLUMBUS, O. Traces of gold paint remain. Extraordinary piece, without damage (information and photograph courtesy of Kyle Johnson, Arizona). 1888. 7 x 6¼ x ⅜" without feet. *$225.00*

God Bless Our Home, 1887 GL. CI, noteworthy antique horseshoe plaque trivet, unsigned on reverse. On face: GOD BLESS OUR HOME, 1887, and GL. Traces of gold paint remain. On reverse: Smooth and flat, with two hooks to accommodate a hanging wire. I have not yet been able to determine what the letters GL stand for. 1887. 6 x 6⅜", without feet. *$85.00*

God Bless Our Home, Sailor's House Blessing. CI, noteworthy antique horseshoe plaque trivet, unsigned on reverse. On face: GOD BLESS OUR HOME and the symbols of heart, anchor, and cross. On reverse: smooth and flat. Heavy. Painted silver and gold. I'm unsure if the paint is original to this trivet. Late 1800s (E). 6 x 6" without feet. *$75.00*

Good Luck, Cat. British, brass, noteworthy vintage horseshoe trivet, unsigned on reverse. On face: GOOD LUCK. Heavy for size. Mitchell (*British Iron Stands*) shows a version of this trivet with the Rd number 727536, which would originally register this design to 1927. After 1927. 6⅜ x 5 x 1¼ " with four legs. *$75.00*

Good Luck, Flowers and Berries. Brass, more desirable vintage horseshoe trivet, unsigned on reverse. On face: GOOD LUCK. Pattern of flowers and berries. Hanging hole at center top. 1910 to 1940 (E). 5¾ x 5" without feet. *$45.00*

Good Luck, Jenny Jones. British or Welsh, brass, more desirable antique or vintage horseshoe trivet, unsigned on reverse. On face, in small letters along her skirt: JENNY JONES. Nineteenth century Welsh legend tells of this girl from Llangollen, Wales, who walked 26 miles to buy a Bible. She is usually pictured in long skirts and a stovepipe hat, knitting as she walks. Late 1800s to early 1900s (E). 4⅞x 3⅝ x ¾" with four feet. *$45.00*

Good Luck, Julia. CI, noteworthy antique horseshoe trivet, unsigned on reverse. On face: GOOD LUCK JULIA. Traces of black paint. Backcoping to sleeves. One small cleat on reverse at top of trivet. Two small gate-marks on bottom edge. Unsure of the significance of this trivet...perhaps a parting gift? Mid to late 1800s (E). 5⅝ x 4⅛ x ⅜" without feet. *$90.00*

Good Luck, No. 12. British, brass, more desirable antique horseshoe trivet, signed on reverse. On face: stable gate and the wording GOOD LUCK. On reverse: No. 12. Heavy for size. Late 1800s (E). 6 x 5⅜ x 1⅛ with three cleated legs. *$65.00*

Good Luck, Pat'd 1885. CI, more desirable antique horseshoe trivet, unsigned on reverse. On face: GOOD LUCK PAT'D 1885. Gate-mark on front cleat edge. Lovely little dated casting. 1885. 5 x 3¾ x ½" with three cleated feet. *$50.00*

Good Luck, Pixie. British, Brass, noteworthy antique or vintage horseshoe trivet, unsigned on reverse. On face: GOOD LUCK. Backcoping on reverse. Depicts the Dartmoor Pixie. 1900s to 1930s (E). 6½ x 5 x 1⅜" with four cleated legs. *$80.00*

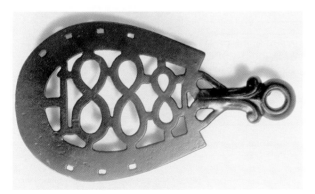

Horseshoe, 1888. CI, noteworthy antique horseshoe trivet, unsigned on reverse. On face: 1888. Filed gate-mark along side. These horseshoe trivets were released yearly from 1880 through 1894. 1888. 7⅞ x 4⅛ x ¾" with three cleated feet. *$75.00*

Horseshoe, 1889. CI, more desirable antique horseshoe trivet, unsigned on reverse. On face: 1889. Filed gate-mark along the edge of one of the rear cleats. Interesting variation, without a handle. Mine is slightly devalued due to one full surface and two partial cracks along the upper round part of the 9. 1889. 5⅛ x 4¼ x ¾" with three cleated feet. $55.00

Horseshoe, 1894. CI, more desirable antique horseshoe trivet, unsigned on reverse. On face: 1894. Two smoothed gate-marks on side. 1894. 7½ x 4⅛ x ¾" with three cleated feet. $75.00

Horseshoe, Good Luck Stand. CI, plentiful antique horseshoe trivet, unmarked on reverse. On face: GOOD LUCK. On reverse: PAT APPL'D FOR on reverse. Machine-filed gate marks on rim. 1880s and beyond. 7⅞ x 4⅝ x ¾" with three cleated feet. $25.00

Horseshoe, Good Luck To All Who Use This Stand. CI, plentiful antique horseshoe trivet, signed on reverse. On face: GOOD LUCK TO ALL WHO USE THIS STAND. PAT APPL'D FOR on reverse. This stand was known to have been produced in 1888 by Wing Manufacturing Company (p. 50, Kelly & Ellwood's (*Trivets & Stands*). Note: Wilton made a signed reproduction. 1880s to early 1900s. 7⅞ x 4⅝ x ¾" with three cleat feet. $40.00

Plaque Trivet, Ancient Order of Foresters. CI, more desirable antique horseshoe plaque trivet, unsigned on reverse. On face: A. O. OF F., signifying the Ancient Order of Foresters. At the top of the arch are the letters U B & C, which stands for unity, benevolence, and concord. Backcoping to horseshoe reverse. Mid 1860s to 1874, at which time they changed their name to the Independent Order of Foresters. 6½ x 4⅛" without feet. *$65.00*

Plaque Trivet, Ancient Order of Foresters with Flag. CI, more desirable antique horseshoe plaque trivet, unsigned on reverse. On face: A. O. OF F., signifying the Ancient Order of Foresters. Backcoping to horseshoe reverse. Smooth, gate-mark at base of horseshoe. Mid 1860s to 1874, at which time they changed their name to Independent Order of Foresters. 6½ x 3¾" without feet. *$65.00*

Plaque Trivet, Birds on a Branch (LR). CI, noteworthy antique horseshoe plaque trivet, unsigned on reverse. Residual traces of paint: burgundy and gold to the birds, gold to the eagle, and gold highlights to the horseshoe. Backcoping to horseshoe and birds. Small defect at center back of horseshoe where hanger was once attached. Mid to late 1800s (E). 6½ x 4⅛" without feet. *$90.00*

Plaque Trivet, Eagle & Horseshoe. CI, antique casting, item is broken, unsigned on reverse. This was sold to me as an unbroken trivet, but there are some rough projections inside the horseshoe that would suggest that quite a bit might be missing. Hanging hole at center top. Backcoping to horseshoe reverse. Mid to late 1800s (E). 6⅞ x 4¼" without feet. *$20.00*

Plaque Trivet, Equestrian. CI, more desirable antique or vintage horseshoe plaque trivet, unsigned on reverse. Long smoothed gate-mark along one side. Backcoping to horseshoe reverse. I have never seen another like this horseshoe, and am not sure whether it is truly antique or perhaps vintage. 1890s to 1930s (E). 8½ x 4¼" without feet. *$45.00*

Plaque Trivet, Forget Me Not. Brass, noteworthy antique horseshoe plaque trivet, unsigned on reverse. On face: GOOD LUCK and FORGET ME NOT. Backcoping to horseshoe reverse. This is a brass horseshoe that has been painted silver; one of the few situations in which I would consider removing the paint. I can't imagine this paint is original to the trivet. 1880s and beyond. 6 x 3⅜" without feet. *$70.00*

Plaque Trivet, Free & Accepted Masons. CI, more desirable antique horseshoe plaque trivet, unsigned on reverse. On face: F&AM and the letter G. Backcoping to horseshoe reverse. This is a Masonic trivet, the letters standing for God or geometry and Free & Accepted Masons. Still has some of the original gold paint and sparkles. Small hanging hook on the reverse. Mid to late 1800s. 6⅝ x 4⅛" without feet. *$60.00*

Plaque Trivet, GAR (Grand Army of the Republic). CI, noteworthy antique horseshoe plaque trivet, signed on reverse. On face: GAR (Grand Army of the Republic). On reverse: PAT APL'D FOR. Backcoping to horseshoe reverse. Some of these GAR trivets still show the original paint, especially the red, white, and blue on the American flag. 1870s and beyond. 6⅜ x 4" without feet. *$90.00*

Plaque Trivet, Good Luck K of L. CI, rare antique horseshoe plaque trivet, unsigned on reverse. On face: IN GOD WE TRUST, GOOD LUCK, and K OF L. Some old paint and glitter remains. Backcoping to horseshoe reverse. The eagle appears to be an older version. The Knights of Labor were founded in 1869, peaked in 1886, and were dissolved by 1900. This trivet dates to the 1880s. 8 x 6½" without feet. *$150.00*

Plaque Trivet, Good Luck Star. Brass, more desirable antique horseshoe plaque trivet, unsigned on reverse. On face: GOOD LUCK. Backcoping to the horseshoe reverse. Three small mounting holes have been drilled into my plaque, which devalues it slightly. 1880s and beyond. 6⅝ x 4⅛" without feet. *$60.00*

Plaque Trivet, Good Luck with Doves. CI, rare antique horseshoe plaque trivet, unsigned on reverse. On face: GOOD LUCK. Still has quite a bit of the original gold paint remaining. All wingtips intact. Backcoping to horseshoe reverse. 1880s and beyond. 8 x 6" without feet. *$140.00*

Plaque Trivet, Good Luck with Eagle. CI, more desirable antique horseshoe plaque trivet, unsigned on reverse. On face: GOOD LUCK. Gold painted. Backcoping to horseshoe reverse. Cast through base of horseshoe. I have also seen this same design cast in brass and copper. 1880s and beyond. 6¼ x 4" without feet. *$55.00*

Plaque Trivet, Handshake. CI, more desirable antique horseshoe plaque trivet, unsigned on reverse. Traces of gold paint. Backcoping to horseshoe reverse. Mid to late 1800s (E). 6¾ x 4⅛" without feet. *$50.00*

Plaque Trivet, Home Sweet Home. Brass, noteworthy antique horseshoe plaque trivet, unsigned on reverse. On face: HOME SWEET HOME. Backcoping to horseshoe reverse. 1880s and beyond. 6 x 3⅞" without feet. *$75.00*

Plaque Trivet, Junior Order United American Mechanics. CI, noteworthy antique horseshoe plaque trivet, unsigned on reverse. On face: JR.O.U.A.M. and VLP. Backcoping and hanging wire on reverse. The initials stand for Junior Order United American Mechanics and their principles of virtue, liberty, and patriotism. This society was established in 1853. Mid to late 1800s. 6 x 3⅞" without feet. *$90.00*

Plaque Trivet, Junior Order United American Mechanics (reverse). On reverse: Close-up of the stiff hanging wire, for wall mounting.

Plaque Trivet, Knights of Pythias. CI, more desirable antique horseshoe plaque trivet, unsigned on reverse. On face: KNIGHTS OF PYTHIAS and FCB, which stands for their principles of friendship, charity, and benevolence. Gold painted. Backcoping to horseshoe reverse. Knights of Pythias was founded in Washington, DC in 1864. Mid to late 1800s. 6⅝ x 4¼" without feet. *$70.00*

Plaque Trivet, Loyal Order of Moose. CI, noteworthy antique horseshoe plaque trivet, unsigned on reverse. On face: GOOD LUCK. Small metal hanging loop on reverse. Backcoping to horseshoe reverse. Represents the Loyal Order of Moose, founded in 1888, and still active today with well over a million members worldwide. Late 1800s and beyond. 8 x 5¾" without feet. *$90.00*

Plaque Trivet, Masonic Cross. Brass, more desirable antique or vintage horseshoe plaque trivet, unsigned on reverse. On face: G for God or geometry. Different from the rest in that the back is flat and smoothly cast. This may be a vintage paperweight rather than the older and more traditionally designed plaque trivets meant for wall display. 1900s to 1940 (E). 6 x 3⅞" without feet. *$50.00*

Plaque Trivet, Odd Fellows Heart in Hand (Independent Order of Odd Fellows). CI, rare antique horseshoe plaque trivet, unsigned on reverse. Independent Order of Odd Fellows symbols on face include: three linked rings of friendship, love, and truth; heart in hand; all-seeing eye; quiver of arrows; and Moses' rod. Backcoping to horseshoe reverse. Rarely found with the two ends of Moses' rod intact. Mid to late 1800s. 7¼ x 5¾" without feet. I've also seen a similar IOOF trivet with a bow rather than Moses' rod. *$110.00*

Plaque Trivet, Odd Fellows No. 2. CI, more desirable antique horseshoe plaque trivet, unsigned on reverse. On face: FLT and I.O.O.F., signifying Friendship, Love, & Truth and the Independent Order of Odd Fellows. Symbols: the Fraternal Handshake and the All-Seeing Eye. The original gold and black paint is intact. Came in original box. Backcoping to reverse. Late 1880s to early 1890s. 6½ x 4⅛" without feet. *$55.00 for trivet alone; $100.00 for both trivet and original box*

Plaque Trivet, Odd Fellows No. 2 Box. On box top: T. Jones & Sons, Sole Manufacturers of Beautiful Emblematic Ornaments. Followed by a complete listing of their 39 different horseshoe plaque trivet designs. Late 1880s to early 1890s. 7 x 4½" cardboard box. More information can be found on pages 27 – 28.

Plaque Trivet, Odd Fellows No. 2, C. J. Hoag. CI, noteworthy antique horseshoe plaque trivet, signed on reverse. On face: IOOF and FLT. An earlier version of the IOOF trivet, this one has the patent application signature on the reverse: DESIGN PAT APLD FOR BY C. J. HOAG. Backcoping to horseshoe reverse. 6⅜ x 4⅛" without feet. Mid to late 1800s. *$75.00*

Plaque Trivet, Odd Fellows No. 2, C. J. Hoag, reverse. On reverse: the patent application signature DESIGN PAT APLD FOR BY C. J. HOAG.

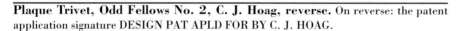

Plaque Trivet, Patriotic Order Sons of America. CI, noteworthy antique horseshoe plaque trivet, unsigned on reverse. On front: P O S of A. GOD, COUNTRY, ORDER OUR CODE. Gold painted. Backcoping to horseshoe reverse. POS of A was an anti-Catholic, anti-immigration, and anti-Irish group. 1870s and beyond. 6½ x 4¼" without feet. *$85.00*

Other Shapes

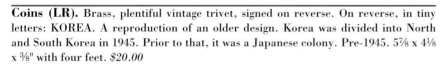

Cathedral, Rectangular. CI, more desirable antique casting, unsigned on reverse. Unusual cathedral variation. Quarter-inch railing around platform. Backcoping on reverse. Mid to late 1800s (E). 8¼ x 3½ x 1⅛" with four legs. *$65.00*

Coins (LR). Brass, plentiful vintage trivet, signed on reverse. On reverse, in tiny letters: KOREA. A reproduction of an older design. Korea was divided into North and South Korea in 1945. Prior to that, it was a Japanese colony. Pre-1945. 5⅞ x 4⅛ x ⅜" with four feet. *$20.00*

Early American Eagle (LR). Brass, noteworthy antique casting, unsigned on reverse. Quality casting with nice detail. Traces of blue and red enamel on shield. Sprue mark in center of reverse. It's unusual to find the remains of a sprue mark on a brass trivet, since casting marks were more easily removed on brass. Early to mid 1800s. Trivets with a sprue mark generally predate 1865. 7½ x 7¾ x ⅝" with three feet. *$90.00*

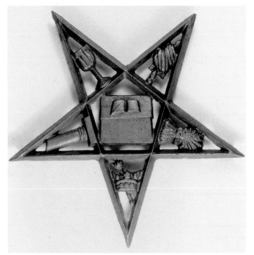

Eastern Star Pentagram (LR). CI, more desirable vintage trivet, unsigned on reverse. On face: the Altar and Bible is in the center, with each star point containing a different symbol. The Order of the Eastern Star, an offshoot of the Masons, was founded in 1876. This casting feels to be of vintage issue but may be more recent. 1910s to 1940 (E). 8⅛" along each edge of star, five ⅛" feet. *$45.00*

Fighting Gamecocks (LR). CI, more desirable older contemporary casting, signed on reverse. Gothic typeface of the lettering HEARTH and number 11 on the trivet reverse. Rough gate-mark on side. 1920s to 1940s (E). 7¾ x 5 x ¾" with four feet. *$45.00*

Flower & Triangles (LR). Brass, noteworthy antique casting, unsigned on reverse. Beautiful design. Mid to late 1800s (E). 9⅞ x 5½ x 1⅜ " with three legs. *$85.00*

Forest City Foundries Fancy Grapes & Scrolls (LR). CI, more desirable vintage trivet, signed on reverse. Reminiscent of the Grapes & Scrolls pattern, but more elaborate. On reverse: THE FOREST CITY FOUNDRY CO. CLEVELAND and NIAGARA FURNACES. Filed gate-mark on side. I've documented this company from 1890s to early 1970s. Foundry property is now vacant. 1940 or before. Might be a more recent casting. 8¼ x 5¼ x ⅞" with four feet. *$55.00*

GAR 2nd Corp Trivet. CI, museum quality antique commemorative, unsigned on reverse. On face: GAR. Second Corp insignia motif with centered GAR (Grand Army of the Republic) membership medal. Painted black. Photograph courtesy of Kyle Johnston, Arizona. 1890s (according to Kyle Johnson). 8½ x 7 x 1" with three legs. *$175.00*

Handyman (LR). Brass, more desirable vintage trivet, signed on reverse. On face: THE HANDYMAN. Cleated corners form feet. Centrally bowed from age. Backcoping on reverse. Looks like a small 684 and an asterisk on the reverse. Manufacturer and exact age of this item unknown. 1920s to 1940 (E). Might be more recent. 5⅞" square. *$45.00*

J.H.D. Cupids (LR). CI, rare antique casting, signed on reverse. Rough casting with finning; shallow backcoping. On reverse: three large embossed initials, J.H.D. Covered with a thick coat of black paint. Mid to late 1800s. 8½ x 5¼ x 1⅜" with four legs. *$135.00*

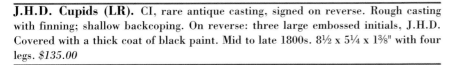

J.H.D. Cupids, reverse (LR). On reverse: detail of the embossed J.H.D. initials.

Jenny Lind Portrait (LR). CI, rare antique casting, unsigned on reverse. Gorgeous casting. On this trivet, the handle appears to have been inserted into the base; I'm unsure if it is original to the trivet. Writing on the loop handle hard to read: ENC or ENG and JEIN? 1850s to 1860s. A souvenir of Jenny Lind's American tour with P.T. Barnum. 4¾" square trivet body and 2⅝" handle with four 1" legs. *$125.00*

Kenrick No. 4 Plate Stand, brass. More desirable antique plate stand, Rd diamond on reverse. On face: EAST OR WEST HAME'S BEST. On reverse: AK (stands for Archibald Kendrick) & Sons, No 4 as well as Rd 257282. Rd number dates this trivet to 1895. 9 x 4⅞ x 4¼" with four ornamental leg supports, attached by nuts and screws. *$60.00*

Kenrick No. 4 Plate Stand, cast iron. More desirable antique plate stand, Rd number on reverse. On face: EAST OR WEST HAME'S BEST. On reverse: AK (stands for Archibald Kendrick) & Sons, No 4 as well as Rd 257282. Rd number dates this trivet to 1895. 9 x 4⅞ x 4¼" with four ornamental leg supports, attached by nuts and screws. *$50.00*

Moon Phases (LR). CI, rare vintage casting, Rd number on reverse. The seven sides of this trivet represent the seven phases of the moon. The moon is in the center (Mitchell p. 136). Rough gate-mark on side. On reverse: Rd No 617458 and the model number 2470. 1913 by Rd number. 9⅛ x 5½ x 1¼" with three legs and one center bracket support which can attach this trivet to a fireplace firebar. *$115.00*

National Emblems (LR). CI, rare antique trivet, Rd number on reverse. Features the national emblems of England, Ireland, Scotland, and Wales in the center circle. Along the outer circle, clockwise from top, are the national flowers of England, Ireland, Wales, Wales, and Scotland (Mitchell, p. 91). On reverse: No 331413. 1899 by Rd number. 9⅞ x 6½ x 1¼" with four legs and one center bracket support which can attach this trivet to a fireplace firebar. *$125.00*

Ornate Filigree (LR). Brass, More desirable antique or vintage trivet, unsigned on reverse. Delicate casting, slight coppery hue to brass. Late 1800s to early 1900s (E). 7¼ x 4¼ x ⅝" with three legs. *$45.00*

Ornate Floral, Brass (LR). More desirable antique casting, unsigned on reverse. Surface wear from use and age. Backcoping under petals on reverse. Early to mid 1800s. 8¾ x 4¾ x 1¼" with three legs. *$65.00*

Ornate Floral, Cast Iron (LR). Noteworthy antique trivet, unsigned on reverse. Backcoping under petals on reverse. Beautiful trivet. Cast through the rim. Early to mid 1800s. 9⅛ x 5⅛ x 1⅞" with three legs. *$75.00*

Queen Victoria Union (LR). Brass, rare antique trivet, signed on reverse. On face: UNION and a portrait of Queen Victoria. On reverse: ETNA GLASGOW and REGISTERED. According to Mitchell (p. 71) this stand commemorated both the 190th anniversary of the union of England and Scotland, as well as Queen Victoria's Diamond Jubilee. The Etna Foundry operated in Glasgow, Scotland, from 1854 to 1923. 1897. 9¾ x 4⅞ x 1¼" with four cleated legs. *$120.00*

R & B Trivet (LR). CI, rare antique trivet, unsigned on reverse. On face: R and B. Roughly cast trivet with unfiled gate-marks on either side. Finning present. Three-dimensional hands. This would appear to be a marriage trivet, considering the symbols (initials, lovebirds, shaking hands). I have seen a smaller version cast in brass, probably a copy. Mid to late 1800s. 8½ x 5⅜ x 1" with three legs. *$110.00*

Rectangular Scrolls (LR). Brass with wooden handle, noteworthy antique trivet, probably British, unsigned on reverse. Slight damage to the turned wooden handle. Cut from ¼" thick sheet brass with tapered, button like feet. 1820 (age guaranteed by seller at time of purchase). 9¾ x 5¼ x 1⅛" with four legs. Length includes handle. *$80.00*

Rocaille Spade Jenny Lind. Brass, rare antique trivet, unsigned on reverse. On face: JENNY LIND. Unusual thumbhole handle. I've also seen this design in cast iron. Pictured in *Spinning Wheel's* "Collectible Iron, Tin, Copper, & Brass," p. 31. Another souvenir of Jenny Lind's American tour with P.T. Barnum. 1850s to 1860s. 7¼ x 4½ x1" with three legs. *$120.00*

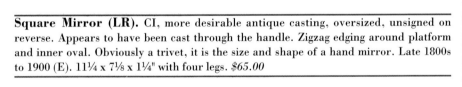

Spread Eagle and Stars (LR). CI, more desirable antique or vintage casting, unsigned on reverse. Backcoping to eagle and ribbons. Machine-filed gate-marks on one edge. Late 1800s to early 1900s (E). 7½ x 5⅜ x ¾" with four feet. *$45.00*

Square Eagle. CI, more desirable antique or vintage casting, unsigned on reverse. An extensive machine grinding on one side and backcoping to reverse. Late 1800s to early 1900s. 5 x 4⅝ x ¾" with four cleated feet. *$60.00*

Square Mirror (LR). CI, more desirable antique casting, oversized, unsigned on reverse. Appears to have been cast through the handle. Zigzag edging around platform and inner oval. Obviously a trivet, it is the size and shape of a hand mirror. Late 1800s to 1900 (E). 11¼ x 7⅛ x 1¼" with four legs. *$65.00*

St. Andrew's Cross (LR). Scottish, brass, noteworthy casting, Rd number on reverse. On face: the Scottish thistle and leaves encircling the cross of St. Andrew, the patron saint of Scotland. (Mitchell p. 102). On reverse: Rd 352431, dating this trivet to 1900. This trivet design was cast in versions both with and without a handle. 5⅜ x 4½ x ¾" with four feet. *$85.00*

Traditional Jenny Lind (LR). CI, noteworthy antique casting, unsigned on reverse. On face: JENNY LIND. Two gate-marks on rim. Heavy casting, Yet another souvenir of Jenny Lind's American tour with P.T. Barnum. 1850s to 1860s. 9¾ x 4½ x 1½" with three legs. *$100.00*

Urn & Fern No.1. CI, noteworthy antique casting, unsigned on reverse. Thin casting. Sprue mark on reverse. Very early version of this design. Early to mid 1800s (E). 8¾ x 5½ x 1⅜" with three legs. *$90.00*

Urn with Fern No. 2. CI, more desirable antique or vintage casting, painted. Tassels at top of trivet different from usual design. Gate-mark on rim. Old script number 14 on reverse. Probably an early reproduction. Early 1900s (E). 7⅝ x 5½ x 1⅜" with three legs. *$45.00*

CONTEMPORARY CASTINGS

JZH Alphabet Series

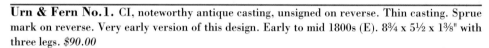

A 1944 J.Z.H. Alphabet trivet. CI, scarce older contemporary casting, signed J.Z.H. On reverse: J.Z.H. 1944 A. Old German design featuring decorative chasing; substantial in size and weight. 1944. 7⅞" diameter with four feet. *$50.00*

B 1944 J.Z.H. Alphabet trivet. CI, scarce older contemporary casting, signed J.Z.H. On reverse: J.Z.H. 1944 B. Compass design with central rosette. 1944. 7" diameter with three feet. *$45.00*

C 1945 J.Z.H. Alphabet trivet. CI, plentiful older contemporary casting, signed J.Z.H. On reverse: J.Z.H. 1945 C. Lightweight, delicate casting. (NOTE: Reissued as 1945 C Ring T-36 in an identical casting @ $15.00.) 1945. 7⅜ x 5½" with three feet. *$20.00*

D 1945 J.Z.H. Alphabet trivet. CI, plentiful older contemporary casting, signed J.Z.H. On reverse: J.Z.H. 1945 D. This design has been called Star, Eastern Star, Western Star, or Star in a Circle. 1945. 7½ x 5" with three legs. *$20.00*

E 1945 J.Z.H. Alphabet trivet. CI, less common older contemporary casting, signed J.Z.H. On reverse: J.Z.H. 1945 E. Reproduction of one of the many 1850s era Jenny Lind, the Swedish Nightingale, souvenir trivets that commemorated her American tour with P.T. Barnum. 1945. 8¾ x 4½" with three feet. *$35.00*

F 1945 J.Z.H. Version No.1. Alphabet trivet. CI, scarce older contemporary casting, signed J.Z.H.. On reverse: J.Z.H. 1945 F. This is the most difficult to acquire of all the alphabet trivets. It took me 2½ years to locate mine! 1945. 10¼ x 6⅝" with three feet. *$70.00*

F 1945 J.Z.H. Version No.2. Alphabet trivet. CI, scarce older contemporary casting, signed J.Z.H. On reverse: J.Z.H. 1945 F. A second version of F, this time without a handle. 1945. 6⅝" in diameter with three feet. *$45.00*

G 1948 J.Z.H. Alphabet trivet. CI, less common older contemporary casting, signed J.Z.H. On reverse: J.Z.H. 1948 G. This is an old William Rimby design from the 1840s called Twelve Hearts. Wilton also made a contemporary signed reproduction. 1948. 13 x 8" with three legs. *$35.00*

H 1955 J.Z.H. Version No.1. Alphabet trivet. CI, less common older contemporary casting, signed J.Z.H. On reverse: J.Z.H. 1955 H. Version No. 1 has an open center. The pinwheel design, referred to as the Chinese swastika or Ying-yang, is a symbol representing the four winds of the earth. 1955. 6⅛" diameter with three feet. *$25.00*

H 1955 J.Z.H. Version No. 2. Alphabet trivet. CI, less common older contemporary casting, signed J.Z.H. On reverse: J.Z.H. 1955 H. Version No. 2 has a closed center and is less commonly found. 1955. 6⅛" diameter with three feet. *$30.00*

I 1948 J.Z.H. Alphabet trivet. CI, plentiful older contemporary casting, signed J.Z.H. On reverse: J.Z.H. 1948 I. This trivet features a compass and rosette variation. The designs on the rings alternate. It is very similar in appearance to the Z trivet. 1948. 5¾" diameter with three legs. *$20.00*

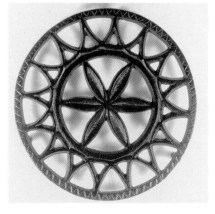

J 1948 J.Z.H. Alphabet trivet. CI, plentiful older contemporary casting, signed J.Z.H. On reverse: J.Z.H. 1948 J. Called Petals and Arches, this trivet features a central rosette and zigzag chasing to the outer circle. Often seen accent painted. 1948. 6½" diameter with three legs. *$20.00*

K 1948 J.Z.H. Alphabet trivet. CI, plentiful older contemporary casting, signed J.Z.H. On reverse: J.Z.H. 1948 K. There is zigzag chasing to the outer circle. This trivet was often accent painted to emphasize either the seven flowers or the six-pointed star. 1948. 6½" diameter with three legs. *$15.00*

L 1948 J.Z.H. Alphabet trivet. CI, less common older contemporary casting, signed J.Z.H. On reverse: J.Z.H. 1948 L. No backcoping on reverse. 1948. 8⅞ x 4¾" with three feet. *$35.00*

L 1955 J.Z.H. Reissue. CI, plentiful older contemporary casting, re-issued Alphabet trivet, signed J.Z.H. On reverse: J.Z.H. 1955 L Cupids T-11. Backcoping on reverse. This is the reissue of 1948 L; notice that the design has been altered and the date is different. 1955. 8⅞ x 4¾" with three feet. *$15.00*

M 1948 J.Z.H. Alphabet trivet. CI, less common older contemporary casting, signed J.Z.H. On reverse: J.Z.H. 1948 M. This design is known as Lyre, Heart, or Heart & Urn. Unusual handle. (NOTE: Reissued as 1948 M Lyre T-35 in identical design @ $15.00.) 1948. 8⅝ x 4" with three legs. *$25.00*

N 1948 J.Z.H. Alphabet trivet. CI, scarce older contemporary casting, signed J.Z.H. On reverse: J.Z.H. 1948 N. Features zigzag chasing and an unusual handle. 1948. 7½" diameter with 1" handle and three feet. *$45.00*

O 1948 J.Z.H. Alphabet trivet. CI, less common older contemporary casting, signed J.Z.H. On reverse: J.Z.H. 1948 O. There is a sawtooth edge and zigzag chasing. The center hole lends itself to adaptations (lamps, candleholders, etc.). 1948. 5¾" diameter with three feet. *$25.00*

P 1948 J.Z.H. Version No. 1. Alphabet trivet. CI, plentiful older contemporary casting, signed J.Z.H. On reverse: J.Z.H. 1948 P. Thinner and lighter weight than version #2. (NOTE: Reissued as 1948 P Hex T-9 in identical design @ $10.00.) 1948. 9¼ x 5⅞" with three legs. *$15.00*

P 1948 J.Z.H. Version No. 2. Alphabet trivet. CI, less common older contemporary casting, signed J.Z.H.. On reverse: J.Z.H. 1948 P. Longer legs and heavier than version #1 or the reissued version #1; different diameter circle on handle. 1948. 9⅜ x 5⅞ " with three legs. *$25.00*

Q 1948 J.Z.H. Alphabet trivet. CI, less common older contemporary casting, painted, signed J.Z.H. On reverse: J.Z.H. 1948 Q. Alternating heart & keys design with decorative scalloped edge and center pinwheel. This pattern is called Heart & Keys. 1948. 6¾" diameter with three feet. *$25.00*

R 1948 J.Z.H. Alphabet trivet. CI, less common older contemporary casting, signed J.Z.H. On reverse: J.Z.H. 1948 R. (NOTE: Reissued as 1955 R Cathedral T-12 in an identical design, with a different date, @ $15.00.) 1948. 9 x 4" with three feet. *$30.00*

S 1948 J.Z.H. Alphabet trivet. CI, less common older contemporary casting, signed J.Z.H. On reverse: GEO WASHINGTON and J.Z.H. 1948 S. Brass original was souvenir of 1876 Grand Centennial Exposition in Philadelphia, Pennsylvania. 1948. 9½ x 4½" with three feet. *$35.00*

T 1948 J.Z.H. Alphabet trivet. CI, less common older contemporary casting, signed J.Z.H. On reverse: J.Z.H. 1948 T. This trivet features an ornamental, three-dimensional handle. 1948. 10½ x 5¼" with three legs. *$25.00*

U 1948 J.Z.H. Alphabet trivet. CI, plentiful older contemporary casting, signed J.Z.H. On reverse: J.Z.H. 1948 U. Called Sunburst or Order of Cincinnati. (NOTE: Reissued as J.Z.H. 1948 U Sunburst in identical casting @ $15.00.) 1948. 9 x 5⅛" with three feet. *$20.00*

V 1948 J.Z.H. Alphabet trivet. CI, less common older contemporary casting, signed J.Z.H. (NOTE: Reissued as 1948 V Sm. Cathedral T-46 in identical casting @ $15.00.) On reverse: J.Z.H. 1948 V. 1948. 7¾ x 3½" with three feet. *$25.00*

W 1948 J.Z.H. Alphabet trivet. CI, less common older contemporary casting, signed J.Z.H. On reverse: J.Z.H. 1948 W. Dick Hankenson named this pattern Geometric #1. The original antique trivet was cast in 1879 and has PATD MAY 27, 79 embossed on the handle face. 1948. 8 x 5¼" with three feet. *$25.00*

X 1948 J.Z.H. Alphabet trivet. CI, less common older contemporary casting, signed J.Z.H. On reverse: J.Z.H. 1948 X. This design is called Double Hearts. 1/16" railing edging the two longer sides and smooth on reverse. 1948. 7⅝ x 4" with three feet. *$35.00*

Y 1948 J.Z.H. Alphabet trivet. CI, plentiful older contemporary casting, signed J.Z.H. On reverse: J.Z.H. 1948 Y. The pinwheel handle has additional cast iron reinforcement on the reverse to stabilize it. Entire surface accented with decorative chasing. 1948. 10⅛ x 4¾" with three legs. *$20.00*

Z 1948 J.Z.H. Alphabet trivet. CI, plentiful older contemporary casting, signed J.Z.H. On reverse: J.Z.H. 1948 Z. Decorative chasing on face. This trivet looks very much like the I alphabet trivet. 1948. 5¼" diameter with three legs. *$15.00*

Reproductions and Original Designs

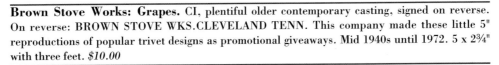

Brown Stove Works: Grapes. CI, plentiful older contemporary casting, signed on reverse. On reverse: BROWN STOVE WKS.CLEVELAND TENN. This company made these little 5" reproductions of popular trivet designs as promotional giveaways. Mid 1940s until 1972. 5 x 2¾" with three feet. *$10.00*

Bureau of Mines: First Cast 1964. CI, scarce older contemporary casting, signed on reverse. Grape pattern. On reverse: FIRST CAST, BUREAU OF MINES, HIGH-PRESSURE BLAST FURNACE, BRUCETON, PA. MARCH, 1964. More elaborate design than the previous smaller brown Stove Works trivet. 1964. 7¾ x 4½" with four feet. *$45.00*

Bureau of Mines: First Cast 1964, reverse. On reverse: FIRST CAST, BUREAU OF MINES, HIGH-PRESSURE BLAST FURNACE, BRUCETON, PA. MARCH, 1964.

Cross Publishing Company: God Is Great. CI, copyrighted design, less common older contemporary casting, motto trivet, signed Cross Publ. Co. On face: GOD IS GREAT GOD IS GOOD AND WE THANK HIM FOR OUR FOOD. On reverse: T2, CROSS PUBL. CO. ELIZABETH N.J, copyright circle, and MADE IN U.S.A. 1940s to 1950s (E). May be older. 5⅜" square with four feet. *$25.00*

Cross Publishing Company: Jesus Never Fails. CI, copyrighted design, less common older contemporary casting, motto trivet, signed Cross Publ. Co. On face: JESUS NEVER FAILS. On reverse: T5, CROSS PUBL. CO. ELIZABETH N.J, copyright circle, and MADE IN U.S.A. 1940s to 1950s (E). May be older. 8 x 5⅞" with four feet. *$30.00*

Cross Publishing Company: The Lord Is My Shepherd. CI, copyrighted design, less common older contemporary casting, motto trivet, signed Cross Publ. Co. On face: THE LORD IS MY SHEPHERD. On reverse: T4, CROSS PUBL. CO. ELIZABETH N.J, copyright circle, and MADE IN U.S.A. I've been unsuccessful in finding any information on this company, which I assume was a publisher of religious books. 1940s to 1950s (E). May be older. 9 x 4½" with three feet. *$30.00*

Dalecraft: Boy Walking. CI, painted, plentiful older contemporary trivet, signed Dalecraft. On reverse: DALECRAFT and 408. Dalecraft was located in Reading, Pennsylvania. 1960s or earlier (E). 8 x 4¾" with three feet. *$15.00*

Dalecraft: Girl with Flowers. CI, painted, plentiful older contemporary trivet, signed Dalecraft. On reverse: DALECRAFT and 409. 1960s or earlier (E). 8 x 4¾" with three feet. *$15.00*

Dalecraft: God Bless Our Home. CI, motto trivet, painted, plentiful older contemporary trivet, signed Dalecraft. On face: GOD BLESS OUR HOME. On reverse: DALECRAFT. 1960s or earlier (E). 8⅛ x 4¾" with three feet. *$15.00*

EFM: 1972. CI, less common recent contemporary casting, painted or plated. On face: EFM 1947 and GROSS DONK 25-YEARS 1972. EFM stands for Electric Furnace Man Division, General Machine Corporation, Emmaus, Pennsylvania. Gross Donk means "Many Thanks" in PaDutch. Translation of the EFM trivets courtesy of Jim Greenawalt. 1972. 6⅛ x 3⅞". Flat on reverse. *$20.00*

EFM: 1993. CI, painted, plentiful recent contemporary casting. On face: EFM 1993 and UFF DER ALT BAUEREI which is PaDutch for "Down on the old farm." 1993. 6¼ x 4". Flat on reverse. *$15.00*

EFM: 1993, with Calendar. A disposable EFM calendar fit with brads through the two holes at the trivet bottom.

EFM: 1994. CI, painted, plentiful recent contemporary casting. On face: EFM 1994 and DU LIEGST MIR IM HERZEN, whose literal translation is: "You lay in my heart." However, "You are my sweetheart" is the everyday meaning. 1994. 6¼ x 4". Flat on reverse. *$15.00*

EFM: 2001. CI, painted, plentiful recent contemporary casting. On face: EFM 2001 and UND NOCH EENS, which means "And one more" in PaDutch. 2001. 6⅛ x 3⅞". Flat on reverse. *$10.00*

Emig: T 55. CI, plentiful older contemporary casting, signed Emig. On reverse: EMIG T 55. The Robert Emig Products Company was based in Reading, Pennsylvaina. 1950 to 1960s. 9⅛ x 4" with three feet. *$15.00*

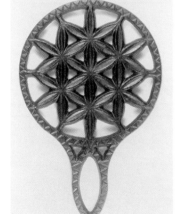

Emig: T 58. CI, Plentiful older contemporary casting, signed Emig. On reverse: EMIG T 58. 1950 to 1960s. 8⅝ x 5⅝" with three feet. *$15.00*

Emig: T 48. CI, plentiful older contemporary casting, signed Emig. On reverse: EMIG T 48. Cast through the rim. 1950 to 1960s. 7⅛ x 4⅛" with three feet. *$15.00*

Emig: T 51. CI, plentiful older contemporary casting, signed Emig. On reverse: EMIG T 51. 1950 to 1960s. 9⅜ x 4½" with three feet. *$15.00*

Fine: Masonic Star and Ladder, Version No.1 (LR). CI, less common older contemporary casting. Signed on reverse: The number 98, and R. FINE and SON, which stands for Richard Fine & Son of Boston, Massachusetts. This is the most common of the Masonic designs. G stands for God or geometry. Varies slightly from the JZH version. 1940s to early 1950s (I've seen a different trivet labeled R. Fine & SONS {plural} dated 1954). 7⅞ x 4⅛" with three feet. *$30.00*

Harvin: Leaves, Pair (LR). Brass, less common vintage or contemporary trivets, signed on reverse. These were sold as a pair. On reverse: the word HARVIN, their logo, and the number 3803. Virginia Metalcrafters purchased the Harvin Company of Baltimore, Maryland, makers of fireplace equipment and decorative accessories for the home, in 1953; so this trivet dates prior to 1953. Each trivet is 8⅜ x 4½" with three feet. *$30.00 per pair.*

Imported from England: Queen Elizabeth's Silver Jubilee (LR). British, chrome, plentiful recent contemporary trivet, unsigned on reverse. On face: SILVER JUBILEE 1952 1977. Hang tag says "A Mayell Product CLASSIC Stainless Chromium Plate." Cut and stamped from sheet chromium plate. 1977. 5⅜" round with four splayed foot supports. *$20.00*

Imported from India: Cats and Dog (LR). Brass, older casting, novelty trivet. On face: top surfaces die stamped with a fancy leaf and flower pattern. On reverse: INDIA. Postdates 1947. Each trivet is 3⅞" in diameter with three splayed feet. *$15.00 each*

Imported from India: Lyre (LR). Brass, made in India, plentiful older contemporary trivet, signed on reverse. Stamped pattern on top. On reverse: INDIA and a signature in illegible script. Postdates 1947. 6 x 4¼" with three feet. *$15.00*

Imported from India: Sarna Bell (LR). Brass, less common older contemporary trivet, made in India, possibly a vintage item, signed on reverse. Made of a sheet of stamped brass. On reverse: BELLS OF SARNA INDIA T 112 A. Foot supports bolted to trivet bottom. Bells of Sarna is S.S. Sarna Inc. and features imported Indian brassware and other collectibles. Bells of Sarna items date from the 1920s; since this is signed "India" it post dates 1947. 6½ x 4⅛" with three curved feet. *$30.00*

Imported from Israel: Shalom Jerusalem (LR). Brass, less common older contemporary casting, made in Israel, signed on reverse. On face: SHALOM JERUSALEM. On reverse: MADE IN ISRAEL. Beautiful casting. 1950s to 1960s (E). 9⅜ x 6" with three splayed feet. *$25.00*

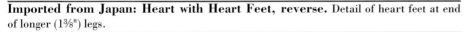

Imported from Japan: Heart with Heart Feet (LR). Brass, Japanese, plentiful older contemporary trivet, signed on reverse. On reverse: JAPAN. Nice quality item with unique heart feet. 1950 to 1960s (E). 5½ x 4 x 1⅜" with three legs that have heart-shaped feet. *$15.00*

Imported from Japan: Heart with Heart Feet, reverse. Detail of heart feet at end of longer (1⅜") legs.

Imported from Taiwan: Turtle. CI, recent contemporary casting, signed on reverse. On reverse: Taiwan. Heavily reproduced design. 1950s to 1960s (E). 6¾ x 5½" with four turtle feet. *$10.00*

Metropolitan Museum of Art: Good Luck For Us All, Version #2 (LR). CI, less common recent contemporary casting, signed on reverse. On face: GOOD LUCK FOR US ALL. On reverse: a copyright circle and MMA. The Metropolitan Museum of Art is located in New York City, and operates a gift shop. 1970s and beyond (E). 7½ x 3⅝" with four legs. *$25.00*

Murrell Dobbins: American Foundrymen's Society 1957 (LR). Aluminum, limited issue, older contemporary casting. On face: AMERICAN FOUNDRYMEN'S SOCIETY MARCH 8, 1957 and MURRELL DOBBINS VOCATIONAL-TECHNICAL SCHOOL (a vo-tech high school in Philadelphia). Roughly cast. Probably made as a speaker's award or as a remembrance piece for attendees at an AFS activity. 1957. 8⅞ x 4½" with three feet. *$25.00*

Portland Stove Factory: Maine. CI, less common older contemporary casting, signed Portland Stove Fdry. On front: the outline of the state of Maine and the White Pine, the state tree. On reverse: PORTLAND STOVE FDRY PORTLAND ME, a shamrock, and the letter C. 1950s to 1970 (E). 7⅛ x 5¼" with four feet. *$20.00*

Portland Stove Factory: New Hampshire. CI, less common older contemporary casting, signed Portland Stove Fdry. On front: the outline of the state of NH and its emblem, The Old Man of the Mountain. On reverse: PORTLAND STOVE FDRY PORTLAND ME, a shamrock, and the letter E. The value should increase considering the 5/3/03 natural destruction of this landmark. 1950s to 1970 (E). 7⅛ x 5¼" with four feet. *$25.00*

Sexton: Butcher (LR). Aluminum, copyrighted design, less common older contemporary casting, signed Sexton. On reverse: SEXTON and the copyright circle. 1960s. 8⅜ x 3½" with four feet. *$20.00*

Sexton: Butcher's Wife (LR). Aluminum, copyrighted design, less common older contemporary casting, signed Sexton. On reverse: SEXTON and the copyright circle. 1960s. 8⅝ x 3⅝" with four feet. *$20.00*

Sexton: Left Facing Gamecock (LR). Aluminum, copyrighted design, less common older contemporary casting, signed Sexton. On reverse: SEXTON and the copyright circle. 1960s. 9⅞ x 5⅞" with four feet. *$20.00*

Sexton: Right Facing Gamecock (LR). Aluminum, copyrighted design, less common older contemporary casting, signed Sexton. On reverse: SEXTON and the copyright circle. 1960s. 9⅞ x 5⅞" with four feet. *$20.00*

Trafford Foundry: EPGH Family Day 1953. CI, plentiful older contemporary casting, signed Trafford Foundry. On face: E PGH DIVISIONS FAMILY DAY 1953. On reverse: TRAFFORD FOUNDRY. Refers to the East Pittsburgh division of Westinghouse; a corporate memento. 1953. 8⅜ x 4¾" with three feet. *$15.00*

Unicast Company: 1991 Baerricks Fersommling. CI, painted, plentiful recent contemporary casting, signed on reverse. On face: BAERRICKS FERSOMMLING 1991. On reverse: D.M.L. and ES FATZEEHT FUN DIE BIGGELEISE DREIFIESSE SCHEE SACHS DEA DISCHTELFINCK, EN TULIP, UN EN HATZ which translates: "The 14th Iron Rest with the Nice Things, the Distelfink, the Tulip, and a Heart." 1991. The Unicast Company is still in business in Boyertown, Pennsylvania. 10 x 6" with four legs. *$15.00*

Unicast Company: Hopewell. CI, plentiful recent contemporary casting, signed Hopewell. On reverse: HOPEWELL on a raised plate. Very heavy for size. Gift shop item from the Hopewell Furnace National Historical Site in Elverson, Pennsylvania. Late 1980s to 1995. 8 x 5¾" with four legs. *$15.00*

Unicast Division, Berkmont Industries (formerly Union Mfg. Co. / JZH): 1978 Baerricks Fersommling. CI, Plentiful recent contemporary casting, signed on reverse. On face: BAERRICKS FERSOMMLING 1978. On reverse: ARSHT-KOURT-HAUS, which translates "Berks County Gathering" and "The First Court House." Also on reverse: the number 1 and D.M.L. (translation of the Fersommling trivets courtesy of Jim Greenawalt). BAERRICKS FERSOMMLING translates "Berks County Gathering" on all these Fersommling trivets. 1978. 10 x 5⅞" with six feet. *$15.00*

Unicast Division, Berkmont Industries (formerly Union Mfg. Co. / JZH): 1979 Baerricks Fersommling. CI, plentiful recent contemporary casting, signed on reverse. On face: BAERRICKS FERSOMMLING 1979. On reverse: D.M.L. and ES ZWEET ORD FUN DIE BIGELEISE DRY FUSSE — STOUDT'S DACHBRICK, which translates "The second kind of three legged iron trivet — Stoudt's Covered Bridge." 1979. 10 x 5⅞" with six feet. *$15.00*

Unicast Division, Berkmont Industries (formerly Union Mfg. Co. / JZH): TPA. CI, less common older contemporary casting, signed on reverse. On face: 1969 and TPA, which stands for the Telephone Pioneers of America. On reverse: JUMBO TULIP. This trivet is similar to another of their castings, the 1956 Grundsow Lodge Groundhog trivet. 1969. 12 x 7¾" with three feet. *$35.00*

Union Manufacturing Company / JZH: Ephrata. CI, plentiful older contemporary casting, unsigned on reverse. On face: ZION EFRATA. Two filed gate-marks on rear edge of platform; backcoping. Sold in the Ephrata Cloister Museum store, Ephrata, Pennsylvania, in the late 1950s through 1960s. Design based on an Ephrata Community Paper Mill watermark, circa 1745. Late 1950s through 1960s. 5½ x 4¼" with three feet. *$20.00*

Union Manufacturing Company / JZH: Tulip Boy (LR). CI, accent painted, plentiful older contemporary casting, signed J.Z.H. On reverse: J.Z.H. 1952 and the numbers 20 and 1. 1952. 9½ x 6" with four feet. *$15.00*

Union Manufacturing Company / JZH: Tulip Girl (LR). CI, accent painted, plentiful older contemporary casting, signed J.Z.H. On reverse: J.Z.H. 1952 and the numbers 21 and 4. 1952. 9½ x 6" with four feet. *$15.00*

Union Manufacturing Company / JZH: 1956 Grundsow Lodge Groundhog. CI, less common older contemporary casting, oversized, signed on reverse. Old German on face, as translated by Jim Greenawalt, reads: "20th Annual Festival of the Grundsow Lodge Number One, On the Lehigh (a river), February 1956 in Northampton, Pa." On reverse: JUMBO TULIP. 900 of these were made by JZH. 1956. 12 x 7½" with three feet. *$35.00*

Union Manufacturing Company / JZH: Butterfly. CI, plentiful older contemporary casting, Signed J.Z.H. On reverse: J.Z.H. 1949 and the number 5. Some come with hanging hooks. 1949. 9½ x 6¼" with three legs. *$15.00*

Union Manufacturing Company / JZH: Five petals (LR). CI, less common older contemporary casting, signed J.Z.H. On reverse: J.Z.H., 1948, and the number 2. Filed gate-mark on side. 1948. 7⅜ x 3¼" with three feet. *$25.00*

Union Manufacturing Company / JZH: Grain & Tassel or Lincoln Drape. CI, plentiful older contemporary casting, signed J.Z.H. On reverse: J.Z.H. 1951 and the number 10. 1951. 8½ x 5⅜" with four feet. *$10.00*

Union Manufacturing Company / JZH: Jester (LR). CI, less common older contemporary casting, signed J.Z.H. On reverse: J.Z.H. 1952 and the number 16. Interesting casting featuring six jester faces and two animal faces. 1952. 9½ x 4¾" with four feet. *$25.00*

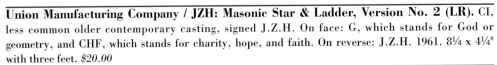

Union Manufacturing Company / JZH: Masonic Star & Ladder, Version No. 2 (LR). CI, less common older contemporary casting, signed J.Z.H. On face: G, which stands for God or geometry, and CHF, which stands for charity, hope, and faith. On reverse: J.Z.H. 1961. 8¼ x 4¼" with three feet. *$20.00*

Union Manufacturing Company / JZH: Pair: Ach Don't Talk So Dumb. Plentiful older contemporary casting, signed J.Z.H. On face: ACH DON'T TALK SO DUMB. On reverse: J.Z.H. 1952 and the number 18. This also was available accent painted. 1952. 6¼ x 4¼" with three feet. *$15.00*

Union Manufacturing Company / JZH: Pair: I Speak English Yet. CI, plentiful older contemporary casting, signed J.Z.H. On face: I SPEAK ENGLISH YET. On reverse: J.Z.H. 1952 and the number 19. This also was available accent painted. 1952. 6¼ x 4¼" with three feet. *$15.00*

Union Manufacturing Company / JZH: Tear Drop. CI, plentiful older contemporary casting, signed J.Z.H. On reverse: J.Z.H. 1952 T-18 Teardrop and the number 17. 1952. 9 x 3½" with three feet. *$15.00*

Union Manufacturing Company / JZH: Tulip. CI, plentiful older contemporary casting, signed J.Z.H. On reverse: JZH 1952 and 12. 1952. 9⅜ x 5⅞" with four legs. *$10.00*

Unknown, Novelty: "Behind Every Man…." Aluminum, motto trivet, painted, plentiful older contemporary casting, unsigned on reverse. On face: BEHIND EVERY SUCCESSFUL MAN STANDS A WOMAN TELLING HIM THAT HE'S WRONG! Typical of trivets available in roadside giftshops since the 1950s. Manufacturer unknown. 1950s and beyond. 4¾" round with three feet. *$7.50*

Unknown, Novelty: "If More Husbands…." Aluminum, motto trivet, painted, plentiful older contemporary casting, unsigned on reverse. On face: IF MORE HUSBANDS WERE SELF-STARTERS THE WIFE WOULDN'T HAVE TO BE A CRANK. Backcoping on reverse behind man's figure. Manufacturer unknown. 1950s and beyond. 4½ x 5" with three feet. *$7.50*

Unknown: "A Merry Heart Doeth Good." Aluminum, motto trivet, painted, plentiful older or recent contemporary casting, unsigned on reverse. On face: A MERRY HEART DOETH GOOD LIKE A MEDICINE. Two mounting holes at top of trivet. Manufacturer unknown. 1950s and beyond. 6 x 7" with three feet. $7.50

Unknown: "East Or West Campbell's Soups Are Best." CI, older contemporary casting, signed on reverse. On reverse: East or West, Campbell's Soups Are Best. Small filed gate-marks on one side. Manufacturer unknown. 1950s (E). 4½" square with four small feet. *$20.00*

Unknown: 1962 Girl Scout 50th Anniversary. CI, less common older contemporary casting, motto trivet. On front: 1912 – 1962 50th ANNIVERSARY GIRL SCOUTS OF THE USA HONOR THE PAST SERVE THE FUTURE. Painted in green and gold; number 1 on reverse. Prized by collectors of Girl Scout memorabilia. Manufacturer unknown. 1962. 7 x 7¼" with three peg legs. *$35.00*

Unknown: 1965 Pottstown Commemorative. CI, plentiful older contemporary casting, unsigned on reverse. On face: POTTSTOWN PENNSYLVANIA SESQUICENTENNIAL 1815 – 1965. Manufacturer unknown. 1965. 9 x 4" with three legs. *$20.00*

Unknown: CF (LR). CI, less common older contemporary casting, unsigned on reverse. On face: CF. Two prominent, filed gate-marks on side. Meaning of "CF" and manufacturer unknown. 1950s (E). Might be older. 9⅛ x 5⅞" with three feet. *$20.00*

Unknown: Easel, Plain (LR). CI, less common older contemporary casting, numbered on the reverse. On reverse: A12. Manufacturer unknown.1950s (E). 10¼ x 5" with four feet. *$20.00*

Unknown: Florida Symbols (LR). Aluminum, older contemporary casting, painted, unsigned on reverse. On face: FLORIDA and the state symbols of the Seminole Indian, the alligator and flamingo, sunshine, and the sabal palm tree. Typical of souvenir trivets available in Florida roadside giftshops since the 1950s. Manufacturer unknown. 1950s and beyond. 7⅞ x 5⅜" with four feet. *$15.00*

Unknown: Good Luck For Us All, Version #1. CI, less common older contemporary casting, Signed on reverse. On face: GOOD LUCK FOR US ALL. On reverse: A13. Manufacturer unknown. 1940s to 1950s (E), might be older. 7⅛ x 4¼" with four feet. *$25.00*

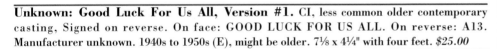

Unknown: Missouri. CI, less common older contemporary casting, numbered on the reverse. On face: MISSOURI and SHOW ME STATE. Gate-mark on side roughly broken off. Decorative rope edging. On reverse: 26 in larger, older looking numerals. 1940s to 1950s, may be older. 7½ x 4½" with three feet. *$20.00*

Unknown: Open Book (LR). Brass, less common older contemporary casting, unsigned on reverse. Roughness to casting. One foot still had the black rubber end cap attached, a clue that this trivet is post 1945. Manufacturer unknown. Late 1940s to 1960s (E). 7⅝ x 4½ x ½" with three small feet. *$20.00*

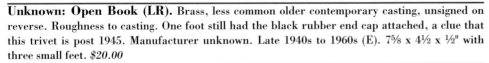

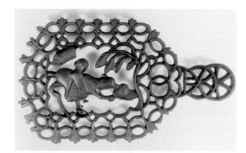

Unknown: Red Riding Hood (LR). CI, less common older contemporary casting. unsigned on reverse. Backcoping on reverse of figures. Gate-marks on edges of four circles nearest handle. Manufacturer unknown. This design was also reproduced by Virginia Metalcrafters; those trivets are signed VM on the reverse. This trivet was shown in a 1950s era Guilford Forge catalog. Priced at $0.95 in "Smoky Black Iron." 1950s. 11 x 6¼ x 1" with four legs. *$25.00*

Unknown: Red Riding Hood, reverse. Reverse of trivet, showing the backcoping to the figures that identifies this as a reproduction. Remember, the old original is flat on the reverse, without any backcoping and has 1¼" legs.

Unknown: Sid Gordon. Aluminum, plentiful older contemporary casting, painted, unsigned on reverse. On front: COMPLIMENTS OF SID GORDON. There was a famous baseball player by this name who played for four different professional teams from 1941 to 1955, including the New York Giants. Could this have been a publicity giveaway? 1940s to 1950s (E). 9½ x 4½" with three feet. *$20.00*

Vermont Castings: 1978. CI, plentiful recent contemporary casting, signed VC on reverse. On face: 1978 VERMONT CASTINGS INC. RANDOLPH, VERMONT. On back: VC on reverse of handle. The company has reorganized and is now known as Canadian Fireplace Manufacturers of Mississauga, Ontario. 1978. 12 x 6⅞" with three feet. *$20.00*

Vermont Castings: Spring. CI, less common recent contemporary casting, signed on reverse. On face: VERMONT CASTINGS SPRING 1983. On reverse: 3312, 4, and 0423. Heavy for its size. 1983. 5⅞" square with three feet. *$25.00*

Vermont Castings: Summer. CI, less common recent contemporary casting, signed on reverse. On face: VERMONT CASTINGS SUMMER. On reverse: 7/20/83. Heavy for its size. 1983. 5⅞" square with three feet. *$25.00*

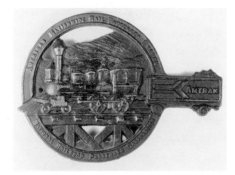

Virginia Metalcrafters: Amtrak. CI, plentiful older contemporary casting, Signed VaMetalcrafters. On face: AMERICAS NATIONWIDE RAIL PASSENGER SYSTEM, AMTRAK, and NATIONAL RAILROAD PASSENGER CORPORATION. On reverse: 9-40, VA. METALCRAFTERS, and the VM Betty Lamp logo. Amtrak service began in May 1971. VM featured several railroads in this series. 1971 and beyond. 6⅝ x 4¾" with three feet. *$15.00*

Virginia Metalcrafters: Colonial Williamsburg Cypher. CI, copyrighted design, plentiful older contemporary casting, signed VaMetalcrafters. On face: W. On reverse: 10-14, Colonial Williamsburg Cypher, copyright legend, and VM trademark. Postdates 1946. Copyrighted by Colonial Williamsburg Foundation. 6 x 6" with four feet. *$20.00*

Virginia Metalcrafters: Confederate States (LR). CI, copyrighted design, plentiful older contemporary casting, signed VaMetalcrafters. On face: 1861 1865 THE CONFEDERATE STATES OF AMERICA: 22 FEBRUARY 1862 and DEO VINDICE. On reverse: 10-18, C.S.A. TRIVET, COPYRIGHT 1952, VA.METALCRAFTERS, and the VM trademark. 1952. 5¼" round with three feet. *$20.00*

Virginia Metalcrafters: Dogwood No. 1. CI, copyrighted design, scarce older contemporary casting, signed VaMetalcrafters. Unusual trivet. On reverse: 9-27, COPYRIGHT 1949, H. BURNS, DOGWOOD, VA. HARDWARE SHOW MARCH 21-23, 1950 ROANKE, VA., RIFE-LOTH CORP. WAYNESBORO, VA. 1950. 5¾ x 4¼" with three feet. *$45.00*

Virginia Metalcrafters: Dogwood No. 2. CI, copyrighted design, plentiful older contemporary casting, signed VaMetalcrafters. On reverse: 10-12, COPYRIGHT 1950 BY H. BURNS, DOGWOOD, and the VM trademark. 1950. 4⅞" round with three feet. *$15.00*

Virginia Metalcrafters: King George. CI, copyrighted design, plentiful older contemporary casting, signed VaMetalcrafters. On face: GR. On reverse: CW 10-9, KING GEORGE, COPYRIGHT 1949, and VM trademark. Copyrighted by Colonial Williamsburg Foundation. 1949. 3¼ x 5" with four feet. *$15.00*

Virginia Metalcrafters: Kings Arms. CI, copyrighted design, plentiful older contemporary casting, signed VaMetalcrafters. On face: DIEU DROIT ET MON, French for "God and My Right," the motto of the Sovereign beginning with England's King Henry V in 1413. On reverse: CW 10-17, KINGS ARMS TRIVET, VA. METALCRAFTERS, COPYRIGHT and the VM Betty Lamp logo. Copyrighted by Colonial Williamsburg Foundation. 1953. 6" round with four feet. *$20.00*

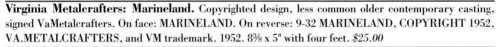

Virginia Metalcrafters: Marineland. Copyrighted design, less common older contemporary casting, signed VaMetalcrafters. On face: MARINELAND. On reverse: 9-32 MARINELAND, COPYRIGHT 1952, VA.METALCRAFTERS, and VM trademark. 1952. 8⅜ x 5" with four feet. *$25.00*

Virginia Metalcrafters: Natural Bridge. CI, copyrighted design, less common older contemporary casting, signed VaMetalcrafters. On face: NATURAL BRIDGE, VIRGINIA. On reverse: COPYRIGHT 1953, VA.METALCRAFTERS, 9-37, and the VM logo. Natural Bridge is one of the seven natural wonders of the world. 1953. 7⅝ x 4⅝" with four feet. *$25.00*

Virginia Metalcrafters: Old Sturbridge. CI, less common older contemporary casting, signed VaMetalcrafters. On reverse: 5-21, the VM logo, and the OSV logo of a grasshopper within a circle with the letters OSV. The antique version can be seen on p. 31 of *Spinning Wheel's* "Collectible Iron, Tin, Copper & Brass." Sold in the giftshops of Old Sturbridge Village. 1960s. 10½ x 4¼" with three feet. *$25.00*

Virginia Metalcrafters: Silver Springs. CI, copyrighted design, less common older contemporary casting, signed VaMetalcrafters. On face: FLORIDA'S SILVER SPRINGS and NATURE'S UNDERWATER FAIRYLAND. On reverse: 9-30, WATER OF SILVER SPRINGS 80 MILLION GALS. DAILY 72 DEGREES YEAR ROUND 400 FT WIDE 80 FT DEEP, COPYRIGHT 1951, VA.METALCRAFTERS, and VM trademark. 1951. 7⅞ x 4" with four legs. *$25.00*

Virginia Metalcrafters: Skyline Drive. CI, copyrighted design, less common older contemporary casting, signed VaMetalcrafters. On face: SKYLINE DRIVE and SHENANDOAH NATIONAL PARK VA. On reverse: SKYLINE DRIVE with map, COPYRIGHT 1951, VA.METALCRAFTERS, 9-28, and VM trademark. The Skyline Drive in Virginia was constructed during the Great Depression. 1951. 7⅞ x 4¼" with four feet. *$25.00*

Virginia Metalcrafters: St. Augustine. CI, copyrighted design, less common older contemporary casting, signed VaMetalcrafters. On face: THE OLDEST HOUSE ST. AUGUSTINE, FLORIDA. On reverse: 1513 PONCE DE LEON DISCOVERED FLORIDA. 1565 PEDRO MENENDEZ FOUNDED ST. AUGUSTINE. 1821 SPAIN CEDED FLORIDA TO USA. On reverse: 9-26, VM logo, COPYRIGHT 1951, and VA.METALCRAFTERS. 1951. 8 x 4⅝" with four feet. *$25.00*

Walker: ABA. CI, limited issue, noteworthy older contemporary casting, signed R. Walker. On face: ABA, for the American Bell Association. Accent painted in shades of green and gold. "Ralph Walker" etched on back of handle. Only 154 were made by the Walker family, and most of those are probably owned by bell collectors. The story of this trivet begins on p. 18. 1966. 9¼ x 5½ x ¾" with three feet. *$75.00*

Walker: ABA trivet, reverse of handle. Reverse: Each of the 154 ABA trivet handles was hand etched by Mr. Walker with his signature.

Wilton: "A Stitch In Time." CI, copyrighted design, motto trivet, plentiful older contemporary casting, signed Wilton. On face: A STITCH IN TIME SAVES NINE. On reverse: WILTON, copyright symbol, and the number 4. The Wilton Company, now known as Wilton Armetale, still operates in Mount Joy, Pennsylvania. 1950s to 1960s. 9 x 5⅜" with three feet. *$20.00*

Wilton: "Bless This House" Version No. 1. CI, motto trivet, painted, plentiful older contemporary casting, signed Wilton. On face: BLESS THIS HOUSE OH LORD WE PRAY MAKE IT SAFE BY NIGHT AND DAY. On reverse: WILTON. 1950s to 1960s. 7½ x 6¾" with four feet. *$15.00*

Wilton: "God Bless Our Mortgaged Home." CI, copyrighted design, less common older contemporary trivet, motto trivet, painted, signed Wilton. On face: GOD BLESS OUR MORTGAGED HOME. On reverse: Wilton and the copyright symbol. 1950s to 1960s. 6½ x 5¼" with three feet. *$15.00*

Wilton: "Bless This House" Version No. 2. CI, motto trivet, plentiful older contemporary casting, signed Wilton. On face: BLESS THIS HOUSE OH LORD WE PRAY MAKE IT SAFE BY NIGHT AND DAY. On reverse: WILTON. 1950s to 1960s. 7⅜ x 6½" with four feet. *$12.50*

Wilton: "Give Us This Day Lord Our Daily Bread." CI, copyrighted design, less common older contemporary casting, motto trivet, painted, signed Wilton. On face: GIVE US THIS DAY OUR DAILY BREAD. On reverse: WILTON and the copyright symbol. 1950s to 1960s. 7 x 6⅛" with four feet. *$20.00*

Wilton: "God Is Great, God Is Good." CI, copyrighted design, less common older contemporary trivet, motto trivet, painted, signed Wilton. On face: GOD IS GREAT GOD IS GOOD AND WE THANK HIM FOR OUR FOOD. On reverse: WILTON and the copyright symbol. 1950s to 1960s. 6 x 7¾" with four feet. *$20.00*

Wilton: "God Is Love." CI, copyrighted design, motto trivet, older contemporary trivet, painted, signed Wilton. On face: GOD IS LOVE. On reverse: WILTON and the copyright symbol. 1950s to 1960s. 8⅜ x 5¼" with three feet. *$20.00*

Wilton: "Kissin' Don't Last." CI, copyrighted design, motto trivet, plentiful older contemporary casting, signed Wilton. On face: KISSIN DON'T LAST COOKIN DO. On reverse: WILTON, the number 4, and the copyright symbol. 1950s to 1960s. 8⅞ x 5½" with three feet. *$15.00*

Wilton: "My Kitchen." CI, copyrighted design, less common older contemporary casting, motto trivet, signed Wilton. On face: NO MATTER WHERE I SERVE MY GUESTS IT SEEMS THEY LIKE MY KITCHEN BEST. On reverse: WILTON and the copyright symbol. 1950s to 1960s. 6½ x 7" with four feet. *$20.00*

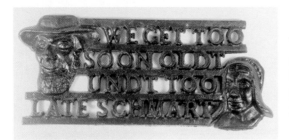

Wilton: "We Get Too Soon Oldt." CI, copyrighted design, less common older contemporary casting, motto trivet, signed Wilton. On face: WE GET TOO SOON OLDT UND TOO LATE SCHMART. On reverse: WILTON, the number 2, and the copyright symbol. 1950s to 1960s. 8¼ x 3½" with four feet. *$15.00*

Wilton: 1894. CI, collectible casting, plentiful trivet, signed Wilton. On face: 1894. On reverse: WILTON. Extensive backcoping. 1950s to 1960s. 8⅝ x 3¾" with three feet. *$15.00*

Wilton: Cupid. CI, plentiful older contemporary casting, signed Wilton. On reverse: WILTON. Legs are an extension of the body. Beautiful casting. 1950s to 1960s. 9 x 4" with four legs. *$20.00*

Wilton: Distelfink. CI, plentiful older contemporary casting, signed Wilton. On reverse: WILTON. The distelfink is the Pennsylvania Dutch bird of good luck and happiness. 1950s to 1960s. 8¾ x 5¼" with three feet. *$15.00*

Wilton: Dumb Dutch. CI, plentiful older contemporary casting, signed Wilton. On reverse: WILTON on a raised plate. Three areas of reinforcing iron on reverse. 1950s to 1960s. 8¾ x 4⅜" with three feet. *$15.00*

Wilton: Dutch Tulip. CI, less common older contemporary casting, oversized, signed Wilton. On reverse: WILTON. Beautifully cast. 1950s. 12¼ x 7⅝" with three feet. *$25.00*

Wilton: Eagle & Serpent (LR). CI, limited issue, oversized, scarce older contemporary casting, signed Wilton. On reverse: WILTON. Beautiful, impressive trivet; a limited issue casting which was not illustrated in the Wilton catalogs. 1950s. 12 x 7" with four legs. *$50.00*

Wilton: Eagle & Shield (LR). CI, limited issue, oversized, scarce older contemporary casting, signed Wilton. On reverse: WILTON. Beautiful, impressive trivet; a limited issue casting which was not illustrated in the Wilton catalogs. 1950s. 12 x 7⅜" with three legs. *$50.00*

Wilton: Heart in Hand. CI, less common older contemporary trivet, signed Wilton. This trivet design is also called Oddfellows, which refers to a fraternal society formed in 1810. 1950s to 1960s. 8 x 5¼" with four legs. *$20.00*

Wilton: Hearts and Flowers. CI, painted, plentiful older contemporary casting, signed Wilton. On reverse: WILTON. Accent painting was contracted out to individuals in the community. Many of Wilton's reproduction designs were offered in either flat black or accent painted. 1950s to 1960s. 9⅜ x 4¼" with three feet. *$20.00*

Wilton: Horseshoe. Brass, plentiful older contemporary casting, signed Wilton. On face: GOOD LUCK TO ALL WHO USE THIS STAND. On reverse: WILTON. As with most Wilton trivets, this design was available in both cast iron and brass. 1950s to 1960s. 8 x 4¾" with three cleated legs. *$25.00*

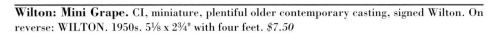

Wilton: Mini Grape. CI, miniature, plentiful older contemporary casting, signed Wilton. On reverse: WILTON. 1950s. 5⅛ x 2¾" with four feet. *$7.50*

Wilton: Mini Bellows. CI, miniature, plentiful older contemporary casting, signed Wilton. On reverse: WILTON. 1950s. 5¼ x 3⅛" with three feet. *$7.50*

Wilton: Mini Butterfly. CI, miniature, plentiful older contemporary casting, signed Wilton. On reverse: WILTON. 1950s. 5¼ x 4⅛" with three feet. *$7.50*

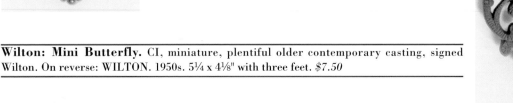

Wilton: Mini Cupid. CI, miniature, plentiful older contemporary casting, signed Wilton. On reverse: WILTON. Feet are an extension of the body. 1950s. 5¼ x 3" with four feet. *$7.50*

Wilton: Mini Dewdrop. CI, miniature, plentiful older contemporary casting, signed Wilton. On reverse: WILTON. 5⅜ x 2½" with three feet. 1950s. *$7.50*

Wilton: Mini Dumb Dutch. CI, miniature, plentiful older contemporary casting, signed Wilton. On reverse: WILTON. 1950s. 5⅜ x 3" with four feet. *$7.50*

Wilton: Mini Dutch Tulip. CI, miniature, plentiful older contemporary casting, signed Wilton. On reverse: WILTON. (Hanging ribbon at bottom.) 1950s. 5⅜ x 2⅞" with four feet. *$7.50*

Wilton: Mini Eagle. CI, miniature, plentiful older contemporary casting, signed Wilton. On reverse: WILTON. 1950s. 5¼ x 3⅛" with four feet. *$7.50*

Wilton: Mini Family Tree. CI, miniature, plentiful older contemporary casting, signed Wilton. On reverse: WILTON. 1950s. 5⅛ x 3⅛" with four feet. *$7.50*

Wilton: Mini Grain & Tassel. CI, miniature, plentiful older contemporary casting, signed Wilton. On reverse: WILTON. This design is also called Lincoln Drape. 1950s. 5¼ x 3⅜" with four feet. *$7.50*

Wilton: Mini Handled Lantz. CI, miniature, plentiful older contemporary casting, signed Wilton. On reverse: WILTON. I have not seen this design in a full-sized Wilton trivet — only in the 5" size. 1950s. 5½ x 3⅛" with three feet. *$7.50*

Wilton: Mini Hex. CI, miniature, plentiful older contemporary casting, signed Wilton. On reverse: WILTON. 1950s. 5¼ x 3" with three feet. *$7.50*

Wilton: Mini Military. CI, miniature, plentiful older contemporary casting, signed Wilton. On reverse: WILTON. 1950s. 5¼ x 3⅛" with three feet. *$7.50*

Wilton: Mini Peacock. CI, miniature, plentiful older contemporary casting, signed Wilton. On reverse: WILTON. 1950s. 5⅜ x 3" with three feet. *$7.50*

Wilton: Mini Reverse Cathedral. CI, miniature, plentiful older contemporary casting, signed Wilton. On reverse: WILTON. Might have been the companion trivet to a toy Wilton sadiron. 1950s. 5⅝ x 2¼" with three feet. *$7.50*

Wilton: Mini Rings. CI, miniature, plentiful older contemporary casting, signed Wilton. On reverse: WILTON and the number 9. 1950s. 5¼ x 3¼" with three feet. *$7.50*

Wilton: Mini Sunburst. CI, miniature, plentiful older contemporary casting, signed Wilton. On reverse: WILTON. 1950s. 5½ x 3⅛" with three feet. *$7.50*

Wilton: Mini Tulip in Motion. CI, miniature, plentiful older contemporary casting, signed Wilton. On reverse: WILTON. 1950s. 5½ x 3⅛ with three feet. *$7.50*

Wilton: Plume. CI, painted, plentiful older contemporary casting, signed Wilton. On reverse: WILTON. Slight backcoping along reverse of handle; accent painted. 1950s to 1960s. 8⅝ x 3⅝" with three feet. *$17.50*

Wilton: Rooster, Left Facing. CI, plentiful older contemporary casting, signed Wilton. On reverse: Wilton and L. 1950s to 1960s. 8¾ x 5⅜" with three feet. *$17.50*

Wilton: Rooster, Right Facing. CI, plentiful older contemporary casting, signed Wilton. On reverse: WILTON and R. 1950s to 1960s. 8¾ x 5⅜" with three feet. *$17.50*

Wilton: Rosette. CI, painted, plentiful older contemporary casting, signed Wilton. On reverse: WILTON, and the numbers 14 and 4. Accent painted. 1950s to 1960s. 8¼ x 3½" with three feet. *$15.00*

Wilton: Snowflake. CI, plentiful older contemporary casting, signed Wilton. On reverse: WILTON. 1950s to 1960s. 7⅞ x 4¾" with three feet. *$12.50*

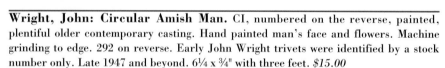

Wright, John: Circular Amish Man. CI, numbered on the reverse, painted, plentiful older contemporary casting. Hand painted man's face and flowers. Machine grinding to edge. 292 on reverse. Early John Wright trivets were identified by a stock number only. Late 1947 and beyond. 6¼ x ¾" with three feet. *$15.00*

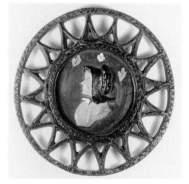

Wright, John: Circular Amish Woman. CI, numbered on reverse, painted, plentiful older contemporary trivet. Hand painted woman's face and flowers. Machine grinding on side. 293 on reverse. (The John Wright Company is still active in Wrightsville, Pennsylvania.) Late 1947 and beyond. 6¼ x ¾" with three feet. *$15.00*

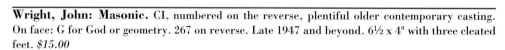

Wright, John: Masonic. CI, numbered on the reverse, plentiful older contemporary casting. On face: G for God or geometry. 267 on reverse. Late 1947 and beyond. 6½ x 4" with three cleated feet. *$15.00*

Glossary

Alloy – An alloy is formed by the mixture, by melting together, of two or more metals.

Aluminum – A silvery, lightweight metal that resists corrosion.

Antique – In the 1930s the U.S. Customs Office declared that an antique is any item greater than 100 years old.

Backcoping – Refers to the process of routing out portions of the trivet reverse, in order to reduce the heaviness of the trivet or to equalize the weight of the casting.

Bracket – A wing nut assembly on the reverse of a trivet that allowed it to be attached within a fireplace to the firebar.

Brass – A yellowish metal that is an alloy of copper and zinc.

British Rd Number – Found on the reverse of English trivets, signifying date of patent.

Bronze – A reddish-brown metal that is an alloy of copper and tin.

Casting – The process of pouring molten metal into a mold and allowing it to harden.

Cast Iron (CI) – Very fluid when molten, it is an alloy of iron, carbon, and silicon.

Cereal or Stove Trivets – These trivets were designed to slightly elevate a pan off the hot stovetop in order to prevent scorching while cooking easily ruined gravies or cereals. Many featured openings for a stove-lid lifter.

Chasing – Refers to a decorative grooved or furrowed ornamentation of the trivet's metal surface.

Cleats – Can be seen either as guides for an iron on the top of a sadiron stand, or formed into leg supports, which are often an extension of the rim of the trivet.

Coffee, Tea, or Table Stands – These were smaller stands, without handles, that were reserved for supporting lighter items. Most were delicate in construction and decorative, as well as functional.

Commemorative Trivets – Decorative trivets or stands that were produced to memorialize a specific person or event. They usually include an inscription of some type.

Compass design – Refers to a sequence of intersecting circles, as if drawn by a compass.

Contemporary Casting – A casting produced since 1940.

Copper – A reddish-brown decorative metal that is corrosion-resistant.

Distelfink – The Pennsylvania Dutch bird of good luck and happiness.

Embossed – Raised above the surface, or raised in relief.

Feet – Trivet or sadiron supports less than one inch in height, as measured from the table surface to the top of the trivet.

Fins – Rough projections on the finished product, caused by a shifting of the pattern during casting.

Fluter – A special iron used to produce uniform pleats in a fabric.

Foundry – A place where metal is cast. Foundries were established in America by the mid 1800s.

Fraternal Order Trivets – Decorative trivets featuring symbols, such as Masonic or Odd Fellows.

Gate-mark – The rectangular casting mark on the rim of a trivet or stand.

Horseshoe Trivets – Decorative trivets that prominently feature the horseshoe shape, and may include an eagle and/or other forms of ornamentation. Some versions had legs and were intended for utilitarian duty. Others had no feet, and were actually plaques meant for decorative use.

Japanned – A cast iron finish achieved by the application of lacquer over black paint.

Kitchen Trivet – A larger, heavier stand that could support larger pots, kettles, or large sadirons.

Lantz Trivets – A style of round trivets featuring three to six little paw feet.

Laundry Stove – A stove specifically intended to heat sadirons for ironing.

Legs – Trivet or sadiron supports equal to or greater than one inch in height, as measured from the table surface to the top of the trivet.

Motto Trivets – These were decorative trivets featuring Bible verses, proverbs, or familiar sayings. Most had small feet so that they could be wall mounted. They came with and without handles.

Nickel – A hard, silver-white metal that is resistant to oxidation, and therefore to rust.

Novelty Trivets – These trivets postdate 1950, and were mass produced of either aluminum or pot metal. They featured sayings that they were cute, but often politically incorrect by today's standards.

Older Contemporary Casting – A casting produced from 1940 to 1970.

Pan Handle – A type of long, narrow handle with a hanging hole in a round or diamond shape.

Paw Feet – Small feet supports that resemble animal paws.

Pennsylvania Dutch – This term, often shortened to PaDutch, refers to the descendents of early German immigrants who settled in eastern Pennsylvania. The term also refers to their carved, painted, or stenciled forms of folk art.

Rails – Projections around the rim of the sadiron stand that helped to keep the iron in position.

Recent Contemporary Casting – A casting produced after 1970.

Reverse Cathedral – The point of the decorative heart is oriented towards the handle.

Rosette – Resembling a six petal flower or star, it is a Pennsylvania Dutch symbol said to have the power to keep away all ill or bad luck.

Rust – Reddish-brown coating on iron formed after exposure to air and moisture.

Sadiron – A solid metal iron, heated on a traditional or a laundry stove. "Sad" means heavy.

Souvenir Trivets – These were specially commissioned, decorative trivets. They could commemorate a specific event, or advertise a particular place or attraction.

Stand – More commonly used to refer to trivets used specifically for supporting irons.

Sprue-mark – A round casting mark on the reverse center of a trivet, probably predating 1865.

Trivet – A large three-legged stand, originally used to hold pots over or near a fire. It evolved into a smaller stand (with a varying number of legs) that was used to protect and support hot pans, coffee pots, or irons above a surface. Some trivets with very small feet were of decorative use only.

Vintage Casting – A casting produced prior to 1940, but less than 100 years old.

Wedge-mark – A rectangular casting mark on the reverse center of a trivet, likely predating 1865.

Wrought – Wrought iron is produced by the process of heating, then shaping, a piece of iron into a particular shape or pattern by hammering. It is totally different from the casting process.

END NOTES

Reference category, if other than books, is given in parenthesis.

1. National Park Service, Statue of Liberty National Monument (Internet)
2. Hopewell Furnace National Historic Site (Internet)
3. Old Sturbridge Village (Internet)
4. Virginia Metalcrafters (Internet)
5. The Wilton Line 1953 (catalog)
6. 1974 John Wright General Store (catalog)
7. American Bell Association. Membership Information (Internet)
8. Kelly & Ellwood 87
9. Cavanah; Schultz
10. Kelly & Ellwood 241
11. Axelrod 123
12. Foresters Friendly Society, History Page (Internet)
13. Axelrod 88
14. Axelrod 249
15. Catholic Encyclopedia: Temperance Movements (Internet)
16. Axelrod 90 – 97
17. Sons of Union Veterans of the Civil War: Brief History of the Grand Army of the Republic (Internet)
18. Axelrod 116
19. Axelrod 206 – 208; Phoenixmasonry Masonic Museum: Improved Order of Red Men (Internet)
20. Axelrod 186 – 187
21. Axelrod 142
22. Axelrod 153 – 154
23. Axelrod 173 – 175
24. Tri-Counties Genealogy & History Sites: Commemorative Plaques & Flagholders of Military and Organizations, POS of A (Internet)
25. Axelrod 264 – 265
26. Drexel Grapevine Antiques. English Registry Marks (Internet)
27. The British Library© (Internet)
28. Ames 132
29. Ames 131 – 132
30. Isle of Man (Internet) and Isle of Man Government (Internet)
31. Berney 89; Smith and Wafford 296 – 297
32. American Beauty Electric Irons, 9/47 (catalog)
33. American Beauty Electric Iron, Cat. No. 33-AB, Information for Consumers (booklet)
34. American Beauty Electric Iron, Cat. No. 79-AB, Information for Consumers (booklet)
35. American Beauty Electric Irons, 9/47 (catalog)
36. American Beauty Electric Irons, 1958 (catalog)
37. American Beauty Electric Heating Devices, 1927 (catalog)
38. Hirshey 4 – 5 (magazine)

BIBLIOGRAPHY

Magazine and Newspaper Articles

- Condensation from June 1952. "Trivets." *Spinning Wheel*, September 1961: 14.
- Darmstaetter, Hugo. "Cast and Wrought Iron Beauty in Trivets for Flat-Irons and Other Hot Items." *Spinning Wheel*, September 1950: 10 – 12.
- Hankenson, Dick. "Handwrought Iron Trivets." *Spinning Wheel*, September 1962: 30.
- Hankenson, Dick. "Old and New Cast Iron Trivets." *Spinning Wheel*, June 1962: 16.
  _____. "Trivets Other than Iron." *Spinning Wheel*, March 1963: 32.
- Hirshey, Gerri. "Together, They Collect Memories." *Parade Magazine*, 11 May 2003: 4 – 5.
- Jessup, Grace. "Trivets as My Hobby." *Hobbies*, November 1950: 107 – 109.
- Koehler, Margaret H. "Toy Trivets to Treasure." *Spinning Wheel*, July – August 1969: 22 – 23.
- Menard, Gene. "Trivets." *Hobbies*, October 1938: 63.
- Paley, William. "Trivets Had It Hot." *Hobbies*, September 1971: 48 – 49.
  _____. "Birds and Animals in Trivets." *Spinning Wheel*, September 1967: 20.
  _____. "Brass Trivets: The Old and the New." *Spinning Wheel*, October 1969: 60 – 61.
  _____. "Circles In...Trivet Designs." *Spinning Wheel*, June 1968: 22 – 23, 50.
  _____. "Flowers and Vines in Trivets." *Spinning Wheel*, September 1973: 30 – 31.
  _____. "Heart Designs in Trivets." *Spinning Wheel*, May 1966: 14.
  _____. "Trivets from A – Z." *Spinning Wheel*, March 1971: 40 – 41.
  _____. "Unusual Features in Gadget Trivets." *Spinning Wheel*, June 1977: 28 – 30.
- Richter, Frances R. "Susan-Jane's Flat-iron Trivets Were Fancy!" *Hobbies*, March 1946: 17.
- Tarter, Jabe. "Fraternal Emblems Capture the Fancy of Many Collectors." *Akron (Ohio) Beacon Journal* December 27, 1975.
- Ware, W. Porter. "Jenny Lind's Trail: Hot Pursuit." *Antiques Journal*, July 1968: 10 – 13.

Books

- Ames, Alex. *Collecting Cast Iron*. Derbyshire, England: Mooreland Publishing Co. Ltd., 1980.
- Axelrod, Daniel. *The International Encyclopedia of Secret Societies and Fraternal Orders*. New York: Checkmark Books, 1997.
- Barlow, Ronald S. *Victorian Houseware: Hardware and Kitchenware*. El Cajon, California: Windmill Publishing, 1992.
- Berney, Esther S. *A Collector's Guide to Pressing Irons and Trivets*. New York: Crown Publishers, Inc., 1977.
- Bowlin, Opal M. *Antique Sad Irons*. Yucca Valley, California: self-published, 1965.
- Cavanah, Frances. *Jenny Lind's America*. Philadelphia: Chilton Book Company, 1969.
- Cheadle, Dave. *Victorian Trade Cards*. Paducah, Kentucky: Collector Books, 1996.
- Clemens, Terri. *American Family Farm Antiques*. Iola, Wisconsin: Krause Publications, 1994.
- Cosentino, Geraldine & Regina Stewart. *Kitchenware*. Racine, Wisconsin: Golden Press, 1977.
- D'Allemagne, Henry Rene. *Decorative Antique Ironwork*. New York: Dover Publications, 1968.
- DiNoto, Andrea, ed. *The Encyclopedia of Collectibles: Telephones to Trivets*. Alexandria, Virginia: Time Life Books, 1980.
- Franklin, Linda Campbell. *From Hearth to Cookstove: Collectibles of the American Kitchen. 1700 – 1930*. Florence, Alabama: House of Collectibles, 1976.
- Glissman, A.H. *The Evolution of the Sad Iron*. Carlsbad, California: Self-published, 1970.
- Goyer, Jane. *Essays on Antique Collecting*. Cape Cod, Massachusetts: Nauset Weekly Calendar, 1978.
- Hankenson, Dick. *Trivets*. Maple Plain, Minnesota: self-published, 1963.
  _____. *Trivets Old and Re-Pro*. Maple Plain, Minnesota: self-published, 1968.
  _____. *Trivets Book 1*. Des Moines, Iowa: Wallace-Homestead Book Co. 1972.
  _____. *Trivets Book 2*. Des Moines, Iowa: Wallace-Homestead Book Company. 1972.
- Harner, John Z. and Alliene Saeger DeChant. *Seedtime to Harvest*. Kutztown, Pennsylvania: The Kutztown Publishing Company, 1957.
- Hunting, Jean & Franklin. *Collectible Match Holders*. Atglen, Pennsylvania: Schiffer Publishing Ltd., 1998.
- Husfloen, Kyle, ed. *Antique Trader's Antiques & Collectibles 2000 Price Guide*. Iola, Wisconsin: Krause Publications, 2001.
- Huxford, Sharon & Bob, Editors. *Schroeder's Antique Price Guide, 2002*. Paducah, Kentucky: Collector Books, 2002.
- Irons, David. *Irons by Irons*. Self-published: 1994.
- Kelly, Rob Roy and James Ellwood. *A Collector's Guide to Trivets and Stands*. Lima, Ohio: Golden Era Publications, 1990.
- Lantz, Louise K. *Old American Kitchenware, 1725 – 1925*. Jointly published by New York: Thomas Nelson Inc. and Hanover, Pennsylvania: Everybody's Press, 1972.
- *Legendary Hex Signs*. Paradise, Pennsylvania: Will Char-The Hex Place, 1999.
- Lichten, Frances. *Folk Art of Rural Pennsylvania*. New York: Charles Scribner's Sons, 1946.
- Lifshey, Earl. *The Housewares Story*. Chicago: National Housewares Manufacturers Assoc., 1973.
- Marshall, Jo. *Collecting for Everyone: Kitchenware*. Radnor, Pennsylvania: Chilton Book Company, 1976.
- McClinton, Katharine. *Antique Collecting for Everyone*. New York: Bonanza Books, 1951.

- McNerney, Kathryn. *Antique Iron Identification and Values*. Paducah, Kentucky: Collector Books, 1996.
  _____. *Kitchen Antiques 1790 – 1940*. Paducah, Kentucky: Collector Books, 1991.
- McQuary, Jim & Cathy. *Collector's Guide to Advertising Cards*. Gas City, Indiana: L-W Productions, 1975.
- Mitchell, Hazel. *British Iron Stands*. Kent, England: self-published, 1991.
- Politzer, Judy. *Early Tuesday Morning: More Little Irons and Trivets*. Walnut Creek, California: self-published, 1986.
  _____. *Tuesday's Children: Collecting Little Irons and Trivets*. Walnut Creek, California: self-published, 1977.
- Rankin, Margaret Cuthbert. *The Art and Practice of Laundry Work*. London: Blackie And Son Limited, (undated) circa 1910 – 1920.
- Revi, Albert Christian, ed. *Spinning Wheel's Collectible Iron, Tin, Copper & Brass*. Hanover, Pennsylvania: Everybody's Press, 1974.
- Schultz, Gladys Denny. *Jenny Lind, The Swedish Nightingale*. Philadelphia: J.B. Lippincott Company, 1962.
- Shull, Thelma. *Victorian Antiques*. Rutland, Vermont: Charles E. Tuttle Company, 1963.
- Smith, David G. and Wafford, Charles. *The Book of Griswold and Wagner*. Atglen, Pennsylvania: Schiffer Publications, 1995.
- Smith, Elmer L. *Early Iron Ware*. Lebanon, Pennsylvania: Applied Arts Publishers, 1971.
- Stoneback, Diane. *Kitchen Collectibles: The Essential Buyers Guide*. Radnor, Pennsylvania: Wallace-Homestead Books, 1994.
- Werner, M.R. *Barnum, a Biography*. New York: Harcourt, Brace and Company, 1923.
- Zook, Jacob and Jane Zook. *Hexology: The History and Meaning of Hex Symbols*. Paradise, Pennsylvania: self-published, 1968.

Internet Information

- AAA Historical Americana – World Exonumia. Complete listing of fraternal organizations, A – L & M – Z.
  http://www.exonumia.com/art/society.htm, 5/2003
- American Beauty Irons
  http://www.jitterbuzz.com/indirn.html, 3/2003
- American Bell Association. Membership Information
  www.americanbell.org, 7/2002
- American Foundry and Manufacturing Company
  http://www.firehydrant.org/pictures/american_foundry_mfg.html, 1/2003
- Amish Country News. The Story of the Hex Sign
  http://www.amishnews.com/featurearticles/Storyofhexsigns.htm, 7/2002
- Antiques Cellar. Registration Marks
  http://www.antiquescellar.com/help/chronology.htm, 10/2002
- The British Library. Searching for British Designs by Number
  http://www.bl.uk/services/information/patents/designs.html, 2/2003
- Brockville Tourism Guide. About Brockville History
  http://www.brockville.com/master.cfm?ID=84&TL=Yes, 12/2002
- Bush & Wilton Valves Limited. About Us
  http://www.bushwiltonvalves.com/company.htm, 1/2003
- Catholic Encyclopedia. Temperance Movements
  www.newadvent.org, 5/2003
- Drexel Grapevine Antiques. English Registry Numbers
  http://www.drexelantiques.com/englishregistry.html, 11/2002
- E-zine. "Antique Pyrography."
  http://carverscompanion.com/Ezine/Vol2Issue1/Menendez/Antiquep2.html, *WWWoodc@rver*, 12/2002
- Foresters Friendly Society. History Page
  http://www.foresters.ws/Fred%20Website/History/History.htm#, 1/2003
- The Improved Order of Red Men. Who are the Red Men?
  http://www.redmen.org, 11/2002
- Indiana Historical Society. Manuscripts and Archives. Historical Sketch – Jenny Lind
  http://www.indianahistory.org/library/manuscripts/collection_guides/barnum.html, 10/2002
- Isle of Man. Welcome to the Isle of Man
  http://www.isleofman.com/about/, 12/2002
- Isle of Man Government. Background to the Isle of Man
  http://www.gov.im, 12/2002
- JOUAM. Junior Order United American Mechanics
  http://www.bessel.org/jouam.htm, 12/2002
- Lucky Mojo Curio Company. The Swastica
  http://www.luckymojo.com/swastika.html, 2/2003

- Masonic Symbols and their Meaning
  www.home.earthlink.net/~jackjoy777/symbols.html, 5/2003
- National Park Service. Hopewell Furnace National Historic Site
  http://www.nps.gov/hofu, 12/2002
- National Park Service. Statue of Liberty National Monument
  http://www.nps.gov/stli, 12/2002
- News India. Obituary for Jaswant Singh Sarna, of Bells of Sarna fame.
  http://www.newsindia-times.com/2002/05/24/dias39-top.html, 1/2003
- Old Capitol Artifacts. Auditor's Office – Iron Stove (Portland Stove Foundry information).
  http://www.uiowa.edu/~oldcap/tour/artifacts/aud_stove.html, 1/2003
- Old Sturbridge Village
  http://www.osv.org, 12/2002
- Oxton Decorative Arts. Registered Design Numbers
  http://dspace.dial.pipex.com/oxton.decart/regdesign.htm, 6/2002
- Phoenixmasonry Masonic Museum. Improved Order of Red Men.
  http://www.phoenixmasonry.org/masonicmuseum/fraternalism/red_men.htm, 11/2002
- Sons of Union Veterans of the Civil War. Brief History of the Grand Army of the Republic
  http://suvcw.org/gar.htm, 11/2002
- Tri-Counties Genealogy & History Sites. Commemorative Plaques & Flagholders of Military and Organizations, Patriotic Order, Sons of America POS of A
  http://www.rootsweb.com/~srgp/flaghold/flag034.htm, 11/2002
- Virginia Metalcrafters. Company History
  www.vametal.com, 05/2003

Catalogs and Brochures

- American Beauty Electric Heating Devices. Sales catalog. Detroit, Michigan: published by the American Heater Company, 1927. Contains 8 pages: 6¾" x 9¾".
- American Beauty Electric Irons. Sales catalog. Detroit, Michigan: published by the American Heater Company, 1947. Contains 12 pages: 8½" x 11".
- American Beauty Electric Irons. A hangtag brochure for the 79-AB iron. Detroit, Michigan: published by the American Heater Company, 1947.
- American Beauty Electric Irons. A hangtag brochure for the 33-AB iron. Detroit, Michigan: published by the American Heater Company, 1951.
- Art Objects in Cast Iron. A 1957 – 1958 sales catalog. Phillipsburg, New Jersey: published by the Iron Art Company, 1958. Contains 10 pages: 6" x 9".
- Catalogue of Hardware Specialties. Sales and recipe catalog. Philadelphia, Pennsylvania: published by the American Machine Company, 1890. Contains 48 pages: 4½" x 7¾".
- Descriptive Catalog of Patented Hardware Specialties. Philadelphia, Pennsylvania: published by the Enterprise Manufacturing Company of Pennsylvania, 1906. Contains 128 pages: 4" x 6".
- The Wilton Line. A 1953 catalog of Distinctive Giftwares. Wrightsville, Pennsylvania: published by the Wilton Company, 1953. Contains 11 pages: 8½" x 11".
- John Wright General Store Booklet. A catalog of John Wright items, circa 1910 – 1974. Wrightsville, Pennsylvania: published by the John Wright Company, 1974. Contains 35 pages: 8½" x 11".

POSTSCRIPT

I hope you have enjoyed reading this book as much as I did writing and compiling it. As I worked, I tried to think of all the things I would want to share with you if you were over for a visit, and we were exchanging information on trivets and trivet collecting.

My late father was a mining engineer in the southern United States. It was not uncommon for him to unearth old Civil War artifacts during excavations, especially in the states of Virginia and Georgia. I can clearly remember the old cannonballs and other battle artifacts he would bring home to show us. So now you can appreciate where at least some of my interest in relics of the past and "old iron" originates.

I've been a registered nurse for over thirty years now, having specialized in both Intensive Care and Labor & Delivery. So, it will come as no surprise to you that, besides collecting trivets, stands, and sadirons, I collect Dionne Quintuplet memorabilia. I also have a growing collection of antiquarian nursing and medical books from the 1800s and early 1900s. I consider these old reference books fascinating ... I've loved them ever since my late godmother, Primrose Bache, gave me her 1919 copy of *Studies in Ethics for Nurses*, which she herself used in nursing school.

My husband Ed is an electrical engineer in a systems and management position. In his spare time, he pursues several interests. Woodworking is one of his hobbies, and he has built a twelve-string guitar as well as a roll top desk, a dining table, and other furniture for our home. He also hand turns beautiful fountain pens on his home lathe. Nature photography is another of his hobbies and, as you know, he took all of the photographs of my trivet collection for this book. He is also active in the SETI@home program (The Search For Extraterrestrial Intelligence), and has completed more work units than 99.001% of the other computer users enrolled.

Ed and I have been married for thirty years, and we have two wonderful adult children, Mike and Mary Katherine. Mike just completed his computer science degree at Georgia Tech, and lives and works in Atlanta, Georgia. Mary-Kate is in her last year of college at the University of Florida, where she will earn a degree in advertising with a minor in French. Neither one seems to have much of an interest in trivets (yet), but hopefully that will develop over the coming years as they mature, make homes of their own, acquire an appreciation for older things, and eventually inherit some of these trivets.

I hope that this book has provided answers to many of the questions you may have had about trivets and trivet collecting. I've commented before that I realize my collection may be modest in comparison to some of you out there. I am continually searching for unfamiliar trivets and stands, and learning something new every day. That is the most wonderful aspect of any hobby...the thrill of the hunt, accompanied by the acquisition of new information.

The facts in this book are accurate to the best of my knowledge. If you should have some additional information to share, want to correct or clarify anything as presented in this book, or have any questions or comments, I would certainly welcome your correspondence. You can reach me through my publisher, and I will try to personally answer all letters.

Regards,
Lynn Rosack

Technical Notes

Technical Notes: Most of the photographs were taken with a Minolta Dimage 7Hi digital camera. The trivets were placed on a copy stand on a white felt background. The camera's highest resolution (2560x1920 pixels) was used, along with aperture priority (at f9.5), manual focus, and low compression to maximize sharpness. The camera's manually operated zoom ring and selectable viewfinder grid helped to precisely frame and align each trivet. Most exposures were on the order of $\frac{1}{15}$ second, set with the camera's automatic exposure mode. Adobe Photoshop Elements was used to process the pictures. Normal steps were color correction (using the white background), rotation (if required), and level adjustment. Level adjustment is necessary to bring out detail in the trivets in the high contrast images. Ulead™ PhotoImpact Album was used to catalog the photos. A custom database records information about each trivet, and makes it easy to keep track of hundreds of photos. PhotoImpact Album can export the database information into Word and Excel formats, which made preparing the text for the User Guide to Trivets and Stands easier.

Regards,
Ed Rosack